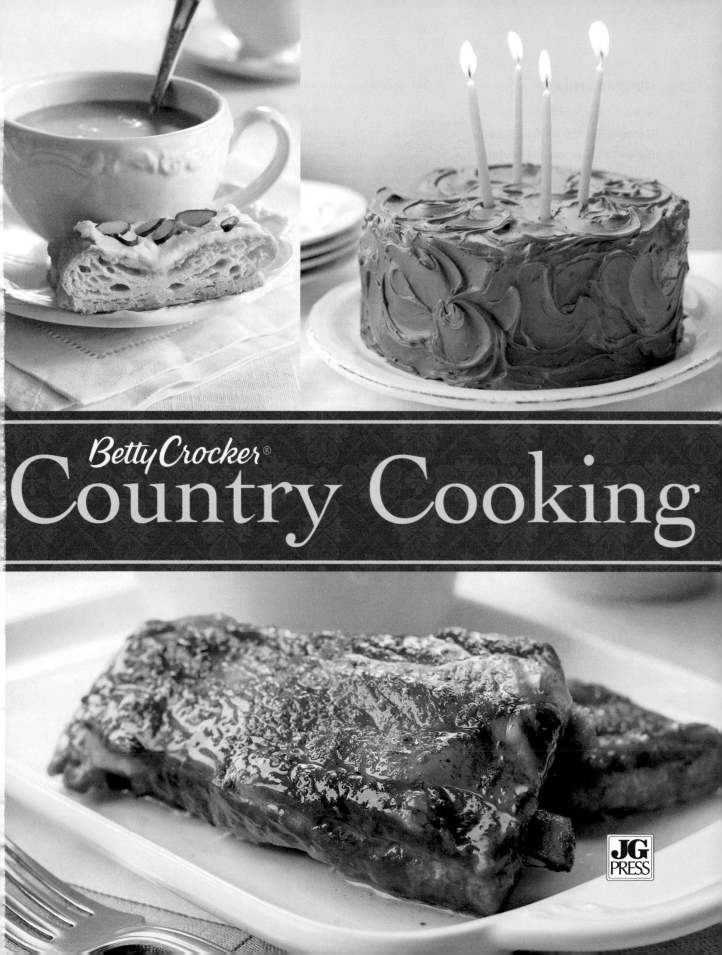

Betty Crocker®
Country Cooking

JG
PRESS

GENERAL MILLS

Editorial Director: Jeff Nowak

Manager, Cookbooks: Lois Tlusty

Recipe Development and Testing:
Betty Crocker Kitchens

Photography: General Mills
Photography Studios and
Image Library

JOHN WILEY & SONS, INC.

Publisher: Natalie Chapman

Executive Editor: Anne Ficklen

Senior Editorial Assistant:
Charleen Barila

Senior Production Editor:
Amy Zarkos

Cover Design: Suzanne Sunwoo

Art Director and Interior Design:
Tai Blanche

Interior Layout: Indianapolis
Composition Services

Manufacturing Manager: Kevin Watt

The **Betty Crocker Kitchens** seal guarantees success in your kitchen. Every recipe has been tested in America's Most Trusted Kitchens™ to meet our high standards of reliability, easy preparation and great taste.

FIND MORE GREAT IDEAS AT
Betty Crocker.com

This book is printed on acid-free paper. ♾

Published by World Publications Group, Inc., 140 Laurel Street, East Bridgewater, MA 02333, www.wrldpub.com

For general information about our other products and services, please contact our Customer Care Department within the United States at (877) 762-2974, outside the United States at (317) 572-3993 or fax (317) 572-4002.

Wiley publishes in a variety of print and electronic formats and by print-on-demand. Some material included with standard print versions of this book may not be included in e-books or in print-on-demand. If this book refers to media such as a CD or DVD that is not included in the version you purchased, you may download this material at http://booksupport.wiley.com. For more information about Wiley products, visit www.wiley.com.

Library of Congress Cataloging-in-Publication Data is available upon request.

ISBN: 978-1-4643-0100-1

Printed in China

10 9 8 7 6 5 4 3 2 1

Dear Friends,

Sipping cold lemonade on the front porch, nibbling Grandma's peach pie on the veranda and enjoying chicken-fried steak in the midst of a family gathering—all of these evoke memories of delicious days gone by. And just because our lives are more technological and faster paced than before, it doesn't mean our food must come from a drive-thru window. We can still delight in the flavors of a slower time while maintaining our modern-day lives. Taking the time to enjoy preparing these nostalgic favorites for our families is comforting and rejuvenating. Share these time-honored classic dishes with your family and create some heartwarming memories of your own.

In Betty Crocker Country Cooking *you'll find 350 recipes focusing on good ole down-home cooking, including fried chicken and fish; soups and stews; breads and muffins; cakes, cookies and pies—even trifles and homemade ice creams. With each one you prepare the memories will flood in as will the smiles on your family's faces.*

In addition, Country Cooking Wisdom will share with you the secrets our grandmothers used for preparing delicious meals. Look for tips on how to make the perfect meringue, prepare fresh chestnuts, or get a glossy crust on fresh baked bread.

This book is filled with delectable delights from across the country. So whether you're from the North, South, East or West of this great country, these recipes are sure to bring back memories while creating new ones.

Warmly,

Betty Crocker

Cranberry-Apple Pie (page 301)

Contents

Glazed Baked Ham (page 187)

Country Favorite Menus

Whether it's casual or elegant, entertaining family and friends is at the heart of the country kitchen. Here's a selection of delicious meal ideas for any occasion. Follow the menus exactly or use them as a jumping-off point, picking only your favorite choices and adding to them as desired.

New Year's Lunch

Honey-Mustard Ham 185

Hoppin' John 209

Spinach Gourmet 193

Hush Puppies 197

Lemon-Filled Coconut Cake 270

Last-Minute Dinner Guests

Classic Beef Stroganoff 161

Avocado-Citrus Salad 226

Bread Pudding with Whiskey Sauce 292

Valentine's Dinner for Two

Chicken in Cream 107

Duchess Potatoes 204

Broccoli with Pine Nuts 192

Hot-Fudge Sundae Cake 290

Mexican Night

Fajitas 160

Spanish Rice 213

Chocolate Hazelnut Tart 315

Bread Pudding with Whiskey Sauce (page 292)

Easy Easter Dinner

Birthday Brunch

Neighborhood Barbecue

Farmers' Market Menu

Chicago Deep-Dish Pizza (page 96)

Pizza Party

Ice Cream Social

Chocolate Chip Cookies (page 216)

CHAPTER ONE

Rise-and-Shine Breakfasts

WHETHER LINGERING OVER COFFEE OR HOSTING A BRUNCH, NOTHING BEATS A NOURISHING, WHOLESOME BREAKFAST.

It's a wonderful way to start the day with your family or friends. Any day of the week, breakfast time is something to look forward to. And if it's the weekend, all the better! Lounge and enjoy the fat Sunday paper. It's one of the week's high points, an occasion that calls for a treat. Pancakes, waffles and French toast fit the bill. Dressed up or down, eggs are glorious in every guise. Here they are, all your favorite recipes—along with a host of ideas for sweet breads, coffee cakes and sticky rolls to accompany any midmorning break, especially alongside a steaming cup of coffee or cocoa.

Ham and Egg Brunch Bake

8 servings | Prep Time: 15 minutes | Start to Finish: 1 hour 5 minutes

This dish is certain to be a real crowd-pleaser when served for breakfast or brunch. For a cheesier flavor, you might want to try a sharp cheddar. To enhance the smoky flavor of the ham, use smoked Gouda.

- 6 cups frozen hash brown potatoes
- 2 cups diced fully cooked ham
- 2 cups shredded Swiss cheese (8 oz)
- 1 jar (7 oz) roasted red bell peppers, drained and chopped
- 1 jar (4¹/₂ oz) sliced mushrooms, drained
- 6 eggs
- ¹/₃ cup milk
- 1 cup small curd creamed cottage cheese
- ¹/₄ teaspoon pepper

1 Heat oven to 350°F. Grease rectangular baking dish, 13 × 9 inches.

2 Sprinkle 3 cups of the potatoes evenly in baking dish. Layer with ham, Swiss cheese, bell peppers and mushrooms. Sprinkle remaining potatoes over mushrooms.

3 Beat eggs, milk, cottage cheese and pepper with fork or wire whisk until blended; pour over potatoes. Bake uncovered 45 to 50 minutes or until light golden brown and set in center.

1 Serving: Calories 310 (Calories from Fat 145); Fat 16g (Saturated 8g); Cholesterol 210mg; Sodium 800mg; Carbohydrate 19g (Dietary Fiber 2g); Protein 25g

Ham and Cheddar Strata

6 servings | Prep Time: 15 minutes | Start to Finish: 1 hour 35 minutes

Choose this recipe if you want to make a dish the night before, then pop it in the oven while the guests arrive. Feel free to use any kind of bread here—a whole-grain bread will add a nice texture to the dish.

12 slices bread

2 cups cut-up fully cooked smoked ham

2 cups shredded Cheddar cheese (8 oz)

4 medium green onions, sliced (1/4 cup)

2 cups milk

1 teaspoon dry mustard

1/4 teaspoon red pepper sauce

6 eggs
Paprika

1 Trim crusts from bread. Arrange 6 bread slices in greased rectangular baking dish, 13 × 9 inches. Layer ham, cheese and onions on bread in dish. Cut remaining bread slices diagonally into halves; arrange on onions.

2 Beat milk, mustard, pepper sauce and eggs until smooth; pour evenly over bread. Sprinkle with paprika. Bake immediately, or cover and refrigerate up to 24 hours.

3 Heat oven to 300°F. Bake uncovered until center is set and bread is golden brown. Let stand 10 minutes before cutting.

1 Serving: Calories 475 (Calories from Fat 225); Fat 25g (Saturated 12g); Cholesterol 285mg; Sodium 1,280mg; Carbohydrate 31g (Dietary Fiber 2g); Protein 33g

Potatoes and Eggs Sunny-Side Up

6 servings | Prep Time: 15 minutes | Start to Finish: 40 minutes

Show your sunny side by serving this filling favorite on a weekend morning when you have a little extra time to relax with your family. What's best—this is baked, making it easy to fix and serve.

12 oz bulk pork sausage

1 small onion, chopped (1/3 cup)

3 cups frozen shredded hash brown potatoes

1 teaspoon herb-seasoned salt

1 1/2 cups shredded Swiss cheese (6 oz)

6 eggs
Pepper, if desired

1 Heat oven to 350°F.

2 Cook and stir sausage and onion in 10-inch skillet over medium heat, stirring frequently, until sausage is brown; drain. Stir in frozen potatoes and herb-seasoned salt. Cook, stirring constantly, about 2 minutes, just until potatoes are thawed. Remove from heat; stir in cheese. Spread in ungreased rectangular baking dish, 11 × 7 inches.

3 Make 6 indentations in potato mixture with back of spoon; break 1 egg into each indentation. Sprinkle with pepper. Bake uncovered 20 to 25 minutes or until eggs are desired doneness.

1 Serving: Calories 355 (Calories from Fat 190); Fat 21g (Saturated 9g); Cholesterol 260mg; Sodium 730mg; Carbohydrate 23g (Dietary Fiber 2g); Protein 21g

Brunch Oven Omelet with Canadian Bacon

Linger over your morning cup of coffee with your guests while the maple-flavored bacon and golden omelet tend themselves in the oven.

Oven Canadian Bacon
(below right)

1/4 cup margarine or butter

18 eggs

1 cup sour cream

1 cup milk

2 teaspoons salt

4 medium green onions, chopped (1/4 cup)

Chopped fresh parsley

1   Heat oven to 325°F.

2   Make Oven Canadian Bacon; set aside. Melt margarine in rectangular baking dish, 13 × 9 inches, in oven; tilt dish to coat bottom.

3   Beat eggs, sour cream, milk and salt with fork or wire whisk until blended. Stir in onions. Pour into baking dish.

4   Bake omelet mixture and bacon about 35 minutes or until eggs are set but moist and bacon is hot. Arrange omelet and bacon on large platter. Sprinkle with parsley.

Oven Canadian Bacon

1   pound Canadian-style bacon, cut into twenty-four 1/8-inch slices

1/4 cup maple-flavored syrup

Reassemble slices of bacon on aluminum foil. Pour syrup over bacon. Wrap in foil; place in shallow baking pan.

1 Serving: Calories 265 (Calories from Fat 160); Fat 18g (Saturated 7g); Cholesterol 350mg; Sodium 1,030mg; Carbohydrate 6g (Dietary Fiber 0g); Protein 18g

COUNTRY COOKING WISDOM

Back Bacon

Canadian bacon, called *back bacon* in Canada, is more like ham than bacon. This lean, tender meat is the cured, smoked tender eye of the pork loin. It comes in rolls that make it easy to slice. Try it in soups, sandwiches and salads as well at breakfast.

Cheese and Egg Pie with Bacon

6 servings   Prep Time: 15 minutes   Start to Finish: 30 minutes

We've used an easy-to-make cornflake crust for this savory pie. The wonderful corn flavor complements the cheese and smoky bacon in this egg dish.

- 1 cup coarsely crushed cornflakes
- 2 tablespoons margarine or butter, melted
- $1/4$ cup margarine or butter
- 8 eggs
- $1/2$ cup milk
- 1 tablespoon chopped fresh chives
- $1/2$ teaspoon seasoned salt
- $1/8$ teaspoon pepper
- 6 slices bacon, crisply cooked and crumbled
- 3 slices American cheese, cut diagonally into halves

1 Heat oven to 375°F.

2 Mix cornflakes and 2 tablespoons melted margarine; reserve $1/4$ cup. Spread remaining cornflake mixture in ungreased pie plate, 9 × $1^{1}/4$ inches, or quiche dish, 9 × $1^{1}/2$ inches. Heat $1/4$ cup margarine in 10-inch skillet over medium heat until melted.

3 Beat eggs, milk, chives, seasoned salt and pepper in large bowl with fork or whisk until blended. Pour egg mixture into skillet; add bacon. Cook over low heat, stirring gently, until eggs are almost set. Quickly spoon into pie plate. Arrange cheese, overlapping slightly, around edge of plate. Sprinkle with reserved cornflake mixture.

4 Bake uncovered 10 to 15 minutes or until cheese is melted and eggs are firm.

1 Serving: Calories 225 (Calories from Fat 145); Fat 16g (Saturated 6g); Cholesterol 300mg; Sodium 450mg; Carbohydrate 6g (Dietary Fiber 0g); Protein 14g

COUNTRY COOKING WISDOM

Crushed Cornflakes

The easiest way to crush cornflakes, or any cookie or cracker, is to place them in a resealable food-storage plastic bag, release any air and then seal the bag. Using a rolling pin or glass, roll over the bag to crush the cornflakes.

Spring Vegetable Frittata

6 servings   Prep Time: 20 minutes   Start to Finish: 35 minutes

The frittata comes to us from Italy. The golden brown crust helps keep the inside of the frittata moist.

¹/₂ cup chopped onion

1 clove garlic, finely chopped

2 tablespoons margarine or butter

1 green or red bell pepper, chopped

¹/₄ teaspoon salt

¹/₄ teaspoon pepper

1 small tomato, chopped

2 small zucchini, chopped

6 eggs, beaten

¹/₄ cup grated Parmesan cheese

1 Heat oven to 375°F.

2 Cook onion and garlic in margarine in 10-inch ovenproof skillet over medium-high heat 3 minutes, stirring frequently. Add bell pepper and cook over medium heat about 2 minutes or until crisp-tender. Add salt, pepper, tomato and zucchini and cook 4 minutes, stirring occasionally. Add eggs.

3 Bake uncovered 10 to 12 minutes or until set in center. Sprinkle top with cheese.

1 Serving: Calories 140 (Calories from Fat 90); Fat 10g (Saturated 3g); Cholesterol 215mg; Sodium 280mg; Carbohydrate 5g (Dietary Fiber 1g); Protein 9g

Baked Vegetable Omelet

6 servings   Prep Time: 15 minutes   Start to Finish: 1 hour 10 minutes

What a great way to eat a serving of vegetables. Make this for breakfast or even for dinner—you'll love the results.

1 cup shredded Monterey Jack cheese (4 oz)

1¹/₂ cups chopped broccoli or 1 package (10 oz) frozen chopped broccoli, thawed and drained

2 medium tomatoes, coarsely chopped

2 cups shredded Cheddar cheese (8 oz)

1 cup milk

¹/₄ cup all-purpose flour

¹/₂ teaspoon salt

3 eggs

1 Heat oven to 350°F.

2 Layer Monterey Jack cheese, broccoli, tomatoes and Cheddar cheese in ungreased square baking dish, 8 × 8 inches. Beat milk, flour, salt and eggs in a medium bowl until smooth; pour over cheese.

3 Bake uncovered 40 to 45 minutes or until egg mixture is set. Let stand 10 minutes before cutting.

1 Serving: Calories 315 (Calories from Fat 200); Fat 22g (Saturated 13g); Cholesterol 165mg; Sodium 610mg; Carbohydrate 10g (Dietary Fiber 1g); Protein 20g

Country Egg Scramble

Scramble up this morning-time favorite and top it with salsa, hot sauce or a dollop of sour cream.

1 pound new red potatoes, cubed (6 small)

6 eggs

1/3 cup milk

1/4 teaspoon salt

1/8 teaspoon pepper

2 tablespoons margarine or butter

4 medium green onions, sliced (1/4 cup)

6 slices bacon, crisply cooked and crumbled

1 Heat 1 inch water to boiling in 2-quart saucepan. Add potatoes. Cover and heat to boiling; reduce heat to medium-low. Cover and cook 6 to 8 minutes or until potatoes are tender; drain.

2 Beat eggs, milk, salt and pepper in medium bowl with fork or wire whisk until a uniform yellow color; set aside.

3 Melt margarine in 10-inch skillet over medium-high heat. Add potatoes and cook, turning occasionally, 3 to 5 minutes or until light brown. Stir in onions. Cook 1 minute, stirring constantly.

4 Pour egg mixture into skillet. As mixture begins to set at bottom and side, gently lift cooked portions with spatula so that thin, uncooked portion can flow to bottom. Avoid constant stirring. Cook 3 to 4 minutes or until eggs are cooked throughout but still moist. Sprinkle with bacon.

1 Serving: Calories 320 (Calories from Fat 160); Fat 18g (Saturated 6g); Cholesterol 330mg; Sodium 480mg; Carbohydrate 26g (Dietary Fiber 2g); Protein 15g

Tomato-Basil Omelet

This savory omelet, filled with vine-ripened tomatoes and sweet basil, bursts with summertime flavor.

1 teaspoon olive or vegetable oil

4 medium green onions, chopped (1/4 cup)

1 medium tomato, chopped (3/4 cup)

1 tablespoon chopped fresh or 1 teaspoon dried basil leaves

4 eggs or 1 cup fat-free cholesterol-free egg product

Freshly ground pepper

1 Heat oil in 8-inch nonstick skillet over medium heat. Cook onions in oil 2 minutes, stirring occasionally. Stir in tomato and basil. Cook about 1 minute, stirring occasionally, until tomato is heated through. Beat eggs thoroughly in medium bowl with fork or wire whisk and pour over tomato mixture.

2 As mixture begins to set at bottom and side, gently lift cooked portions with spatula so that thin, uncooked portion can flow to bottom. Avoid constant stirring. Cook 3 to 4 minutes or until eggs are thickened throughout but still moist. Sprinkle with pepper.

1 Serving: Calories 190 (Calories from Fat 115); Fat 13g (Saturated 4g); Cholesterol 425mg; Sodium 140mg; Carbohydrate 6g (Dietary Fiber 1g); Protein 13g

Tomato-Basil Omelet

Hash Brown Potatoes

You don't have to go to a diner to have delicious hash browns. These are sure to become a favorite in your family.

4 medium Idaho or russet baking potatoes (1½ lb)

2 tablespoons finely chopped onion

½ teaspoon salt

⅛ teaspoon pepper

2 tablespoons vegetable oil

1 Shred enough potatoes to measure 4 cups. Rinse well; drain and pat dry.

2 In large bowl, mix potatoes, onion, salt and pepper. In 10-inch nonstick skillet, heat 1 tablespoon of the oil over medium heat. Pack potato mixture firmly in skillet, leaving ½-inch space around edge.

3 Reduce heat to medium-low. Cook about 15 minutes or until bottom is brown. Drizzle remaining oil evenly over potatoes. Cut potato mixture into fourths and turn over. Cook about 12 minutes longer or until bottom is brown.

1 Serving: Calories 160 (Calories from Fat 65); Fat 7g (Saturated 1g); Cholesterol 0mg; Sodium 300mg; Carbohydrate 22g (Dietary Fiber 2g); Protein 2g

Skillet Hash

4 servings | Prep Time: 10 minutes | Start to Finish: 25 minutes

For extra convenience, substitute 2 cups frozen diced hash browns, partially thawed, for the potatoes.

2 cups chopped cooked lean beef or corned beef

4 small potatoes, cooked and chopped (2 cups)

1 medium onion, chopped (½ cup)

1 tablespoon chopped fresh parsley

½ teaspoon salt

⅛ teaspoon pepper

2 to 3 tablespoons vegetable oil

1 In large bowl, mix beef, potatoes, onion, parsley, salt and pepper.

2 In 10-inch skillet, heat oil over medium heat. Spread beef mixture evenly in skillet. Cook 10 to 15 minutes, turning frequently, until brown.

1 Serving: Calories 310 (Calories from Fat 115); Fat 13g (Saturated 3g); Cholesterol 50mg; Sodium 340mg; Carbohydrate 27g (Dietary Fiber 3g); Protein 22g

COUNTRY COOKING WISDOM

Oven Hash

To prepare this hash in the oven, heat oven to 350°F. Spray a square baking dish, 8 x 8 inches, with cooking spray. Omit the oil. Spread beef mixture evenly in baking dish and bake uncovered about 20 minutes or until hot.

Potato Pancakes

These pancakes are a favorite in German and Jewish homes and restaurants. Traditionally they're served with sour cream or applesauce. Try them with sliced green onions or maple syrup too.

- 4 medium Idaho or russet baking potatoes (1½ lb)
- 4 eggs, beaten
- 1 small onion, finely chopped (¼ cup), if desired
- ¼ cup all-purpose flour
- 1 teaspoon salt
- ¼ cup vegetable oil

1 Shred enough potatoes to measure 4 cups. Rinse well; drain and pat dry.

2 In large bowl, mix potatoes, eggs, onion, flour and salt. In 12-inch skillet, heat 2 tablespoons of the oil over medium heat. Using ¼ cup potato mixture for each pancake, place 4 mounds into skillet. Flatten each with spatula to about 4 inches in diameter.

3 Cook pancakes about 2 minutes on each side or until golden brown. Cover to keep warm while cooking remaining pancakes.

4 Repeat with remaining potato mixture. As mixture stands, liquid and potatoes will separate, so stir to mix as necessary. Add remaining oil as needed to prevent sticking.

1 Pancake: Calories 65 (Calories from Fat 35); Fat 4g (Saturated 1g); Cholesterol 55mg; Sodium 160mg; Carbohydrate 8g (Dietary Fiber 1g); Protein 2g

Ultimate Pancakes

Sixteen 4-inch pancakes   Prep Time: 5 minutes   Start to Finish: 15 minutes

Who doesn't love pancakes? These light, fluffy pancakes are great hot off the griddle. For something special, try these favorite mix-ins: raspberries, blueberries, sliced peaches, chocolate chips, sliced bananas, or toasted nuts. Gently mix them into the batter or sprinkle them on top of the pancake after pouring the batter and before flipping them over.

2 eggs

2 cups Original Bisquick® or Bisquick Heart Smart

1 cup milk

2 tablespoons lemon juice

4 teaspoons sugar

2 teaspoons baking powder

1 Beat eggs in medium bowl with hand beater until fluffy; beat in remaining ingredients just until smooth.

2 Heat griddle or skillet over medium heat or to 375°F. Grease heated griddle, if necessary. To test griddle, sprinkle with a few drops of water. If bubbles skitter around, heat is just right.

3 For each pancake, pour slightly less than $1/4$ cup batter onto hot griddle. Cook until edges are dry. Turn; cook until golden.

1 Pancake: Calories 80 (Calories from Fat 25); Fat 3g (Saturated 1g); Cholesterol 30mg; Sodium 290mg; Carbohydrate 11g (Dietary Fiber 0g); Protein 2g

Buckwheat Pancakes

Ten 4-inch pancakes   Prep Time: 15 minutes   Start to Finish: 15 minutes

Pile these wholesome and hearty pancakes high on your plate and serve with Citrus-Banana Compote (page 48) alongside. You'll find buckwheat flour in the flour section of many supermarkets or natural foods stores.

1 egg

$1/2$ cup buckwheat flour

$1/2$ cup whole wheat flour

1 cup milk

1 tablespoon sugar

3 teaspoons baking powder

2 tablespoons shortening, melted, or vegetable oil

$1/2$ teaspoon salt

Whole bran or wheat germ, if desired

1 Beat egg in medium bowl with hand beater until fluffy. Beat in remaining ingredients, except whole bran, just until smooth.

2 Heat griddle or skillet over medium heat or to 375°F. Grease heated griddle, if necessary. To test griddle, sprinkle with a few drops water. If bubbles skitter around, heat is just right.

3 For each pancake, pour slightly less than $1/4$ cup batter onto hot griddle. Cook pancakes until puffed and dry around edges. Sprinkle each pancake with 1 teaspoon whole bran. Turn and cook other sides until golden brown.

1 Pancake: Calories 90 (Calories from Fat 35); Fat 4g (Saturated 1g); Cholesterol 25mg; Sodium 280mg; Carbohydrate 11g (Dietary Fiber 1g); Protein 3g

Best Buttermilk Pancakes

Nine 4-inch pancakes | Prep Time: 15 minutes | Start to Finish: 15 minutes

Drizzle these tender, golden pancakes with rich chocolate sauce, pile on the fresh juicy red raspberries and top them off with a dusting of powdered sugar. Your family will be in seventh heaven.

1 egg
1 cup all-purpose or whole wheat flour
1 cup buttermilk
1 tablespoon granulated or packed brown sugar
2 tablespoons vegetable oil
1 teaspoon baking powder
$1/2$ teaspoon baking soda
$1/4$ teaspoon salt

1 Beat egg in medium bowl with hand beater until fluffy. Beat in remaining ingredients just until smooth. (For thinner pancakes, stir in 1 to 2 tablespoons milk.)

2 Heat griddle or skillet over medium heat or to 375°F. Grease heated griddle, if necessary. To test griddle, sprinkle with a few drops of water. If bubbles jump around, heat is just right.

3 For each pancake, pour slightly less than $1/4$ cup batter from cup or pitcher onto hot griddle. Cook pancakes until puffed and dry around edges. Turn and cook other sides until golden brown.

1 Pancake: Calories 105 (Calories from Fat 35); Fat 4g (Saturated 1g); Cholesterol 25mg; Sodium 220mg; Carbohydrate 14g (Dietary Fiber 0g); Protein 3g

COUNTRY COOKING WISDOM

Pretty Pancakes

One way to turn ordinary pancakes into something spectacular is with the help of a metal cookie cutter. Place the cutter on the grill pan and pour the batter into the cutter. Just before flipping, remove the cutter. Use holiday cutters for special holiday memories or any cutter to celebrate life—flowers for the first of spring, stars for the Fourth of July or leaves for autumn.

Cocoa Pancakes with Strawberries

Eight 4-inch pancakes | Prep Time: 15 minutes | Start to Finish: 15 minutes

Who can resist chocolate and strawberries together? What is great is that these pancakes are good for you too. They are low in fat and cholesterol!

2 egg whites or ¼ cup fat-free cholesterol-free egg product

¾ cup milk

1 tablespoon margarine or butter, melted

¾ cup all-purpose flour

¼ cup sugar

2 tablespoons baking cocoa

1 teaspoon baking powder

⅛ teaspoon salt

⅛ teaspoon ground nutmeg

1 cup vanilla fat-free yogurt, if desired

1 cup sliced strawberries

1 Beat egg whites in medium bowl with hand beater until foamy. Beat in milk and margarine until smooth. Stir in remaining ingredients except yogurt and strawberries.

2 Spray griddle or skillet with nonstick cooking spray. Heat over medium heat or to 375°F. To test griddle, sprinkle with a few drops of water. If bubbles jump around, heat is just right.

3 For each pancake, pour slightly less than ¼ cup batter onto hot griddle. Cook pancakes until puffed and dry around edges. Turn and cook other sides until golden brown. Serve with yogurt and strawberries.

1 Pancake: Calories 95 (Calories from Fat 20); Fat 2g (Saturated 1g); Cholesterol 2mg; Sodium 140mg; Carbohydrate 17g (Dietary Fiber 1g); Protein 3g

COUNTRY COOKING WISDOM

Beautiful Brunches

The next time you're planning a gathering, why not opt for a brunch buffet? Breakfast and brunch foods are perfect for a buffet. And to decorate the table, go for food items. A glass bowl filled with lemons, oranges or apples makes a lovely centerpiece. A basket of fresh artichokes and lemons; a vase of orange slices and cranberries; or a plate with a tall pillar candle surrounded by whole nuts—each of these easily makes a beautiful table setting.

Oatmeal Pancakes with Strawberry Sauce

Six 4-inch pancakes | Prep Time: 20 minutes | Start to Finish: 20 minutes

Start your day off right with the wholesome goodness of fiber-packed oat pancakes. Topped with strawberries, they're a sweet beginning to any morning.

  1 cup quick-cooking oats

3¹/₂ cups milk

  2 cups all-purpose flour

¹/₄ cup margarine or butter, melted

  3 tablespoons sugar

  1 tablespoon baking powder

  2 eggs

  Strawberry Sauce (below right)

1 Mix oats and milk in large bowl; let stand 5 minutes. Add remaining ingredients except Strawberry Sauce. Beat mixture with electric mixer on medium speed until well blended.

2 Heat griddle or skillet over medium heat or to 375°F. Grease heated griddle, if necessary. To test griddle, sprinkle with a few drops of water. If bubbles jump around, heat is just right. For each pancake, pour 3 tablespoons batter onto hot griddle. Cook pancakes until puffed and dry around edges. Turn and cook other side until golden brown. Serve with warm Strawberry Sauce.

Strawberry Sauce
  1 package (10 oz) frozen sliced strawberries, thawed
  2 teaspoons cornstarch

Drain strawberries; reserve liquid. Combine liquid and cornstarch in small saucepan. Cook over medium heat about 1 minute or until mixture boils. Stir in strawberries; cook 1 minute.

1 Pancake: Calories 320 (Calories from Fat 90); Fat 10g (Saturated 3g); Cholesterol 60mg; Sodium 330mg; Carbohydrate 51g (Dietary Fiber 3g); Protein 10g

Banana-Pecan Pancakes

Twenty-seven 4-inch pancakes   Prep Time: 15 minutes   Start to Finish: 15 minutes

No time for pancakes in the mornings? Try the breakfast-for-dinner approach and make sure these wonderful pancakes are on your menu.

2 eggs

2 cups all-purpose flour

2 cups buttermilk

2 cups mashed ripe bananas (4 medium)

1/4 cup granulated or packed brown sugar

1/4 cup vegetable oil

2 teaspoons baking powder

1 teaspoon baking soda

1/2 teaspoon salt

1 cup chopped pecans, toasted, if desired

3 medium bananas, sliced

3 cups strawberry halves

Maple-flavored syrup

Sweetened whipped cream, if desired

Ground nutmeg, if desired

1 Beat eggs in medium bowl with hand beater until fluffy. Beat in flour, buttermilk, mashed bananas, sugar, oil, baking powder, baking soda and salt just until smooth. Stir in pecans. (For thinner pancakes, stir in additional 1 to 2 tablespoons milk.)

2 Heat griddle or skillet over medium heat or to 375°F. Grease heated griddle, if necessary. To test griddle, sprinkle with a few drops of water. If bubbles jump around, heat is just right.

3 For each pancake, pour slightly less than 1/4 cup batter from cup or pitcher onto hot griddle. Cook pancakes until puffed and dry around edges. Turn and cook other sides until golden brown.

4 Serve pancakes with sliced bananas and strawberry halves. Drizzle with syrup. Top with whipped cream; sprinkle with nutmeg.

1 Pancake: Calories 105 (Calories from Fat 25); Fat 3g (Saturated 1g); Cholesterol 15mg; Sodium 150mg; Carbohydrate 18g (Dietary Fiber 1g); Protein 2g

Cinnamon French Toast

4 servings   Prep Time: 10 minutes   Start to Finish: 10 minutes

French toast doesn't get much better than this! Use cinnamon-raisin bread for a real treat, or sprinkle the golden slices of cinnamon bread with raisins.

3 eggs

³/₄ cup milk

1 tablespoon sugar

¹/₄ teaspoon vanilla

¹/₈ teaspoon salt

8 slices cinnamon or plain sandwich bread

1 Beat eggs, milk, sugar, vanilla and salt in medium bowl with hand beater until smooth.

2 Heat griddle or skillet over medium-low heat or to 375°F. Grease heated griddle, if necessary. To test griddle, sprinkle with a few drops of water. If bubbles jump around, heat is just right.

3 Dip bread into egg mixture, coating both sides. Place on griddle. Cook about 4 minutes on each side or until golden brown.

1 Slice: Calories 105 (Calories from Fat 25); Fat 3g (Saturated 1g); Cholesterol 80mg; Sodium 210mg; Carbohydrate 16g (Dietary Fiber 1g); Protein 5g

Surprise French Toast

4 servings   Prep Time: 25 minutes   Start to Finish: 25 minutes

Add an extra "surprise" to your French toast. Spread some bread slices with tangy orange marmalade and some with chunky peanut butter and serve, along with the cream cheese in the recipe. Or use any of your favorite jams or jellies—they'll work too.

1 package (3 oz) cream cheese

16 slices French bread (¹/₂ inch thick)

1 cup milk

4 eggs

2 tablespoons margarine or butter

Powdered sugar

Maple-flavored syrup

1 Spread 1 tablespoon cream cheese on each of 8 bread slices; top with second bread slice. Whisk together milk and eggs in large bowl.

2 Heat griddle or large skillet over medium heat or to 350°F. Melt margarine.

3 Dip sandwiches in egg mixture and carefully place on griddle. Cook about 8 minutes on each side until golden brown. Sprinkle with powdered sugar; serve with syrup.

1 Slice: Calories 485 (Calories from Fat 205); Fat 23g (Saturated 9g); Cholesterol 240mg; Sodium 820mg; Carbohydrate 54g (Dietary Fiber 3g); Protein 19g

Surprise French Toast

Mom's Best Waffles

Twelve 4-inch waffle squares   Prep Time: 5 minutes   Start to Finish: 10 minutes

Mom, you'll get rave reviews when you serve these waffles. They're perfect for weekend breakfasts. If you have any leftovers, just put them in the freezer or refrigerator, so they are ready to pop in the toaster for another delicious breakfast anytime during the week.

2 eggs

2 cups all-purpose or whole wheat flour

1¾ cups milk

½ cup vegetable oil

1 tablespoon granulated or packed brown sugar

4 teaspoons baking powder

¼ teaspoon salt

1 Spray nonstick waffle iron with cooking spray, if necessary. Heat waffle iron.

2 Beat eggs in large bowl with hand beater until fluffy. Beat in remaining ingredients just until smooth.

3 Pour about ½ cup batter onto center of hot waffle iron. (Waffle irons vary in size; check manufacturer's directions for recommended amount of batter.) Close lid of waffle iron.

4 Bake about 5 minutes or until steaming stops. Carefully remove waffle.

1 Waffle Square: Calories 190 (Calories from Fat 100); Fat 11g (Saturated 2g); Cholesterol 40mg; Sodium 240mg; Carbohydrate 19g (Dietary Fiber 0g); Protein 4g

Nut Waffles

Twelve 4-inch waffle squares   Prep Time: 5 minutes   Start to Finish: 10 minutes

Your family will be nutty for these waffles. The kind of nuts you can use is endless—walnuts, pecans, almonds or even pistachios. They're great!

2 eggs

2 cups all-purpose or whole wheat flour

½ cup vegetable oil or margarine or butter, melted

1¾ cups milk

1 tablespoon granulated or brown sugar

4 teaspoons baking powder

¼ teaspoon salt

2 tablespoons coarsely chopped or broken nuts

1 Spray nonstick waffle iron with nonstick cooking spray, if necessary. Heat waffle iron.

2 Beat eggs with hand beater in large bowl until fluffy. Beat in remaining ingredients just until smooth.

3 Pour about ½ cup batter onto center of hot waffle iron. Immediately sprinkle with nuts. (Waffle irons vary in size; check manufacturer's directions for recommended amount of batter.) Close lid of waffle iron.

4 Bake about 5 minutes or until steaming stops. Carefully remove waffle.

1 Waffle Square: Calories 195 (Calories from Fat 110); Fat 12g (Saturated 3g); Cholesterol 40mg; Sodium 240mg; Carbohydrate 19g (Dietary Fiber 1g); Protein 4g

Rise-and-Shine Waffles

Eight 4-inch waffle squares | Prep Time: 15 minutes | Start to Finish: 25 minutes

You won't believe these flavor-packed waffles are also a low-fat, low-cholesterol breakfast. Top off with a spoonful of creamy maple-flavored yogurt—we're sure you'll love them.

3/4 cup old-fashioned oats

1/4 cup packed brown sugar

1 cup milk

2 egg whites, slightly beaten, or 1/4 cup fat-free cholesterol-free egg product

3 tablespoons margarine or butter, melted

2/3 cup all-purpose flour

2 tablespoons wheat germ

2 teaspoons baking powder

1/4 teaspoon baking soda

1 teaspoon grated orange peel

Maple Yogurt Topping (right)

Grated orange peel, if desired

Chopped cranberries, if desired

1 Mix oats, brown sugar and milk in large bowl; let stand 10 minutes. Stir in egg whites and margarine. Stir in flour, wheat germ, baking powder, baking soda and 1 teaspoon orange peel.

2 Spray nonstick waffle iron with cooking spray. Heat waffle iron.

3 Pour about 1/2 cup batter onto center of hot waffle iron. (Waffle irons vary in size; check manufacturer's directions for recommended amount of batter.) Close lid of waffle iron.

4 Bake 4 to 5 minutes or until steaming stops. Carefully remove waffle. Top with Maple Yogurt Topping. Garnish with orange peel and cranberries.

Maple Yogurt Topping
1 cup plain fat-free yogurt
1/4 cup maple-flavored syrup

Mix ingredients in small bowl until well blended.

1 Waffle Square: Calories 200 (Calories from Fat 55); Fat 6g (Saturated 2g); Cholesterol 5mg; Sodium 270mg; Carbohydrate 31g (Dietary Fiber 1g); Protein 6g

Banana and Chocolate Chip Waffles

Mmmmm! Bananas and chocolate together make a winning breakfast combination. Freeze any over-ripe bananas you might have sitting on your counter and you will always have them on hand when the urge hits to make these luscious pancakes.

2 eggs

2 cups all-purpose flour

$1/2$ cup mashed ripe banana (1 medium)

$1^1/2$ cups milk

$1/3$ cup vegetable oil or $1/3$ cup margarine or butter, melted

1 tablespoon sugar

4 teaspoons baking powder

$1/4$ teaspoon salt

$1/2$ cup miniature semisweet chocolate chips

2 medium bananas, sliced

2 tablespoons miniature semisweet chocolate chips

Strawberry-flavored syrup

1 Spray nonstick waffle iron with cooking spray. Heat waffle iron.

2 Beat eggs in medium bowl with electric mixer on medium speed 1 minute. Beat in flour, mashed banana, milk, oil, sugar, baking powder and salt just until smooth. Stir in $1/2$ cup chocolate chips.

3 Pour about $1/2$ cup batter onto center of hot waffle iron. (Waffle irons vary in size; check manufacturer's directions for recommended amount of batter.) Close lid of waffle iron.

4 Bake about 5 minutes or until steaming stops. Carefully remove waffle.

5 Serve waffles with sliced bananas and 2 tablespoons chocolate chips. Drizzle with syrup.

I Waffle Square: Calories 210 (Calories from Fat 90); Fat 10g (Saturated 4g); Cholesterol 40mg; Sodium 240mg; Carbohydrate 31g (Dietary Fiber 1g); Protein 5g

Maple-Pecan Waffles

Twenty-four 4-inch waffle squares | Prep Time: 5 minutes | Start to Finish: 10 minutes

Waffles are such a treat in the morning. The combination of maple and pecans is hard to beat, especially with Date Butter and sweet syrup cascading down your stack of steaming hot waffles!

4 eggs

4 cups all-purpose flour

2 cups milk

1½ cups maple-flavored syrup

1 cup margarine or butter, melted

¼ cup chopped pecans

2 tablespoons baking powder

Date Butter (below right)

1 Spray nonstick waffle iron with cooking spray; heat waffle iron.

2 Beat eggs in large bowl until fluffy; beat in remaining ingredients except Date Butter just until smooth.

3 Pour about ½ cup batter from cup or pitcher onto center of hot waffle iron. (Waffle irons vary in size; check manufacturer's directions for recommended amount of batter.) Close lid of waffle iron.

4 Bake about 5 minutes or until steaming stops. Remove waffle carefully. Serve with Date Butter.

Date Butter
½ cup margarine or butter
¼ cup chopped dates

Mix margarine and dates in small bowl until well blended.

1 Waffle Square: Calories 265 (Calories from Fat 125); Fat 14g (Saturated 3g); Cholesterol 40mg; Sodium 300mg; Carbohydrate 32g (Dietary Fiber 1g); Protein 4g

Danish Puff

The next time you want to treat your co-workers to a little something special, bring in this puff and watch it disappear!

½ cup margarine or butter, softened

2 cups all-purpose flour

2 tablespoons water

½ cup margarine or butter

1 cup water

1 teaspoon almond extract

3 eggs

Powdered Sugar Glaze (below right)

Sliced almonds or chopped nuts

1 Heat oven to 350°F.

2 Cut ½ cup margarine into 1 cup flour until particles are size of small peas. Sprinkle 2 tablespoons water over mixture; mix with fork. Gather pastry in ball; divide in half. Pat each half into rectangle, 12 × 3 inches, about 3 inches apart on ungreased cookie sheet.

3 Heat ½ cup margarine and 1 cup water to rolling boil in 2-quart saucepan; remove from heat. Quickly stir in almond extract and remaining 1 cup flour. Stir vigorously over low heat about 1 minute or until mixture forms a ball; remove from heat. Add eggs and beat until smooth.

4 Spread half of the topping over each rectangle. Bake about 1 hour or until topping is crisp and brown; cool.

5 Spread with Powdered Sugar Glaze; sprinkle with nuts.

Powdered Sugar Glaze

1½ cups powdered sugar

2 tablespoons margarine or butter, softened

1½ teaspoons vanilla

1 to 2 tablespoons warm water

Mix all ingredients in a medium bowl until smooth and spreadable.

2 Puffs (5–6 slices each): Calories 385 (Calories from Fat 215); Fat 24g (Saturated 14g); Cholesterol 120mg; Sodium 160mg; Carbohydrate 38g (Dietary Fiber 1g); Protein 5g

French Breakfast Puffs

15 puffs | Prep Time: 10 minutes | Start to Finish: 25 minutes

Get ready for oohs and aahs when you serve these heavenly rolls. Coated with cinnamon and sugar, these quick-fix breakfast puffs are a favorite in Betty's Kitchens.

$\frac{1}{3}$ cup shortening

1 cup sugar

1 egg

$1\frac{1}{2}$ cups all-purpose flour

$1\frac{1}{2}$ teaspoons baking powder

$\frac{1}{2}$ teaspoon salt

$\frac{1}{4}$ teaspoon ground nutmeg

$\frac{1}{2}$ cup milk

1 teaspoon ground cinnamon

$\frac{1}{2}$ cup margarine or butter, melted

1 Heat oven to 350°F. Grease 15 regular-size muffin cups.

2 In a large bowl, mix shortening, $\frac{1}{2}$ cup of the sugar and the egg thoroughly. Mix flour, baking powder, salt and nutmeg. Stir into egg mixture alternately with milk.

3 Fill muffin cups two-thirds full. Bake 20 to 25 minutes or until golden brown. Mix remaining $\frac{1}{2}$ cup sugar and cinnamon. Roll hot puffs immediately in melted butter, then in sugar-cinnamon mixture. Serve hot.

1 Puff: Calories 205 (Calories from Fat 100); Fat 11g (Saturated 5g); Cholesterol 30mg; Sodium 180mg; Carbohydrate 24g (Dietary Fiber 0g); Protein 2g

Cinnamon Biscuit Fans

8 biscuits | Prep Time: 20 minutes | Start to Finish: 40 minutes

Looking for a shortcut? A fast and easy way to cut margarine into flour mixture is to slice the margarine into smaller pieces and place all the ingredients into the bowl of a food processor. With a few quick pulses, the flour mixture and margarine will cut in perfectly.

1/3 cup firm margarine or butter

2 cups all-purpose flour

2 tablespoons sugar

3 teaspoons baking powder

1/2 teaspoon salt

About 3/4 cup milk

3 tablespoons margarine or butter, softened

3 tablespoons sugar

1 teaspoon ground cinnamon

Glaze (below right)

1 Heat oven to 425°F. Grease 8 regular-size muffin cups.

2 Cut 1/3 cup margarine into flour, 2 tablespoons sugar, the baking powder and salt in large bowl, using pastry blender or crisscrossing 2 knives, until mixture resembles fine crumbs. Stir in just enough milk so dough leaves side of bowl and forms a ball.

3 Turn dough onto lightly floured surface. Knead lightly 10 times. Roll into rectangle, 12 × 10 inches. Spread 3 tablespoons margarine over rectangle. Mix 3 tablespoons sugar and the cinnamon and sprinkle over rectangle. Cut rectangle crosswise into 6 strips, 10 × 2 inches each. Stack strips; cut crosswise into 8 pieces. Place cut sides up in muffin cups.

4 Bake 16 to 18 minutes or until golden brown. Immediately remove from pan. Drizzle Glaze over warm biscuits. Serve warm.

Glaze

1/2 cup powdered sugar

2 to 2 1/2 teaspoons milk

Mix ingredients in a small bowl until smooth and thin enough to drizzle.

1 Biscuit: Calories 295 (Calories from Fat 115); Fat 13g (Saturated 3g); Cholesterol 2mg; Sodium 480mg; Carbohydrate 41g (Dietary Fiber 0g); Protein 4g

Lemon and Poppy Seed Scones

8 scones   Prep Time: 20 minutes   Start to Finish: 35 minutes

Did you know it takes over 900,000 poppy seeds to make one pound? You'll find their crunchy texture and nutty flavor pleasing in these scones.

2 cups all-purpose flour

3 teaspoons baking powder

1/4 teaspoon salt

1/4 cup sugar

1 tablespoon poppy seed

1/3 cup firm margarine or butter

1/3 cup currants

2 tablespoons lemon juice

3/4 cup milk

Sugar, if desired

1 Heat oven to 425°F. Spray cookie sheet with cooking spray.

2 Mix flour, baking powder, salt, sugar and poppy seed in large bowl. Cut in margarine, using pastry blender or crisscrossing 2 knives, until mixture resembles fine crumbs. Stir in currants. Mix lemon juice and milk in a small bowl, and stir into flour mixture.

3 Turn dough onto lightly floured surface. Knead lightly 10 times. Pat or roll into 9-inch circle on ungreased cookie sheet. Brush with milk and sprinkle with sugar. Cut into 8 wedges, but do not separate.

4 Bake 12 to 15 minutes or until golden brown. Immediately remove from cookie sheet and carefully separate wedges. Serve warm.

1 Scone: Calories 240 (Calories from Fat 80); Fat 9g (Saturated 2g); Cholesterol 2mg; Sodium 360mg; Carbohydrate 37g (Dietary Fiber 1g); Protein 4g

Orange-Currant Scones

| 20 scones | Prep Time: 20 minutes | Start to Finish: 30 minutes |

Currants look like tiny, dark raisins. If they are unavailable, you can always substitute dark or golden raisins. If you want to add a sweet-tart twist, mix in dried cranberries or blueberries with the currants.

$^1/_2$ cup currants

$^1/_3$ cup margarine or butter

1$^3/_4$ cups all-purpose flour

3 tablespoons sugar

2$^1/_2$ teaspoons baking powder

$^1/_4$ teaspoon salt

1 tablespoon grated orange peel

1 egg, beaten

4 to 6 tablespoons half-and-half

1 egg white, beaten

1 Heat oven to 400°F.

2 Soak currants in warm water for 10 minutes to soften; drain. Cut margarine into flour, sugar, baking powder and salt in a large bowl, using pastry blender or crisscrossing 2 knives, until mixture resembles fine crumbs. Stir in orange peel, egg, currants and just enough half-and-half until dough leaves side of bowl.

3 Turn dough onto lightly floured surface. Knead lightly 10 times. Divide dough into 2 parts. Roll or pat into two 6-inch circles about $^1/_2$ inch thick. Place on ungreased cookie sheet and brush with beaten egg white.

4 Bake 10 to 12 minutes or until golden brown. Immediately remove from cookie sheet. Cut into wedges to serve.

1 Scone: Calories 95 (Calories from Fat 35); Fat 4g (Saturated 1g); Cholesterol 10mg; Sodium 140mg; Carbohydrate 13g (Dietary Fiber 0g); Protein 2g

COUNTRY COOKING WISDOM

Herbs for Herb

When planning a summer brunch, why not give a small gift to your guests? Place tiny terra-cotta pots filled with various herbs at each place setting. Add small cards to the pots, and your gift doubles as a place card holder. If some of your guests are meeting for the first time, an alliterative connection between the first name and the herb will help your guests remember who they met. For example, use mint for Michelle or Mike, dill weed for Debbie, basil for Barb and rosemary for, well, Rosemary!

Sweet Breakfast Rolls

15 rolls | Prep Time: 40 minutes | Start to Finish: 3 hours 15 minutes

Let the wake-up call be the smell of freshly baked cinnamon rolls wafting through the house. It will be your little secret that you did not have to get up at the crack of dawn to prepare them.

3¹/₂ to 4 cups all-purpose flour

¹/₃ cup granulated sugar

1 teaspoon salt

2 packages regular active dry yeast

1 cup very warm milk (120°F to 130°F)

¹/₃ cup margarine or butter, softened

1 egg

2 tablespoons margarine or butter, softened

2 tablespoons granulated sugar

2 tablespoons packed brown sugar

1 teaspoon ground cinnamon

Glaze (page 37)

1 Mix 2 cups of the flour, ¹/₃ cup granulated sugar, the salt and yeast in large bowl. Add milk, ¹/₃ cup butter and the egg. Beat with electric mixer on low speed 1 minute, scraping bowl frequently. Stir in enough remaining flour, 1 cup at a time, to make dough easy to handle.

2 Turn dough onto lightly floured surface. Knead about 5 minutes or until smooth and elastic. Place in greased bowl and turn greased side up. Cover and let rise in warm place about 1 hour or until double. (Dough is ready if indentation remains when touched.)

3 Grease rectangular pan, 13 × 9 inches.

4 Punch down dough. Flatten with hands or rolling pin into rectangle, 15 × 10 inches, and spread with 2 tablespoons butter. Mix the sugars and cinnamon in a small bowl. Sprinkle evenly over rectangle. Roll up tightly, beginning at 15-inch side. Pinch edge of dough into roll to seal. Stretch and shape to make even.

5 Cut roll into fifteen 1-inch slices. Place slightly apart in pan. Wrap pan tightly with heavy-duty foil. Refrigerate at least 12 hours but no longer than 48 hours. (To bake immediately, do not wrap. Let rise in warm place about 30 minutes or until double. Bake as directed in step 6.)

6 Heat oven to 350°F. Bake uncovered 30 to 35 minutes or until golden brown. Drizzle rolls with Glaze.

1 Roll: Calories 380 (Calories from Fat 145); Fat 16g (Saturated 3g); Cholesterol 15mg; Sodium 320mg; Carbohydrate 55g (Dietary Fiber 1g); Protein 5g

Chocolate Caramel Rolls

15 rolls | Prep Time: 40 minutes | Start to Finish: 3 hours 15 minutes

Gooey chocolate chips melted in between sweet dough! It doesn't get much better than this. These rolls make a nice treat for coffee break or anytime you want a little snack.

3½ cups all-purpose flour

½ cup baking cocoa

⅓ cup granulated sugar

½ teaspoon salt

2 packages regular active dry yeast

1 cup very warm milk (120°F to 130°F)

⅓ cup margarine or butter, softened

1 egg

1 cup packed brown sugar

½ cup margarine or butter

¼ cup dark corn syrup

¾ cup pecan halves

2 tablespoons margarine or butter, softened

½ cup miniature semisweet chocolate chips

2 tablespoons packed brown sugar

1 teaspoon ground cinnamon

1 Mix 2 cups of the flour, the cocoa, granulated sugar, salt, and yeast in large bowl. Add milk, ⅓ cup margarine and the egg. Beat with electric mixer on low speed 1 minute, scraping bowl frequently. Beat on medium speed 1 minute, scraping bowl frequently. Stir in the remaining flour (dough will be stiff).

2 Turn dough onto lightly floured surface. Knead about 5 minutes or until smooth and elastic. Place in greased bowl and turn greased side up. Cover and let rise in warm place about 1 hour 30 minutes or until double. (Dough is ready if indentation remains when touched.)

3 Heat 1 cup brown sugar and ½ cup margarine to boiling in 2-quart saucepan, stirring constantly; remove from heat. Stir in corn syrup. Pour into ungreased rectangular pan, 13 × 9 inches. Sprinkle with pecan halves.

4 Punch down dough. Flatten with hands or rolling pin into rectangle, 15 × 10 inches, on lightly floured surface. Spread with 2 tablespoons margarine. Mix chocolate chips, 2 tablespoons brown sugar and the cinnamon in a small bowl; sprinkle evenly over margarine. Roll up tightly, beginning at 15-inch side. Pinch edge of dough into roll to seal. Stretch and shape until even.

5 Cut roll into fifteen 1-inch slices. Place slightly apart in pan. Cover and let rise in warm place about 30 minutes or until double.

6 Heat oven to 350°F. Bake uncovered 30 to 35 minutes or until dark brown. Immediately turn pan upside down onto heatproof tray or serving plate. Let stand 1 minute so caramel will drizzle over rolls; remove pan.

1 Roll: Calories 390 (Calories from Fat 160); Fat 18g (Saturated 4g); Cholesterol 15mg; Sodium 260mg; Carbohydrate 54g (Dietary Fiber 3g); Protein 6g

Caramel-Pecan Sticky Rolls

15 rolls | Prep Time: 40 minutes | Start to Finish: 3 hours 15 minutes

Save time tomorrow by preparing these rolls today! Prepare dough as directed, but do not let the dough rise after placing rolls in pan. Just cover the pan tightly with heavy-duty foil and pop it in the refrigerator for at least 12 hours, but no longer than 24 hours. In the morning, bake them as directed in the recipe.

3½ to 4 cups all-purpose or bread flour

⅓ cup granulated sugar

1 teaspoon salt

2 packages regular active dry yeast

1 cup very warm milk (120°F to 130°F)

⅓ cup margarine or butter, softened

1 egg

1 cup packed brown sugar

½ cup margarine or butter, softened

¼ cup dark corn syrup

1 cup pecan halves (4 oz)

2 tablespoons stick margarine or butter, softened

½ cup chopped pecans or raisins, if desired

¼ cup granulated or packed brown sugar

1 teaspoon ground cinnamon

1 Mix 2 cups of the flour, ⅓ cup granulated sugar, the salt and yeast in large bowl. Add warm milk, ⅓ cup margarine and the egg. Beat with electric mixer on low speed 1 minute, scraping bowl frequently. Beat on medium speed 1 minute, scraping bowl frequently. Stir in enough remaining flour to make dough easy to handle.

2 Turn dough onto lightly floured surface. Knead about 5 minutes or until smooth and elastic. Place in greased bowl and turn greased side up. Cover and let rise in warm place about 1 hour 30 minutes or until double. (Dough is ready if indentation remains when touched.)

3 Heat 1 cup brown sugar and ½ cup margarine to boiling in 2-quart saucepan, stirring constantly; remove from heat. Stir in corn syrup. Pour into ungreased rectangular pan, 13 × 9 inches. Sprinkle with pecan halves.

4 Punch down dough. Flatten with hands or rolling pin into rectangle, 15 × 10 inches, on lightly floured surface. Spread with 2 tablespoons margarine. Mix chopped pecans, ¼ cup granulated sugar and the cinnamon in a small bowl and sprinkle evenly over margarine. Roll rectangle up tightly, beginning at 15-inch side. Pinch edge of dough into roll to seal. Stretch and shape until even.

5 Cut roll into fifteen 1-inch slices. Place slightly apart in pan. Cover and let rise in warm place about 30 minutes or until double.

6 Heat oven to 350°F. Bake 30 to 35 minutes or until golden brown. Immediately turn upside down onto heatproof tray or serving plate. Let stand 1 minute so caramel will drizzle over rolls; remove pan. Serve warm.

1 Roll: Calories 370 (Calories from Fat 155); Fat 17g (Saturated 3g); Cholesterol 15mg; Sodium 300mg; Carbohydrate 51g (Dietary Fiber 2g); Protein 5g

Overnight Cinnamon Rolls

24 rolls | Prep Time: 15 minutes | Start to Finish: 15 hours 15 minutes

Don't want to wait all night for these cinnamon rolls? You don't have to. Just skip the part about wrapping them in Step 5. Instead, let the rolls rise in a warm place about 30 minutes or until they double in size. Then, just bake them as directed in Step 6 and enjoy.

2 packages regular active dry yeast

1/2 cup warm water (105°F to 115°F)

2 cups very warm milk (120°F to 130°F)

1/3 cup sugar

1/3 cup vegetable oil or shortening

3 teaspoons baking powder

2 teaspoons salt

1 egg

6 1/2 to 7 1/2 cups all-purpose flour

4 tablespoons margarine or butter, softened

1/2 cup sugar

1 tablespoon plus 1 teaspoon ground cinnamon

Powdered Sugar Frosting (below right)

1 Dissolve yeast in warm water in large bowl. Stir in milk, 1/3 cup sugar, the oil, baking powder, salt, egg and 3 cups of the flour. Beat until smooth. Stir in enough remaining flour, 1 cup at a time, to make dough easy to handle.

2 Turn dough onto well-floured surface. Knead about 10 minutes or until smooth and elastic. Place in greased bowl and turn greased side up. Cover and let rise in warm place about 1 hour 30 minutes or until double. (Dough is ready if indentation remains when touched.)

3 Grease bottom and sides of 2 rectangular pans, 13 × 9 inches.

4 Punch down dough and divide in half. Flatten one half with hands or rolling pin into rectangle, 12 × 10 inches, on lightly floured surface. Spread with 2 tablespoons of the margarine. Mix 1/2 cup sugar and the cinnamon. Sprinkle half of the sugar-cinnamon mixture over rectangle. Roll up, beginning at 12-inch side. Pinch edge of dough into roll to seal. Stretch and shape until even.

5 Cut roll into 12 slices. Place slightly apart in pan. Wrap pan tightly with heavy-duty foil. Repeat with other half of dough. Refrigerate at least 12 hours but no longer than 24 hours. (To bake immediately, do not wrap. Let rise in warm place about 30 minutes or until double. Bake as directed in step 6.)

6 Heat oven to 350°F. Remove foil from pans. Bake 30 to 35 minutes or until golden. Frost with Powdered Sugar Frosting while warm.

Powdered Sugar Frosting

2 cups powdered sugar

2 tablespoons milk

1 teaspoon vanilla

Mix all ingredients in medium bowl until smooth and spreadable.

1 Roll: Calories 250 (Calories from Fat 55); Fat 6g (Saturated 2g); Cholesterol 15mg; Sodium 280mg; Carbohydrate 45g (Dietary Fiber 1g); Protein 5g

Sour Cream Coffee Cake

16 servings | Prep Time: 30 minutes | Start to Finish: 1 hour 50 minutes

Layered with a delicious nut filling and drizzled with a pretty powdered sugar glaze, this coffee cake is an easy and popular cake to serve at morning get-togethers. Choose either the cinnamon or almond filling.

Cinnamon Filling or Almond Filling (below right)

1 1/2 cups sugar

3/4 cup margarine or butter, softened

1 1/2 teaspoons vanilla

3 eggs

3 cups all-purpose or whole wheat flour

1 1/2 teaspoons baking powder

1 1/2 teaspoons baking soda

3/4 teaspoon salt

1 1/2 cups sour cream

1/2 cup powdered sugar

1/4 teaspoon vanilla

1 to 2 teaspoons milk

1 Heat oven to 325°F. Grease tube pan, 10 × 4 inches, or 12-cup bundt cake pan.

2 Make Cinnamon Filling or Almond Filling; set aside.

3 Beat granulated sugar, margarine, vanilla and eggs in 2 1/2-quart bowl with electric mixer on medium speed 2 minutes, scraping bowl occasionally. Beat in flour, baking powder, baking soda and salt alternately with sour cream on low speed.

4 Spread one-third of the batter (about 2 cups) in pan. Sprinkle with one-third of the filling (about 1/3 cup). Repeat 2 times.

5 Bake about 1 hour or until toothpick inserted near center comes out clean. Cool 20 minutes; remove from pan.

6 Mix powdered sugar, vanilla and milk in medium bowl until smooth and of desired consistency. Drizzle over coffee cake.

Cinnamon Filling

1/2 cup packed brown sugar
1/2 cup finely chopped nuts
1 1/2 teaspoons ground cinnamon

Mix all ingredients in a small bowl.

Almond Filling

1/2 package (7- to 8.8-ounce size) almond paste, cut into small pieces
1/2 cup powdered sugar
1/4 cup margarine or butter
1/2 cup sliced almonds

Cook almond paste, powdered sugar and margarine in medium saucepan over medium heat, stirring constantly, until smooth. Stir in almonds.

1 Serving: Calories 340 (Calories from Fat 145); Fat 16g (Saturated 5g); Cholesterol 55mg; Sodium 410mg; Carbohydrate 47g (Dietary Fiber 3g); Protein 5g

Blueberry Buckle Coffee Cake

9 servings   Prep Time: 15 minutes   Start to Finish: 1 hour 15 minutes

This "buckle" is made by tossing summer fruit into a sweet cake batter and sprinkling with a buttery crumb topping. The juicy blueberries will bubble and ooze up through the cake batter and add a bit of summery sweetness in each bite of this delicious cake.

2 cups all-purpose flour

³/₄ cup sugar

2¹/₂ teaspoons baking powder

³/₄ teaspoon salt

¹/₄ cup shortening

³/₄ cup milk

1 egg

2 cups fresh or frozen (thawed and drained) blueberries

Crumb Topping (right)

Glaze (below right)

1 Heat oven to 375°F. Grease square pan, 9 × 9 inches, or round pan, 9 inches.

2 Blend flour, sugar, baking powder, salt, shortening, milk and egg in a large bowl; beat with an electric mixer 30 seconds. Carefully stir in blueberries. Spread butter in pan and sprinkle with Crumb Topping.

3 Bake 45 to 50 minutes or until toothpick inserted in center comes out clean. Drizzle with Glaze. Serve warm.

Crumb Topping

¹/₂ cup sugar

¹/₃ cup all-purpose flour

¹/₂ teaspoon ground cinnamon

¹/₄ cup margarine or butter, softened

Mix all ingredients in small bowl until crumbly.

Glaze

¹/₂ cup powdered sugar

¹/₄ teaspoon vanilla

1¹/₂ to 2 teaspoons hot water

Mix all ingredients in small bowl until drizzling consistency.

1 Serving: Calories 380 (Calories from Fat 110); Fat 12g (Saturated 5g); Cholesterol 40mg; Sodium 390mg; Carbohydrate 65g (Dietary Fiber 2g); Protein 5g

COUNTRY COOKING WISDOM

Bountiful Blueberries

Seasonal blueberries are sweet and flavorful. Whether you've picked them off the vine or supermarket shelf, stock up when they are abundant. Freezing berries for later in the year is a breeze—simply place, unwashed, in a resealable freezer storage bag, label and freeze. Wash them just before using.

Citrus-Banana Compote

6 servings | Prep Time: 10 minutes | Start to Finish: 15 minutes

This sweet compote is wonderful over pancakes or even as a dessert topping spooned over ice cream, pound cake or angel food cake. Even better—the lime juice and oranges keep the sliced banana looking fresh.

1/2 cup sugar

1/2 cup water

2 tablespoons grated orange peel

2 tablespoons grated lime peel

4 bananas, peeled and sliced

2 oranges, peeled and cut into sections

2 tablespoons lime juice

1 Heat sugar and water to boiling in small saucepan over medium heat. Stir in orange peel and lime peel and boil 2 minutes, stirring occasionally. Remove from heat and let mixture stand 5 minutes.

2 Mix bananas and oranges with lime juice in medium bowl. Pour warm syrup over fruit. Serve fruit warm.

1 Serving: Calories 155 (Calories from Fat 0); Fat 0g (Saturated 0g); Cholesterol 0mg; Sodium 0mg; Carbohydrate 41g (Dietary Fiber 3g); Protein 1g

Key West Fruit Salad

8 servings | Prep Time: 25 minutes | Start to Finish: 2 hours 25 minutes

This salad makes about 14 cups, so it's perfect for potlucks, open houses, graduations and showers as well as brunches.

3/4 cup sugar

1/4 cup water

1/4 cup fresh or bottled Key lime juice or regular lime juice

2 to 3 tablespoons tequila or Key lime juice

1 teaspoon grated Key lime peel or regular lime peel

14 cups cut-up fresh fruit (such as pineapple, strawberries, kiwifruit or grapes)

1 Heat sugar and water to boiling in 1 1/2-quart saucepan; reduce heat. Simmer uncovered about 2 minutes, stirring constantly, until sugar is dissolved. Remove from heat. Stir in lime juice and tequila.

2 Let lime dressing stand until room temperature. Cover and refrigerate about 2 hours or until cool.

3 Stir lime peel into dressing. In very large bowl, carefully toss fruit and dressing. Serve immediately.

1 Serving: Calories 65 (Calories from Fat 0); Fat 0g (Saturated 0g); Cholesterol 0mg; Sodium 5mg; Carbohydrate 16g (Dietary Fiber 2g); Protein 1g

Apple-Pear Salad

8 servings | Prep Time: 25 minutes | Start to Finish: 25 minutes

Fruits, veggies and cheese burst with flavor when tossed with this light and natural dressing.

- 1 large red apple, cut into fourths, then cut crosswise into thin slices
- 1 large pear, cut into fourths, then cut crosswise into thin slices
- 1 medium stalk celery, cut diagonally into thin slices (1/2 cup)
- 4 oz Havarti cheese, cut into julienne strips
- 3 tablespoons olive or vegetable oil
- 2 tablespoons frozen (thawed) apple juice concentrate
- 3 tablespoons coarsely chopped honey-roasted peanuts

1 In medium salad bowl, mix apple, pear, celery and cheese.

2 In small bowl, thoroughly mix oil and juice concentrate. Pour over apple mixture and toss to coat. Sprinkle with peanuts.

1 Serving: Calories 150 (Calories from Fat 100); Fat 11g (Saturated 4g); Cholesterol 15mg; Sodium 110mg; Carbohydrate 10g (Dietary Fiber 1g); Protein 3g

Peach and Plum Salad

6 servings | Prep Time: 10 minutes | Start to Finish: 10 minutes

What a beautiful and inviting fruit salad, boasting colorful ingredients and nuts!

- 3 medium plums, sliced
- 3 medium peaches, sliced
- 1/2 cup coarsely chopped walnuts, toasted
- 1/4 cup raspberry preserves
- 2 tablespoons red wine vinegar or white vinegar
- 1 tablespoon vegetable oil

1 Arrange plums and peaches on serving plate. Sprinkle with walnuts.

2 In small bowl, mix remaining ingredients and drizzle over fruit.

1 Serving: Calories 170 (Calories from Fat 80); Fat 9g (Saturated 1g); Cholesterol 0mg; Sodium 5mg; Carbohydrate 21g (Dietary Fiber 2g); Protein 2g

CHAPTER TWO
Blue-Ribbon Lunches and Lighter Fare

SCRUMPTIOUS SANDWICHES, SNAPPY FRESH SALADS AND SOUL-SATISFYING SOUPS ARE RIGHT HERE. THESE ARE YOUR FAVORITE LUNCHTIME MEALS.

Stack them high or wrap them up, you'll find easy-to-make sandwiches that give an irresistible spin to American classics. Robust or delicately flavored, the soups are one-pot meals for every season or mood. A meal in itself, there's nothing like a salad to satisfy our craving for variety, texture and complex flavors. If you "brown bag" it at the office or are looking for great picnic ideas, all your lunch favorites are here, waiting for you to enjoy.

Minestrone with Pesto

6 servings   Prep Time: 15 minutes   Start to Finish: 30 minutes

The great thing about minestrone is that you can use whatever vegetables are in season. White cannellini beans can also be used in place of the kidney beans. The swirl of pesto stirred in before serving is a flavorful, fresh-tasting addition to the soup.

4 cups raw vegetable pieces (carrots, celery, zucchini or yellow summer squash, green beans, cut into 1-inch slices, chopped tomatoes or shelled peas)

1 oz uncooked spaghetti, broken into 2- to 3-inch pieces, or ¹/₂ cup uncooked macaroni

¹/₂ teaspoon dried basil leaves

¹/₂ teaspoon pepper

1 medium onion, chopped (¹/₂ cup)

1 clove garlic, finely chopped

1 can (15 oz) kidney or garbanzo beans, undrained

2 cans (10.5 oz each) condensed beef broth

2 broth cans (10.5 oz each) water

5 oz spinach, cut crosswise into ¹/₄-inch strips

Prepared pesto

Grated Parmesan cheese, if desired

1 Heat all ingredients except spinach, pesto and cheese to boiling in 4-quart Dutch oven; reduce heat.

2 Cover and simmer, about 10 minutes, until vegetables and spaghetti are tender. Stir in spinach until wilted. Serve with pesto and grated Parmesan cheese.

1 Serving: Calories 200 (Calories from Fat 80); Fat 9g (Saturated 2g); Cholesterol 2mg; Sodium 800mg; Carbohydrate 24g (Dietary Fiber 6g); Protein 12g

Great-Tasting Gazpacho

4 servings   Prep Time: 10 minutes   Start to Finish: 1 hour 15 minutes

Gazpacho is a cold tomato-vegetable soup, perfect for sultry summertime weather. Popular garnishes of gazpacho include croutons, a dollop of sour cream or yogurt or chopped hard-boiled eggs.

1 can (28 oz) whole tomatoes, undrained

1 medium green bell pepper, finely chopped (1 cup)

1 cup finely chopped cucumber

1 medium onion, chopped (¹/₂ cup)

1 cup croutons

2 tablespoons dry white wine or chicken broth

2 tablespoons olive or vegetable oil

1 tablespoon ground cumin

1 tablespoon white vinegar

¹/₂ teaspoon salt

¹/₄ teaspoon pepper

1 Place tomatoes, ½ cup of the bell pepper, ½ cup of the cucumber, ¼ cup of the onion, ½ cup of the croutons and the remaining ingredients in blender or food processor. Cover and blend on medium speed until smooth.

2 Cover and refrigerate at least 1 hour. Serve remaining vegetables and croutons as accompaniments.

1 Serving: Calories 150 (Calories from Fat 70); Fat 8g (Saturated 2g); Cholesterol 0mg; Sodium 670mg; Carbohydrate 19g (Dietary Fiber 3g); Protein 4g

Creamy Tomato-Beef Noodle Soup

4 servings | Prep Time: 5 minutes | Start to Finish: 30 minutes

This is a creamy tomato soup that makes a great lunch or light supper. Kids will love slurping up the noodles and dunking in bits of breadsticks.

1 lb ground beef

1 small onion, chopped (¼ cup)

½ cup frozen green peas

2 cups tomato juice

1¼ cups water

¾ teaspoon chopped fresh or ¼ teaspoon dried marjoram leaves

⅛ teaspoon pepper

1 bay leaf

1 can (10.75 oz) condensed cream of celery soup

1 cup uncooked egg noodles (2 oz)

1 Cook beef and onion in Dutch oven over medium heat about 10 minutes, stirring occasionally, until beef is brown; drain.

2 Stir in remaining ingredients except noodles. Heat to boiling. Stir in noodles; reduce heat. Simmer uncovered about 10 minutes, stirring occasionally, until noodles are tender. Remove bay leaf.

1 Serving: Calories 370 (Calories from Fat 180); Fat 20g (Saturated 8g); Cholesterol 85mg; Sodium 1,080mg; Carbohydrate 24g (Dietary Fiber 2g); Protein 25g

Chunky Tomato Soup

8 servings | Prep Time: 20 minutes | Start to Finish: 1 hour 20 minutes

A quick whirl in a blender or food processor will smooth out this soup without sacrificing any flavor. Kids will love it if you stir in some cooked alphabet noodles for some lunchtime fun.

2 tablespoons olive or vegetable oil

2 cloves garlic, finely chopped

2 medium stalks celery, coarsely chopped (1 cup)

2 medium carrots, coarsely chopped (1 cup)

2 cans (28 oz each) whole Italian-style tomatoes, undrained

2 cups water

1 teaspoon dried basil leaves

½ teaspoon pepper

2 cans (14.5 oz each) chicken broth

8 slices hard-crusted Italian or French bread, each 1 inch thick, toasted

Grated Parmesan cheese, if desired

1 Heat oil in Dutch oven over medium-high heat. Cook garlic, celery and carrots in oil 5 to 7 minutes, stirring frequently, until carrots are crisp-tender.

2 Stir in tomatoes, breaking up tomatoes coarsely. Stir in water, basil, pepper and broth. Heat to boiling; reduce heat. Cover and simmer 1 hour, stirring occasionally.

3 Place 1 slice toast in each of 8 bowls. Ladle soup over toast. Sprinkle with cheese. Serve immediately.

1 Serving: Calories 175 (Calories from Fat 55); Fat 6g (Saturated 1g); Cholesterol 0mg; Sodium 840mg; Carbohydrate 26g (Dietary Fiber 3g); Protein 7g

Tomato Vegetable Soup with Yogurt

Yogurt adds a nice creaminess to this soup without adding unwanted calories or fat. The yogurt is added at the end so it doesn't boil or become curdled.

- 1 can (24 oz) tomato juice (3 cups)
- 1/4 to 1/2 teaspoon ground red pepper
- 1/4 teaspoon salt
- 1 package (10 oz) frozen whole kernel corn
- 1 bunch green onions (about 6), sliced
- 1 medium red or green bell pepper, coarsely chopped
- 1 medium zucchini, coarsely chopped
- 1 container (18 oz) plain yogurt
- Cilantro or parsley, if desired

1 Heat all ingredients except yogurt to boiling in 4-quart Dutch oven; reduce heat. Simmer uncovered 7 to 8 minutes, stirring occasionally, until vegetables are crisp-tender. Remove from heat. Cool 5 minutes before adding yogurt.

2 Stir yogurt into soup until smooth. Heat over medium heat, stirring constantly, just until hot (do not boil). Garnish with snipped cilantro or parsley.

1 Serving: Calories 195 (Calories from Fat 45); Fat 5g (Saturated 3g); Cholesterol 15mg; Sodium 880mg; Carbohydrate 32g (Dietary Fiber 4g); Protein 9g

COUNTRY COOKING WISDOM

Cooking Yogurt

When yogurt is added to a hot mixture, it can separate if it gets too hot, looking curdled. To prevent curdling, bring the yogurt to room temperature. Gently stirring the yogurt will help as well as adding it at the last moment and heating the mixture just until hot. Boiling will surely separate the yogurt. If it does separate, stir 1 teaspoon of cornstarch into 2 teaspoons water until dissolved. Stir this into the separated mixture over low heat just until the yogurt is no longer separated.

Tomato Vegetable Soup with Yogurt *(left)* and
Grilled Three-Cheese Sandwiches *(right*, page 83)

Vegetable-Beef Soup

7 servings   Prep Time: 20 minutes   Start to Finish: 3 hours 50 minutes

Want to make this soup in a snap? Use 4 cups canned beef broth and 3 cups cut-up cooked beef for the Beef and Broth. You can also keep it speedy by using 1 cup each frozen corn kernels, peas and green beans for the fresh.

Beef and Broth (right)

1 ear corn

2 medium potatoes, cubed (2 cups)

2 medium tomatoes, chopped (1½ cups)

1 medium carrot, thinly sliced (½ cup)

1 medium stalk celery, sliced (½ cup)

1 cup 1-inch pieces green beans

1 cup shelled green peas

¼ teaspoon pepper

1 Make Beef and Broth. Add enough water to broth to measure 5 cups. Return strained beef and broth to Dutch oven.

2 Cut kernels from corn. Stir corn and remaining ingredients into broth. Heat to boiling; reduce heat to low. Cover and simmer about 30 minutes or until vegetables are tender.

Beef and Broth

2 lb beef shank crosscuts or soup bones

6 cups cold water

1 teaspoon salt

¼ teaspoon dried thyme leaves

1 medium carrot, cut up

1 medium stalk celery with leaves, cut up

1 small onion, cut up

5 peppercorns

3 whole cloves

3 sprigs parsley

1 bay leaf

1 Remove marrow from center of bones. Heat marrow in Dutch oven over low heat until melted, or heat 2 tablespoons vegetable oil until hot. Cook beef shanks over medium heat until brown on both sides.

2 Add water; heat to boiling. Skim foam from broth. Stir in remaining ingredients and heat to boiling. Skim foam from broth. Reduce heat to low; cover and simmer 3 hours.

3 Remove beef from broth. Cool beef about 10 minutes or just until cool enough to handle. Strain broth through cheesecloth-lined sieve. Discard vegetables and seasonings.

4 Remove beef from bones. Cut beef into ½-inch pieces. Skim fat from broth. Use immediately, or cover and refrigerate broth and beef in separate containers up to 24 hours or freeze for future use.

1 Serving: Calories 235 (Calories from Fat 80); Fat 9g (Saturated 4g); Cholesterol 50mg; Sodium 440mg; Carbohydrate 19g (Dietary Fiber 3g); Protein 22g

Chicken Noodle Soup

4 servings | Prep Time: 10 minutes | Start to Finish: 25 minutes

When you're feeling a little under the weather, what's better than a warm, soothing bowl of golden chicken noodle soup? Even better, this soup can be made in under 30 minutes!

- 2 tablespoons olive or vegetable oil
- 2 cloves garlic, finely chopped
- 2 medium green onions, chopped (2 tablespoons)
- 1 medium carrot, sliced ($1/2$ cup)
- 2 cups cubed cooked chicken
- 1 cup 2-inch pieces uncooked spaghetti or 4 oz uncooked egg noodles
- 1 tablespoon chopped fresh parsley or 1 teaspoon dried parsley flakes
- $1/2$ teaspoon ground nutmeg
- $1/4$ teaspoon pepper
- 1 dried bay leaf
- 3 cans (14.5 oz each) chicken broth

1 Heat oil in 3-quart saucepan over medium heat. Cook garlic, onions and carrot in oil about 4 minutes, stirring occasionally, until carrot is crisp-tender.

2 Stir in remaining ingredients. Heat to boiling; reduce heat. Cover and simmer about 15 minutes, stirring occasionally, until spaghetti is tender.

3 Remove bay leaf.

1 Serving: Calories: 360 (Calories from Fat 125); Fat 14g (Saturated 3g); Cholesterol 55mg; Sodium 1,120mg; Carbohydrate 30g (Dietary Fiber 2g), Protein 31g

COUNTRY COOKING WISDOM

Simple Soups

Soups are a staple in the country kitchen—they are the perfect way to use farm-fresh vegetables or leftover meals. Keep broths on hand to make quick homemade soups anytime. Stir bite-size pieces of fresh or frozen vegetables and uncooked pasta or rice into simmering broth. Cook 12 to 15 minutes or until the vegetables and pasta or rice are tender. If you'd like, add small chunks of cooked beef, poultry or fish, and heat through.

Chicken Tortellini Soup

8 servings Prep Time: 5 minutes Start to Finish: 20 minutes

Cheese-stuffed tender pasta floating in steamy chicken broth will provide comfort and warmth to rejuvenate your soul. Some hot, homemade Buttermilk Biscuits (page 254) might help, too.

¼ cup margarine or butter

½ cup finely chopped onion

½ cup finely chopped celery

4 boneless, skinless chicken breast halves, cut into 1-inch pieces (about 1½ lb)

¼ cup all-purpose flour

½ teaspoon pepper

4½ cups chicken broth

1 package (16 oz) cheese-filled tortellini, cooked

Parmesan cheese

1 Melt margarine in large saucepan. Cook onion, celery and chicken in margarine over medium heat about 8 minutes, stirring frequently, or until chicken is done.

2 Stir in flour and pepper. Gradually add chicken broth. Cook over medium heat, stirring constantly until mixture boils; boil 1 minute.

3 Stir in tortellini and heat until warm. Serve with Parmesan cheese.

1 Serving: Calories 245 (Calories from Fat 110); Fat 12g (Saturated 3g); Cholesterol 85mg; Sodium 720mg; Carbohydrate 14g (Dietary Fiber 1g); Protein 21g

New England Clam Chowder

4 servings Prep Time: 5 minutes Start to Finish: 30 minutes

New Englanders claim to have invented this hearty all-white clam chowder. It evolved from a fisherman's dish, made up of layers of salt pork, fish and dough, all cooked up in a large kettle. Later, milk was added to the mixture to make it more of a stew, clams replaced the fish, and potatoes were swapped for the dough.

¼ cup cut-up bacon or lean salt pork

1 medium onion, chopped (½ cup)

2 cans (6.5 oz each) minced clams, drained and liquid reserved

2 cups diced potatoes (3 medium)

Dash of pepper

2 cups milk

1 Cook bacon and onion in 2-quart saucepan over medium heat, stirring frequently, until bacon is crisp.

2 Add enough water, if necessary, to reserve clam liquid to measure 1 cup. Stir clams, liquid, potatoes and pepper into onion mixture. Heat to boiling; reduce heat.

3 Cover and boil about 15 minutes or until potatoes are tender. Stir in milk. Heat, stirring occasionally, just until hot (do not boil).

1 Serving: Calories 215 (Calories from Fat 0); Fat 6g (Saturated 0g); Cholesterol 45mg; Sodium 200mg; Carbohydrate 20g (Dietary Fiber 0g); Protein 20g

Manhattan Clam Chowder

5 servings   Prep Time: 10 minutes   Start to Finish: 30 minutes

I'll take Manhattan . . . chowder, that is! Rich, tomatoey broth, chock-full of smoky bacon, tender potatoes and sweet fresh clams makes this soup the talk of the town.

- $1/4$ cup finely chopped bacon or salt pork
- 1 small onion, finely chopped ($1/4$ cup)
- 1 pint shucked fresh clams with liquor*
- 2 cups finely chopped potatoes
- $1/3$ cup chopped celery
- 1 cup water
- 2 teaspoons chopped fresh parsley
- $1/2$ teaspoon salt
- 1 teaspoon chopped fresh or $1/4$ teaspoon dried thyme leaves
- $1/8$ teaspoon pepper
- 1 can (16 oz) whole tomatoes, undrained

1 Cook bacon and onion in Dutch oven, stirring occasionally, until bacon is crisp and onion is tender.

2 Stir clams and clam liquor, potatoes, celery and water into bacon and onion. Heat to boiling; reduce heat. Cover and simmer about 10 minutes or until potatoes are tender.

3 Stir in remaining ingredients, breaking up tomatoes. Heat to boiling, stirring occasionally.

2 cans (6.5 oz each) minced clams, undrained, can be substituted for fresh clams. Stir in clams with remaining ingredients.

1 Serving: Calories 210 (Calories from Fat 0); Fat 13g (Saturated 0g); Cholesterol 15mg; Sodium 610mg; Carbohydrate 17g (Dietary Fiber 0g); Protein 7g

Cream of Broccoli Soup

For a lighter cream soup, we suggest using half-and-half or milk in place of the whipping cream. Look for broccoli with tight, compact heads and a nice green color throughout. Stay away from broccoli flowerets that are starting to yellow.

1½ lb broccoli

2 cups water

1 large stalk celery, chopped (¾ cup)

1 medium onion, chopped (½ cup)

2 tablespoons margarine or butter

2 tablespoons all-purpose flour

2½ cups chicken broth

½ teaspoon salt

⅛ teaspoon pepper

Dash of ground nutmeg

½ cup whipping cream

Shredded cheese, if desired

1 Remove flowerets from broccoli; set aside. Cut stalks into 1-inch pieces.

2 Heat water to boiling in 3-quart saucepan. Add broccoli flowerets and pieces, celery and onion. Cover and heat to boiling. Boil about 10 minutes or until broccoli is tender (do not drain).

3 Carefully place broccoli mixture in blender. Cover and blend on medium speed until smooth.

4 Melt margarine in 3-quart saucepan over medium heat. Stir in flour. Cook, stirring constantly, until mixture is smooth and bubbly; remove from heat.

5 Stir broth into flour mixture. Heat to boiling, stirring constantly. Boil and stir 1 minute.

6 Stir in broccoli mixture, salt, pepper and nutmeg. Heat just to boiling. Stir in whipping cream. Heat just until hot (do not boil). Serve with cheese.

1 Serving: Calories 105 (Calories from Fat 70); Fat 8g (Saturated 4g); Cholesterol 15mg; Sodium 440mg; Carbohydrate 6g (Dietary Fiber 2g); Protein 4g

Cheesy Cauliflower Soup

5 servings | Prep Time: 5 minutes | Start to Finish: 1 hour 45 minutes

Did you know cauliflower comes in three different colors? The most popular and easy to find is white, but you can also find green and a vibrant purple (which turns pale green when cooked). All three varieties can be used in this recipe, or you can substitute broccoflower—a hybrid of broccoli and cauliflower.

2 cups water

1 small head cauliflower (about 1 lb), broken into large flowerets, or
2 packages (8 oz each) frozen cauliflower

1 medium stalk celery, cut into $1/2$-inch pieces

1 medium carrot, cut into $1/2$-inch pieces

1 small onion, cut into eighths

1 tablespoon instant chicken bouillon (dry)

$1/4$ teaspoon lemon and pepper seasoning salt

1 can (5 oz) evaporated milk

$1^1/2$ cups shredded Harvati or Monterey Jack cheese (6 oz)

1 Cover and cook all ingredients except milk and cheese in 3-quart saucepan over medium-low heat about 1 hour 30 minutes or until vegetables are very tender.

2 Carefully pour mixture into food processor fitting with steel blade or into blender. Cover and process until smooth.

3 Return mixture to saucepan. Stir in milk and cheese. Heat over medium heat, stirring constantly, until cheese is melted and mixture is hot.

1 Serving: Calories 200 (Calories from Fat 115); Fat 13g (Saturated 8g); Cholesterol 40mg; Sodium 1,110mg; Carbohydrate 10g (Dietary Fiber 2g); Protein 13g

Vegetable–Cheddar Cheese Soup

8 servings | Prep Time: 5 minutes | Start to Finish: 20 minutes

For lunch or dinner, this creamy, colorful cheese soup is popular with adults and kids alike. Warm whole-grain bread or rolls are perfect for sopping up and dunking in the soup.

½ cup margarine or butter

2 medium carrots, finely chopped (1 cup)

1 medium onion, finely chopped (½ cup)

1 medium stalk celery, finely chopped (½ cup)

2 medium zucchini, cut into 2-inch strips

½ cup all-purpose flour

1 teaspoon dry mustard

2 cups chicken broth

2 cups half-and-half

3 cups shredded Cheddar cheese

1 Melt margarine in Dutch oven. Cook carrot, onion and celery in margarine until softened. Stir in zucchini and cook about 2 minutes or until crisp-tender. Mix flour and mustard; stir into vegetable mixture.

2 Gradually stir in chicken broth and half-and-half. Cook over medium heat, stirring constantly, until mixture boils; boil 1 minute. Slowly stir in cheese until melted.

1 Serving: Calories 400 (Calories from Fat 295); Fat 33g (Saturated 15g); Cholesterol 65mg; Sodium 710mg; Carbohydrate 13g (Dietary Fiber 2g); Protein 15g

Green Pea Soup

4 servings | Prep Time: 5 minutes | Start to Finish: 20 minutes

For a beautiful color contrast, garnish this bright green soup with a dollop of sour cream or yogurt. If you have any soup left over, reheat it gently over low heat. Avoid boiling this soup once the cream is added so it won't curdle.

1 package (16 oz) frozen green peas

1 cup milk

2 tablespoons margarine or butter

2 tablespoons all-purpose flour

¾ teaspoon salt

⅛ teaspoon pepper

½ cup whipping cream or half-and-half

Mint leaves, if desired

1 Cook peas as directed on package. Reserve ½ cup for garnish, if desired.

2 Place remaining peas and the milk in food processor fitted with steel blade or in blender. Cover and process until of uniform consistency.

3 Melt margarine in 2-quart saucepan. Stir in flour, salt and pepper. Cook, stirring constantly, until smooth and bubbly. Remove from heat; stir in pea mixture.

4 Heat to boiling, stirring constantly. Boil and stir 1 minute. Stir in cream and heat just until hot (do not boil). Garnish each serving with reserved peas and mint leaves.

1 Serving: Calories 225 (Calories from Fat 135); Fat 16g (Saturated 8g); Cholesterol 40mg; Sodium 650mg; Carbohydrate 21g (Dietary Fiber 6g); Protein 8g

Vegetable–Cheddar Cheese Soup

Wild Rice Soup

5 servings | Prep Time: 10 minutes | Start to Finish: 35 minutes

Native Americans called wild rice *mahnomen,* or "precious grain." This delicacy isn't actually rice but is a grain from an aquatic plant. Cooks have used this grain in many recipes. This creamy, chowderlike soup is one of the more popular creations.

2 medium stalks celery, sliced (1 cup)

1 medium carrot, coarsely shredded (1/2 cup)

1 medium onion, chopped (1/2 cup)

1 small green bell pepper, chopped (1/2 cup)

2 tablespoons margarine or butter

3 tablespoons all-purpose flour

1 teaspoon salt

1/4 teaspoon pepper

1 1/2 cups cooked wild rice

1 cup water

1 can (10.5 oz) condensed chicken broth

1 cup half-and-half

1/3 cup slivered almonds, toasted

1/4 cup chopped fresh parsley

1 Cook and stir celery, carrot, onion and bell pepper in margarine in 3-quart saucepan until celery is tender, about 5 minutes.

2 Stir in flour, salt and pepper. Stir in wild rice, water and broth. Heat to boiling; reduce heat. Cover and simmer 15 minutes, stirring occasionally.

3 Stir in remaining ingredients. Heat just until hot (do not boil).

1 Serving: Calories 200 (Calories from Fat 110); Fat 12g (Saturated 4g); Cholesterol 15mg; Sodium 800mg; Carbohydrate 19g (Dietary Fiber 3g); Protein 7g

Basil Rice Soup

Fresh basil adds such a nice flavor to this soup. Any aromatic rice, such as basmati or jasmine, can be used for the regular long-grain rice.

2 tablespoons olive or vegetable oil

2 cloves garlic, finely chopped

2 medium stalks celery, chopped (1 cup)

1 medium onion, chopped ($^1/_2$ cup)

1 medium carrot, chopped ($^1/_2$ cup)

$^1/_4$ cup chopped fresh basil leaves

$^3/_4$ cup uncooked regular long-grain rice

2 medium tomatoes, chopped ($1^1/_2$ cups)

4 cups chicken broth

1 cup water

1 teaspoon salt

$^1/_4$ teaspoon pepper

$^1/_4$ cup grated Romano cheese

1 Heat oil in Dutch oven over medium-low heat. Cover and cook garlic, celery, onion, carrot and basil in oil 10 minutes, stirring occasionally, until vegetables are crisp-tender. Stir in rice and tomatoes. Cook uncovered over medium heat 5 minutes, stirring occasionally.

2 Stir in remaining ingredients except cheese. Heat to boiling; reduce heat. Cover and simmer bout 20 minutes or until rice is tender. Top each serving with cheese.

1 Serving: Calories 185 (Calories from Fat 65); Fat 7g (Saturated 2g); Cholesterol 5mg; Sodium 990mg; Carbohydrate 25g (Dietary Fiber 1g); Protein 7g

COUNTRY COOKING WISDOM

Fresh Flavors

Whether it's tarragon, basil, parsley, rosemary or thyme, fresh herbs add oomph to just about any food. Some herbs grow wild and some are cultivated on herb farms, but you can easily grow kitchen favorites in your garden or in windowsill pots. Since most of them "grow like weeds" it's easy to grow them from seeds or plants. Keep your kitchen scissors on hand to snip herbs for a simple but impressive garnish. Because their flavor isn't as concentrated, you'll need three to four times more fresh herbs than dried for cooking.

Lentil Soup

Vary your lentils. Look for either brown or green lentils to use for this robust soup. Look forward to leftovers, too! This soup tastes even better the second day.

2 tablespoons olive or vegetable oil

2 cloves garlic, finely chopped

1 medium onion, finely chopped (1/2 cup)

1/2 cup diced prosciutto or fully cooked Virginia ham (4 oz)

1/4 cup diced Genoa salami (2 oz)

1 dried bay leaf

4 cups water

2 cups chicken broth

1 1/2 cups dried lentils (8 oz), sorted and rinsed

1/2 teaspoon pepper

1 Heat oil in Dutch oven over medium-high heat. Cook garlic and onion in oil 5 to 7 minutes, stirring frequently, until onion is tender. Stir in prosciutto and salami. Cook over medium heat 10 minutes, stirring frequently.

2 Stir in remaining ingredients. Heat to boiling; reduce heat. Cover and simmer about 1 hour, stirring occasionally, until lentils are tender. Remove bay leaf.

1 Serving: Calories 315 (Calories from Fat 125); Fat 14g (Saturated 4g); Cholesterol 15mg; Sodium 710mg; Carbohydrate 37g (Dietary Fiber 13g); Protein 23g

COUNTRY COOKING WISDOM

Lentil Lesson

Healthful lentils provide all the benefits of legumes—high in fiber and protein and low in fat—but have another benefit over the others: They need no soaking and cook quickly compared to beans. Always rinse and sort through them as small stones could be mixed in with them. Try the many varieties available, including the small French ones and red lentils.

Black Bean Chili

The flavor of cilantro is distinctive and pungent, but it quickly disappears when cooked. That's why we stir the cilantro into the chili after cooking is completed. Serve with flour tortillas and a fresh fruit salad.

- 2 cups water
- 2 cups apple juice
- 1 tablespoon chopped fresh or 1 teaspoon dried oregano leaves
- 2 tablespoons tomato paste
- 1 teaspoon ground cumin
- 1/8 teaspoon ground red pepper (cayenne)
- 1 large onion, chopped (1 cup)

- 2 cans (4 oz each) chopped mild green chiles, drained
- 3 cans (15 oz each) black beans, rinsed and drained
- 1 medium red bell pepper, chopped (1 cup)
- 3 tablespoons chopped fresh cilantro
- 1 cup shredded reduced-fat Cheddar cheese (4 oz)

1 Heat water, apple juice, oregano, tomato paste, cumin, red pepper, onion and chiles to boiling in Dutch oven; reduce heat. Cover and simmer 30 minutes.

2 Stir in beans and bell pepper. Cover and simmer about 10 minutes or until beans are hot. Stir in cilantro. Top each serving with cheese.

1 Serving: Calories 335 (Calories from Fat 45); Fat 5g (Saturated 3g); Cholesterol 10mg; Sodium 920mg; Carbohydrate 65g (Dietary Fiber 14g); Protein 22g

Tarragon Chicken Salad

4 servings   Prep Time: 10 minutes   Start to Finish: 15 minutes

Have some chicken left over from dinner? Try this flavorful salad for lunch the next day. You can even make it the day before—just cover and refrigerate. Stir in honeydew melon balls just before serving.

1/2 cup mayonnaise

1/2 cup plain yogurt

2 tablespoons tarragon vinegar

1 tablespoon chopped fresh or 1 teaspoon dried tarragon leaves

4 cups cut-up cooked chicken

1 cup chopped pecans, toasted

2 cups honeydew balls

Lettuce

Melon slices

1 Mix mayonnaise, yogurt, vinegar and tarragon in large bowl. Toss with chicken, pecans and honeydew balls.

2 Serve salad on lettuce-lined plates with slices of melon.

1 Serving: Calories 710 (Calories from Fat 475); Fat 53g (Saturated 8g); Cholesterol 140mg; Sodium 300mg; Carbohydrate 17g (Dietary Fiber 3g); Protein 44g

Italian Chicken Salad

4 servings   Prep Time: 5 minutes   Start to Finish: 30 minutes

The premixed salad greens give this refreshing pasta salad its Italian flair. If you have some fresh basil growing in your garden, pick a few leaves and thinly slice them for garnishing each serving.

3/4 cup uncooked fusilli or rotini pasta

1/2 cup zesty Italian dressing

1 medium yellow or green bell pepper, chopped (1 cup)

1 medium carrot, shredded (1/2 cup)

4 boneless, skinless chicken breast halves (about 1 lb)

6 cups Italian blend salad mix or 6 cups bite-size pieces mixed salad greens

Pepper, if desired

1 Cook and drain pasta as directed on package. Toss pasta and 1/3 cup of the dressing. Stir in bell pepper and carrot.

2 Heat coals or gas grill. Cover and grill chicken 4 to 6 inches from medium heat 15 to 20 minutes, brushing with remaining dressing and turning occasionally, until juice of chicken is no longer pink when centers of thickest pieces are cut. Cut chicken diagonally into 1-inch strips.

3 Divide salad greens among 4 serving plates. Top with pasta mixture and chicken. Sprinkle with pepper.

1 Serving: Calories 380 (Calories from Fat 160); Fat 18g (Saturated 3g); Cholesterol 60mg; Sodium 300mg; Carbohydrate 27g (Dietary Fiber 2g); Protein 29g

Turkey Taco Salad

4 servings   Prep Time: 10 minutes   Start to Finish: 20 minutes

What a great salad to serve at your next fiesta! For beef lovers, use lean ground beef instead of the turkey. Have colorful bowls of additional toppings, such as sliced black olives, sour cream, and sliced jalapeño peppers for those who like it "hot."

1 lb ground turkey

¾ cup water

2 teaspoons chili powder

½ teaspoon salt

½ teaspoon ground cumin

1 small onion, finely chopped (¼ cup)

1 clove garlic, finely chopped

1 can (11 oz) whole kernel corn, drained

6 cups corn tortilla chips (3 oz)

4 cups shredded iceberg lettuce

1 medium tomato, chopped (¾ cup)

1 cup salsa

1 Cook turkey, water, chili powder, salt, cumin, onion and garlic in 10-inch skillet over medium-high heat 10 to 12 minutes, stirring frequently, until turkey is no longer pink and liquid is absorbed. Stir in corn. Cover and keep warm over low heat.

2 Arrange tortilla chips on large serving plate. Top with lettuce, tomato, turkey mixture and salsa.

1 Serving: Calories 395 (Calories from Fat 160); Fat 18g (Saturated 4g); Cholesterol 75mg; Sodium 1,160mg; Carbohydrate 35g (Dietary Fiber 5g); Protein 28g

Curried Turkey Salad

6 servings   Prep Time: 5 minutes   Start to Finish: 2 hours 20 minutes

Did you know curry isn't just one spice? It's a mixture of up to 20 different spices, including cardamom, nutmeg, cinnamon, cloves, coriander and black pepper. In India, people grind fresh curry powder daily. The flavor of those curries can vary dramatically from region to region.

1½ cups uncooked elbow macaroni (6 oz)

1 package (10 oz) frozen green peas

¾ cup mayonnaise or salad dressing

2 teaspoons curry powder

2 cups cut-up cooked turkey breast

½ cup shredded Cheddar cheese (2 oz)

4 medium green onions, sliced (¼ cup)

1 medium stalk celery, sliced (½ cup)

Lettuce leaves, if desired

1 Cook and drain macaroni as directed on package. Rinse with cold water; drain. Rinse frozen peas with cold water to separate; drain.

2 Mix mayonnaise and curry powder in large bowl. Stir in macaroni, peas and remaining ingredients except lettuce. Cover and refrigerate 2 to 4 hours to blend flavors. Serve on lettuce.

1 Serving: Calories 465 (Calories from Fat 250); Fat 28g (Saturated 6g); Cholesterol 60mg; Sodium 290mg; Carbohydrate 34g (Dietary Fiber 4g); Protein 23g

Pasta Salad with Salmon and Dill

4 servings   Prep Time: 10 minutes   Start to Finish: 20 minutes

You'll be surprised how easy it is to cut carrots and zucchini into thin slices with a vegetable peeler. For more control when cutting, be sure the vegetables are lying on a flat surface, such as a cutting board or countertop.

8 oz uncooked fettuccine

2 medium carrots

2 medium zucchini

1 can (7.5 oz) boneless, skinless red sockeye salmon, drained and flaked

1 container (8 oz) refrigerated dill dip

¾ teaspoon lemon pepper

1 Cook and drain fettuccine as directed on package. Rinse with cold water; drain.

2 Cut carrots and zucchini lengthwise into thin slices, using vegetable peeler.

3 Toss fettucine, vegetables and remaining ingredients in large bowl. Serve immediately or refrigerate 1 to 2 hours or until chilled.

1 Serving: Calories 390 (Calories from Fat 135); Fat 15g (Saturated 7g); Cholesterol 95mg; Sodium 760mg; Carbohydrate 46g (Dietary Fiber 3g); Protein 20g

Shrimp-Pasta Salad Toss

2 servings   Prep Time: 10 minutes   Start to Finish: 10 minutes

If your favorite deli pasta salad is too thick for this recipe, thin it by stirring in a tablespoon of milk until you get the consistency you like. This recipe is perfect to double, or even triple, if you want to serve more people.

6 oz cooked peeled deveined shrimp, thawed if frozen

2 cups bite-size pieces spinach

½ pint deli pasta salad (1 cup)

½ cup cherry tomatoes, cut in half

2 tablespoons sliced ripe olives

Toss all ingredients in large bowl.

1 Serving: Calories 300 (Calories from Fat 115); Fat 13g (Saturated 2g); Cholesterol 175mg; Sodium 630mg; Carbohydrate 26g (Dietary Fiber 3g); Protein 23g

COUNTRY COOKING WISDOM

Lovely Lunches

Don't forget lunch as an option when planning a party. Whether it's a Sunday lunch for family or time with your girlfriends, lunch is a great time for simple yet fun gatherings. Serve two salad offerings like this Shrimp-Pasta Salad Toss and Tarragon Chicken Salad (page 68). Whip up a batch of Buttermilk Biscuits (page 254) and a pitcher of iced tea to serve alongside. In no time, you'll have an impressive meal that everyone will enjoy.

Seafood-Rice Salad

10 servings | Prep Time: 25 minutes | Start to Finish: 25 minutes

Looking for a shortcut? If your supermarket offers a salad bar, you'll find freshly steamed broccoli flowerets waiting for you there. Just purchase the amount you need and toss this fresh, lemony salad together in no time.

2 lb cooked scallops

1 lb medium shrimp, cooked peeled deveined, thawed if frozen

4 cups cooked rice

3 cups broccoli flowerets, cooked (8 oz)

2 packages (6 oz each) frozen ready-to-serve crabmeat, thawed and drained

Lemon Vinaigrette (right)

1 Make Lemon Vinaigrette.

2 Mix all ingredients in large bowl except Lemon Vinaigrette. Toss salad with Lemon Vinaigrette.

Lemon Vinaigrette

$1/2$ cup vegetable oil

$1/2$ cup lemon juice

2 tablespoons chopped fresh chives

1 tablespoon grated lemon peel

1 teaspoon Dijon mustard

1 teaspoon sugar

Mix all ingredients in small bowl.

1 Serving: Calories 295 (Calories from Fat 115); Fat 13g (Saturated 2g); Cholesterol 90mg; Sodium 270mg; Carbohydrate 22g (Dietary Fiber 1g); Protein 24g

Snappy Seafood Salad

4 servings | Prep Time: 15 minutes | Start to Finish: 15 minutes

It's a snap to put this summer seafood salad together. Dress it up and add a nice texture and flavor with tender, young salad greens that you can purchase premixed in place of the lettuce.

2 cups uncooked medium pasta shells (5 oz)

$2/3$ cup mayonnaise or salad dressing

1 tablespoon chili sauce or cocktail sauce

$1/3$ cup small pitted ripe olives

3 cups bite-size pieces lettuce

1 package (8 oz) frozen seafood chunks (imitation crabmeat), thawed

1 small tomato, cut into 8 wedges

1 Cook and drain pasta as directed on package. Rinse with cold water; drain.

2 Mix mayonnaise and chili sauce in large bowl. Add pasta and olives; toss. Add lettuce and seafood; toss. Serve with tomato wedges.

1 Serving: Calories 480 (Calories from Fat 290); Fat 32g (Saturated 5g); Cholesterol 40mg; Sodium 870mg; Carbohydrate 36g (Dietary Fiber 2g); Protein 14g

Pesto Macaroni Salad

6 servings   Prep Time: 5 minutes   Start to Finish: 2 hours 15 minutes

Here's a fresh and tasty twist on traditional macaroni salad. Even better, the oil and vinegar used in place of mayonnaise make it perfect to pack for picnic lunches.

- 3 cups uncooked elbow macaroni (12 oz)
- 1 tablespoon olive or vegetable oil
- 1 container (8 oz) pesto
- 4 plum tomatoes, each cut into 4 wedges
- ½ cup small pitted ripe olives
- ¼ cup white wine vinegar
- 4 cups coarsely shredded spinach
- Grated Parmesan cheese

1 Cook macaroni as directed on package; drain. Rinse in cold water; drain and toss with oil.

2 Mix pesto, tomatoes, olives and vinegar in large bowl. Arrange 2 cups of the macaroni and 2 cups of the spinach on pesto mixture; repeat with remaining macaroni and spinach.

3 Cover and refrigerate at least 2 hours but no longer than 24 hours. Toss; sprinkle with cheese.

1 Serving: Calories 470 (Calories from Fat 215); Fat 24g (Saturated 15g); Cholesterol 150mg; Sodium 220mg; Carbohydrate 56g (Dietary Fiber 5g); Protein 13g

COUNTRY COOKING WISDOM

Presto Pesto

Be sure to have a container of prepared pesto on hand for last minute dishes. For a quick dinner, toss prepared pesto with hot angel hair pasta and a bit of cream or half-and-half. Spread it on toasted Italian bread slices to serve alongside soup or salad. Brush it on chicken or fish before grilling or roasting. Flavorful pesto is a convenient way to turn the ordinary meal into something extraordinary.

Vegetable-Pasta Salad

10 servings   Prep Time: 20 minutes   Start to Finish: 20 minutes

Keep your vegetables fresh and bright by blanching them. It's not hard. Just place vegetables in a wire basket or a blancher, and drop the basket into boiling water. Cover and cook vegetables for about a minute, just until slightly tender. Then remove the basket from the boiling water and immediately plunge the vegetables into iced water to stop cooking.

1 package (16 oz) pasta shells, cooked and drained

1½ lb fresh asparagus, cut into 4-inch pieces

1 lb fresh sugar snap peas, blanched

6 green onions, sliced

1 yellow bell pepper, cut into julienne strips

Lemon Mayonnaise (below right)

1 Cook and drain pasta shells as directed on package. Rinse with cold water; drain.

2 Place asparagus in boiling water. Cover and cook 1 minute; drain. Immediately rinse with cold water; drain.

3 Place snap pea pods in boiling water. Cover and cook 1 minute; drain. Immediately rinse with cold water; drain.

4 Mix pasta, asparagus, snap peas, onions and bell pepper in large bowl; toss. Stir in Lemon Mayonnaise until well mixed. Cover and refrigerate until ready to serve.

Lemon Mayonnaise

1 cup mayonnaise
½ cup plain yogurt
¼ cup lemon juice
2 tablespoons chopped fresh or 2 teaspoons dried tarragon leaves
½ teaspoon salt

Mix all ingredients until well blended.

1 Serving: Calories 365 (Calories from Fat 170); Fat 19g (Saturated 3g); Cholesterol 15mg; Sodium 260mg; Carbohydrate 43g (Dietary Fiber 4g); Protein 10g

Broiled Burgers with Mushrooms and Onions

4 servings   Prep Time: 5 minutes   Start to Finish: 20 minutes

Punch up the flavor of the mushrooms on your burger! Substitute ¼ cup sliced fresh mushrooms—try button, portabella, or shiitake—for the canned.

1 lb ground beef

3 tablespoons finely chopped onion

3 tablespoons water

¾ teaspoon salt

⅛ teaspoon pepper

Mushrooms and Onions (right)

1 Mix ground beef, onion, water, salt and pepper. Shape mixture into 4 patties, each about ¾ inch thick.

2 Set oven control to broil. Place patties on rack in broiler pan. Broil with tops about 3 inches from heat until thoroughly cooked, 5 to 7 minutes on each side for medium. Make Mushrooms and Onions; spoon over hamburgers.

Mushrooms and Onions

1 medium onion, thinly sliced

1 tablespoon margarine or butter

1 can (4 oz) mushroom pieces and stems, drained

½ teaspoon Worcestershire sauce

Cook onion in margarine over medium heat, stirring occasionally, until tender. Stir in mushrooms and Worcestershire sauce and heat until mushrooms are hot.

1 Serving: Calories 275 (Calories from Fat 170); Fat 19g (Saturated 7g); Cholesterol 65mg; Sodium 660mg; Carbohydrate 5g (Dietary Fiber 1g); Protein 22g

Grilled Coney Island Burgers

6 servings   Prep Time: 15 minutes   Start to Finish: 15 minutes

If you can't decide whether you want a chili dog or a burger, here's the recipe for you! It's a hot dog and burger wrapped up in one.

1 lb ground beef

1 can (7.5 oz) chili with beans

1 tablespoon chopped green chiles

6 hot dog buns, split and warmed

1 Shape ground beef into 6 rolls, each about 5 inches long and ¾ inch thick. Mix chili and green chiles in small grill pan. Heat coals or gas grill. Heat chili on grill until hot.

2 Grill ground beef rolls about 4 inches from medium heat 3 to 5 minutes on each side for medium doneness, turning once. Serve in hot dog buns. Spoon about 2 tablespoons chili mixture into each bun.

1 Serving: Calories 310 (Calories from Fat 135); Fat 15g (Saturated 6g); Cholesterol 50mg; Sodium 450mg; Carbohydrate 26g (Dietary Fiber 2g); Protein 20g

Broiled Burgers with Mushrooms and Onions *(bottom)* and Old-Fashioned Coleslaw *(top,* page 223)

Grilled Teriyaki Burgers

4 servings | Prep Time: 5 minutes | Start to Finish: 30 minutes

You'll love how versatile these burgers are since you can also use ground chicken or turkey for the ground beef. The poultry flavor blends nicely with the soy and ginger, making these delightful sandwiches.

- 1 lb ground beef
- 2 tablespoons soy sauce
- 1 teaspoon salt
- 1/4 teaspoon crushed gingerroot or 1/8 teaspoon ground ginger
- 1 clove garlic, crushed

1 Shape ground beef into 4 patties, each about ¾ inch thick. Mix remaining ingredients and spoon onto patties. Turn patties; let stand 10 minutes.

2 Heat coals or gas grill for direct heat. Grill patties about 4 inches from medium heat 5 to 7 minutes on each side for medium doneness, turning once. Serve on toasted sesame seed buns if desired.

1 Serving: Calories 230 (Calories from Fat 145); Fat 16g (Saturated 6g); Cholesterol 65mg; Sodium 1,100mg; Carbohydrate 1g (Dietary Fiber 0g); Protein 21g

COUNTRY COOKING WISDOM

Best Burgers

To keep burgers moist and flavorful, don't press down on them with your spatula while they're cooking (even though it may be tempting). If you do, you'll squeeze out too much of the great-tasting juices that also make the burgers nice and moist.

Hamburgers Parmigiana

4 servings | Prep Time: 15 minutes | Start to Finish: 15 minutes

Parmigiana describes a food made with Parmesan cheese. And who can say no to cheese and tomato sauce? Jazz up your mealtime with these tasty patties.

- 1 lb ground beef
- 1 small onion, chopped (1/4 cup)
- 2 tablespoons grated Parmesan cheese
- 1/2 teaspoon garlic salt
- 1 jar (15.5 oz) chunky-style tomato pasta sauce
- 1/2 cup shredded mozzarella cheese
- 4 slices French bread, toasted, or 2 hamburger buns, split and toasted

1 Mix ground beef, onion, Parmesan cheese and garlic salt. Shape into 4 patties, each about ½ inch thick.

2 Cook in 10-inch skillet over medium heat, turning frequently, until thoroughly cooked; drain.

3 Pour sauce over patties and heat until hot. Top each patty with 2 tablespoons mozzarella cheese. Let stand until cheese begins to melt. Serve on French bread.

1 Serving: Calories 465 (Calories from Fat 215); Fat 24g (Saturated 9g); Cholesterol 75mg; Sodium 980mg; Carbohydrate 35g (Dietary Fiber 2g); Protein 30g

Beef and Veggie Pitas

4 servings   Prep Time: 15 minutes   Start to Finish: 20 minutes

Make one or both of the super-easy sauces to dip or dunk your sandwich in. Of course, these sandwiches are also is delicious with turkey instead of roast beef.

Cheese Sauce or Creamy
Italian Sauce (right)
Lettuce leaves
¾ lb thinly sliced cooked roast beef
1 medium cucumber, thinly sliced
1 medium tomato, thinly sliced
1 medium bell pepper, cut into rings
1 medium zucchini, thinly sliced
4 thin slices red onion
4 pita breads (6 inch), cut in half to form pockets

1 Make Cheese Sauece or Creamy Italian Sauce.

2 Layer lettuce, beef, cucumber, tomato, bell pepper, zucchini and onion in pita bread halves. Serve with sauce.

Cheese Sauce

1 jar (8 oz) process cheese spread
2 tablespoons milk
¼ cup chopped tomato
3 medium green onions, sliced (¼ cup)

Heat cheese spread and milk in 1-quart saucepan over medium heat, stirring constantly, until smooth. Stir in tomato and onions. Serve warm.

Creamy Italian Sauce

½ cup creamy Italian dressing
¼ cup sour cream
¼ cup mayonnaise or salad dressing
¼ cup milk

Mix all ingredients in medium bowl.

1 Serving: Calories 515 (Calories from Fat 160); Fat 18g (Saturated 10g); Cholesterol 105mg; Sodium 1,300mg; Carbohydrate 46g (Dietary Fiber 3g); Protein 45g

Deli Turkey Stacks

4 sandwiches | Prep Time: 10 minutes | Start to Finish: 10 minutes

Here's the secret for those perfect hard-cooked eggs—the ones with a tender white surrounding a golden yellow yolk. Heat the water and eggs to boiling, then remove from heat, cover and let stand 18 minutes. Immediately cool eggs in cold water to prevent further cooking.

8 slices pumpernickel bread, cut in half

Lettuce leaves

12 oz thinly sliced cooked turkey

2 medium tomatoes, cut into wedges

2 hard-cooked eggs, sliced

1/2 cup reduced-fat Thousand Island dressing

Whole ripe olives

1 Top 4 bread halves with one-fourth of the lettuce, turkey, tomatoes, eggs and dressing. Garnish with olives.

2 Top each with remaining slices of bread.

1 Sandwich: Calories 355 (Calories from Fat 100); Fat 11g (Saturated 3g); Cholesterol 175mg; Sodium 790mg; Carbohydrate 34g (Dietary Fiber 4g); Protein 34g

Open-Face Garden Turkey Sandwiches

4 open-face sandwiches | Prep Time: 20 minutes | Start to Finish: 15 minutes

Get out your knife and fork! These succulent sandwiches boast warm turkey breast and peppers and onions on pumpernickel bread, topped with cheese and broiled just until the cheese melts. Yum!

4 cups frozen stir-fry bell peppers and onions (from 16-oz package)

4 uncooked turkey breast slices, about 1/4 inch thick (1 lb)

1/2 cup shredded Cheddar cheese (2 oz)

4 tablespoons sandwich spread, mayonnaise or salad dressing

4 slices pumpernickel bread, toasted

1 Spray 12-inch nonstick skillet with cooking spray and heat over medium-high heat. Cook vegetables in skillet 3 to 5 minutes, stirring frequently, until tender; remove from skillet.

2 In the same skillet, cook turkey 10 to 12 minutes, turning occasionally, until light golden brown and no longer pink in center. Remove from heat.

3 Top each turkey slice with vegetables and cheese. Cover 1 to 2 minutes or until cheese is melted. Spread sandwich spread over toast. Top each slice with turkey topped with vegetables and cheese.

1 Serving: Calories 330 (Calories from Fat 104); Fat 12g (Saturated 4g); Cholesterol 65mg; Sodium 599mg; Carbohydrate 23g (Dietary Fiber 2g); Protein 35g

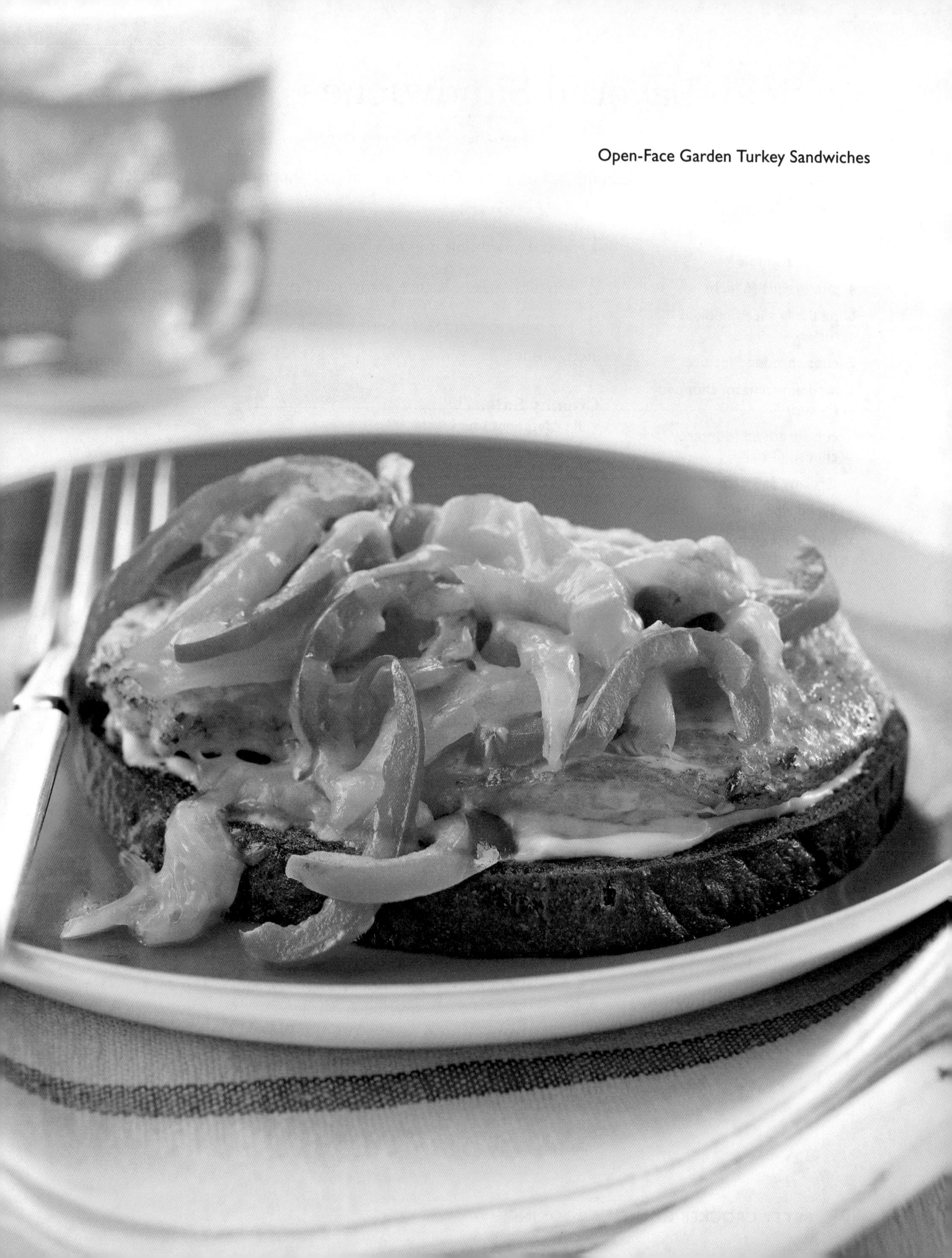

Open-Face Garden Turkey Sandwiches

Mexican Layered Sandwiches

4 sandwiches   Prep Time: 15 minutes   Start to Finish: 15 minutes

You can find prepared guacamole in the deli or frozen-food section of your supermarket. Of course, you can always use your favorite guacamole recipe.

½ cup guacamole

4 pita breads (6 inch)

6 oz thinly sliced cooked turkey

2 cups shredded lettuce

1 medium tomato, chopped (¾ cup)

¾ cup shredded Monterey Jack cheese (3 oz)

Creamy Salsa (right)

Sliced ripe olives, if desired

Chopped green onions, if desired

1 Spread guacamole over pita breads.

2 Top with turkey, lettuce, tomato and cheese.

3 Top with Creamy Salsa. Sprinkle with sliced ripe olives or chopped green onions.

Creamy Salsa
3 tablespoons sour cream
1 tablespoon salsa
1 tablespoon chopped green onions

Mix all ingredients in small bowl.

1 Sandwich: Calories 385 (Calories from Fat 135); Fat 15g (Saturated 7g); Cholesterol 60mg; Sodium 660mg; Carbohydrate 40g (Dietary Fiber 3g); Protein 25g

Rachel Sandwiches

6 sandwiches   Prep Time: 10 minutes   Start to Finish: 10 minutes

Rachel sandwiches could be the sister sandwich to the Reuben, which is topped with sauerkraut instead of coleslaw. For lunch away from home, pack the meat, cheese and coleslaw in separate containers in an insulated lunch bag or cooler and assemble each sandwich just before you're ready to eat!

12 slices dark rye bread

Margarine or butter, if desired

4 oz sliced Swiss cheese

¼ lb sliced corned beef

3 cups deli coleslaw

1 Butter 1 side of each bread slice.

2 Layer cheese, corned beef and coleslaw on buttered side of each of 6 bread slices.

3 Top with remaining bread slices with buttered side down. Cut sandwiches in half.

1 Sandwich: Calories 435 (Calories from Fat 260); Fat 29g (Saturated 8g); Cholesterol 50mg; Sodium 730mg; Carbohydrate 33g (Dietary Fiber 5g); Protein 16g

Egg Salad Stacks

2 servings | Prep Time: 10 minutes | Start to Finish: 10 minutes

Yum! These "stacks" are a nice change from typical egg salad. Mixing yogurt and mayonnaise together reduces the calories and fat but still gives you the great flavor of a creamy egg salad.

4 hard-cooked eggs, chopped

2 medium green onions, sliced (2 tablespoons)

1 small carrot, shredded (1/4 cup)

2 tablespoons mayonnaise or salad dressing

2 tablespoons plain low-fat yogurt

1/4 teaspoon curry powder

1/8 teaspoon salt

Dash of pepper

4 leaves romaine

2 English muffins, split and toasted, or 2 slices bread

4 rings yellow or green bell pepper

2 tablespoons alfalfa sprouts

1 Mix eggs, onions, carrot, mayonnaise, yogurt, curry powder, salt and pepper.

2 Place 1 romaine leaf on each muffin half. Top with egg mixture, bell pepper rings and alfalfa sprouts.

1 Serving: Calories 400 (Calories from Fat 200); Fat 22g (Saturated 5g); Cholesterol 435mg; Sodium 630mg; Carbohydrate 35g (Dietary Fiber 3g); Protein 19g

COUNTRY COOKING WISDOM

Brown Bagging

Bringing lunch to school or work is an age-old tradition. Following these tips will help you assemble the perfect sandwich:

- To prevent soggy sandwiches, spread bread slices with cream cheese, butter or mayonnaise.
- Hold together mixed fillings—such as chopped eggs, cut-up pieces of meat or vegetables—with mayonnaise, salad dressing, cream cheese, barbecue sauce or other sandwich spreads.
- Firm-textured breads work best for sandwiches because they're sturdy enough to hold fillings.

Summertime Shrimp Rounds

8 open-face sandwiches | Prep Time: 15 minutes | Start to Finish: 15 minutes

If you can't find garlic-and-herb spreadable cheese, mix 4 oz softened cream cheese, 1 tablespoon mayonnaise, 1 teaspoon each dried basil and oregano leaves and ¼ teaspoon garlic powder.

1 container (5 oz) garlic-and-herb or herb spreadable cheese

4 onion or plain bagels, cut horizontally in half

32 medium shrimp cooked peeled deveined, thawed if frozen

1 small cucumber, cut lengthwise in half and sliced ¼ inch thick

¼ cup chopped green onions or red onion

8 cherry tomatoes

1 Spread 1 tablespoon cream cheese on each bagel half.

2 Arrange 4 shrimp and 4 cucumber slices on each. Sprinkle with onions.

3 Insert toothpicks into cherry tomatoes. Place in sandwiches.

1 Open-Face Sandwich: Calories 180 (Calories from Fat 55); Fat 6g (Saturated 3g); Cholesterol 125mg; Sodium 320mg; Carbohydrate 17g (Dietary Fiber 1g); Protein 16g

Mozzarella and Tomato Melts

4 open-face sandwiches | Prep Time: 15 minutes | Start to Finish: 15 minutes

You'll be craving these melts in the summer when the tomatoes are so juicy and ripe you'll hardly be able to wait the few minutes it takes to make them.

4 slices Italian bread, 1 inch thick

8 oz part-skim mozzarella cheese, sliced

2 medium tomatoes, thinly sliced

Salt and pepper

½ cup pesto

Fresh basil leaves, if desired

1 Set oven control to broil. Place bread on rack in broiler pan. Broil with tops about 4 inches from heat until golden brown; turn. Divide cheese among bread slices. Broil just until cheese begins to melt.

2 Arrange tomatoes on cheese. Sprinkle with salt and pepper. Top with pesto. Garnish with fresh basil leaves.

1 Open-Face Sandwich: Calories 435 (Calories from Fat 270); Fat 30g (Saturated 10g); Cholesterol 35mg; Sodium 860mg; Carbohydrate 22g (Dietary Fiber 2g); Protein 21g

Grilled Three-Cheese Sandwiches *Photo on page 55*

2 sandwiches   **Prep Time: 15 minutes**   **Start to Finish: 15 minutes**

Grilled cheese sandwiches are always a hit, so why stop at one cheese? If you have a little pesto in the refrigerator, try spreading some between the cheese layers instead of the spicy mustard. Mmmm!

- 2 tablespoons spicy mustard
- 4 slices whole wheat or rye bread
- 1 tablespoon sunflower nuts
- 1 slice mozzarella cheese (1.5 oz), cut in half
- 1 slice Swiss cheese (1.5 oz), cut in half
- 1 slice Cheddar cheese (1.5 oz), cut in half or 2 slices American cheese (.75 oz each)
- 2 tablespoons margarine, butter or spread, softened

1 Spread mustard over 1 side of each bread slice. Sprinkle nuts over mustard on 2 bread slices. For each sandwich, place one half piece each of mozzarella cheese, Swiss cheese and Cheddar cheese on nuts. Top with remaining bread, mustard side down. Spread half of the margarine over tops of bread.

2 Place sandwiches, margarine sides down, in 10-inch skillet. Spread remaining margarine over tops of bread. Cook uncovered over medium heat about 5 minutes or until bottoms are golden brown; turn. Cook 2 to 3 minutes until bottoms are golden brown and cheese is melted.

1 Sandwich: Calories 500 (Calories from Fat 295); Fat 33g (Saturated 14g); Cholesterol 55mg; Sodium 920mg; Carbohydrate 30g (Dietary Fiber 3g); Protein 24g

COUNTRY COOKING WISDOM

Sandwich Lore

The sandwich was named after the Fourth Earl of Sandwich (1718–92) who was too busy with a card game to stop and eat. He didn't want to get his cards sticky from eating meat with his fingers, so he placed the meat between two slices of bread. Today, the sandwich gives us a delicious, portable meal and is one of the world's most popular forms of food.

Pita Sandwiches

The great thing about pita sandwiches is that you can stuff whatever you like inside. For a Mediterranean twist, spoon some prepared hummus into a pita pocket and top with ripe tomatoes, a little red onion, some crumbled feta cheese and lettuce. It's so yummy!

8 pita breads (6 inch)

$\frac{1}{2}$ lb thinly sliced cooked turkey

$\frac{1}{2}$ lb thinly sliced cooked roast beef

8 tomato slices

$\frac{1}{2}$ cup alfalfa sprouts

Peppery Mustard Sauce (right)

Horseradish Sauce (below right)

1 Split each pita bread halfway around edge with knife. Separate to form pocket.

2 Place 2 slices turkey or roast beef in each pocket. Top with tomato slice and sprouts.

3 Serve sandwiches with Peppery Mustard Sauce and Horseradish Sauce.

Peppery Mustard Sauce

$\frac{3}{4}$ cup olive oil

3 tablespoons lemon juice

2 tablespoons coarse-grained mustard

1 teaspoon cracked black pepper

Combine all ingredients in blender or food processor. Cover and blend or process until smooth. Store tightly covered in refrigerator.

Horseradish Sauce

$\frac{1}{2}$ cup sour cream

2 tablespoons prepared horseradish

2 tablespoons apple cider

Mix all ingredients in small bowl. Cover and refrigerate until chilled.

1 Sandwich: Calories 470 (Calories from Fat 235); Fat 26g (Saturated 5g); Cholesterol 55mg; Sodium 420mg; Carbohydrate 37g (Dietary Fiber 2g); Protein 24g

What Makes a Sandwich a Sandwich?

In the United States, we tend to think of a sandwich as a filling between two pieces of bread. Globally, however, this definition is too restrictive. Almost every cuisine has its own version of a sandwich:

- Filled tortillas from Mexico
- Middle Eastern stuffed pitas
- Italian calzones
- Cornish pasties from England
- Chinese pork buns

And the list goes on . . .

Known for their versatility, sandwiches can be served cold or hot, grilled, baked or fried; layered, stacked, rolled or wrapped; and eaten open-face with a fork and knife.

And then, of course, there are wraps, one of the greatest things to happen to American sandwiches in the last fifteen years. Here's all you need to know to turn just about any sandwich or salad into a delicious wrap:

- The bread must be pliable—pitas, tortillas and lahvosh work best. Wrap the bread in foil and warm for a few minutes for the most pliable bread.

- Spreading the bread with mayo, cream cheese, salsa, hummus or a cheese spread helps to hold the sandwich together. Vary the spread for a unique flavor each time.

- Layer vegetables and meats over the spread, leaving about 2 inches all around the edge of the bread. Roll by folding one end of the bread up about 1 inch over the filling; fold the right and left sides over the folded end, overlapping the end. Fold the remaining bread down or roll this end toward the remaining end.

- For the most flavor, seal the wrap in plastic wrap and refrigerate a few hours to allow the flavors to meld.

Roasted Vegetable Wraps with Garlic Mayonnaise

6 wraps | Prep Time: 15 minutes | Start to Finish: 30 minutes

Wrap up lots of flavor in these neat-to-eat sandwiches. Check out the refrigerated section in your grocery store to find different flavored flour tortillas, such as sun-dried tomato or pesto. They're delicious!

I medium bell pepper, cut into
$^1/_2$-inch wedges

I medium red onion, cut into
$^1/_2$-inch wedges

I medium zucchini, cut
lengthwise in half, then cut
crosswise into $^1/_4$-inch slices

$^1/_4$ lb mushrooms, cut into
fourths

3 tablespoons olive or
vegetable oil

$^1/_2$ teaspoon dried basil leaves

$^1/_4$ teaspoon salt

$^1/_4$ teaspoon pepper

Garlic Mayonnaise (right)

6 flour tortillas (8 or 10 inch)

$1^1/_2$ cups shredded lettuce

1   Heat oven to 450°F. Spread bell pepper, onion, zucchini and mushrooms in ungreased jelly roll pan, 15 × 10 inch.

2   Mix oil, basil, salt and pepper. Brush over vegetables. Bake uncovered 12 to 15 minutes or until crisp-tender; cool slightly.

3   Spread about 2 teaspoons Garlic Mayonnaise down center of each tortilla to within 2 inches of bottom. Top with vegetables, spreading to within 2 inches of bottom of tortilla. Top with $^1/_4$ cup lettuce.

4   Fold one end of tortilla up about 1 inch over filling; fold right and left sides over folded end, overlapping. Fold remaining end down.

Garlic Mayonnaise
$^1/_4$ cup mayonnaise or salad dressing
I tablespoon finely chopped fresh parsley
I teaspoon chopped garlic or $^1/_4$ teaspoon garlic powder

Mix all ingredients in small bowl.

I Wrap: Calories 280 (Calories from Fat 155); Fat 17g (Saturated 3g); Cholesterol 5mg; Sodium 360mg; Carbohydrate 29g (Dietary Fiber 2g); Protein 5g

Vegetable Lasagna

8 servings | Prep Time: 10 minutes | Start to Finish: 1 hour 10 minutes

You can also add some shredded carrots, chopped broccoli or sliced mushrooms to this cheesy lasagna to make it even more chock-full of vegetables.

3 cups chunky-style tomato pasta sauce

1 medium zucchini, shredded

6 uncooked lasagna noodles

1 cup ricotta or small curd creamed cottage cheese

1/4 cup grated Parmesan cheese

1 tablespoon chopped fresh or 1 teaspoon dried oregano leaves

2 cups shredded mozzarella cheese (8 oz)

1 Heat oven to 350°F.

2 Mix sauce and zucchini. Spread 1 cup mixture in ungreased rectangular baking dish, 11 × 7 inches. Top with 3 uncooked noodles.

3 Mix ricotta cheese, Parmesan cheese and oregano; spread over noodles in dish. Spread with 1 cup of the sauce mixture.

4 Top with remaining noodles, sauce mixture and the mozzarella cheese. Bake uncovered about 45 minutes or until hot and bubbly. Let stand 15 minutes before cutting.

1 Serving: Calories 290 (Calories from Fat 110); Fat 12g (Saturated 6g); Cholesterol 25mg; Sodium 700mg; Carbohydrate 32g (Dietary Fiber 2g); Protein 16g

COUNTRY COOKING WISDOM

Cheese Lore

Legend has it that cheese was "discovered" by an Arab merchant crossing the desert who was pleased to find that the milk he'd carried all day in a pouch had transformed into dinner: thin, watery whey and thick curds. Although cheese making is a little more scientific today, the process is similar.

Cheesy Lasagna

12 servings   Prep Time: 15 minutes   Start to Finish: 1 hour 5 minutes

It's easy to sing the praises of lasagna—it's cheesy, filling and loved by all ages. And a good lasagna recipe is invaluable when you have to feed a crowd, want a make-ahead meal or need to supply a covered dish.

½ cup margarine or butter

½ cup all-purpose flour

1 teaspoon salt

4 cups milk

1 cup shredded Swiss cheese (4 oz)

1 cup shredded mozzarella cheese (4 oz)

1 cup grated Parmesan cheese

2 cups small curd cottage cheese

¼ cup chopped fresh parsley

1 tablespoon chopped fresh or 1 teaspoon dried basil leaves

1 teaspoon snipped fresh or ½ teaspoon dried oregano leaves

2 cloves garlic, crushed

12 uncooked lasagna noodles

1 Heat oven to 350°F.

2 Melt margarine in 2-quart saucepan over low heat. Stir in flour and ½ teaspoon of the salt. Cook, stirring constantly, until smooth and bubbly. Remove from heat; stir in milk. Heat to boiling, stirring constantly. Boil and stir 1 minute. Stir in Swiss cheese, mozzarella cheese and ½ cup of the Parmesan cheese. Cook and stir over low heat until cheeses are melted.

3 In medium bowl, mix remaining ingredients except noodles and remaining Parmesan cheese.

4 Spread one-fourth of the cheese sauce mixture in ungreased rectangular baking dish, 13 × 9 inches; top with 4 noodles. Spread 1 cup of the cottage cheese mixture over noodles; spread with one-fourth of the of the cheese sauce mixture. Repeat with 4 noodles, the remaining cottage cheese mixture, one-fourth of the cheese sauce mixture, the remaining noodles and remaining cheese sauce mixture. Sprinkle with the remaining Parmesan cheese.

5 Bake uncovered 35 to 40 minutes or until noodles are done. Let stand 10 minutes before cutting.

1 Serving: Calories 325 (Calories from Fat 155); Fat 17g (Saturated 7g); Cholesterol 30mg; Sodium 680mg; Carbohydrate 26g (Dietary Fiber 1g); Protein 18g

Spinach Phyllo Pie

6 servings | Prep Time: 35 minutes | Start to Finish: 1 hour 20 minutes

For best results, be sure the phyllo is completely thawed so each thin layer will easily separate from one another. Also, phyllo dough can dry out easily, so keep any unused dough wrapped tightly.

1 tablespoon olive or vegetable oil

1 medium onion, chopped (½ cup)

1 medium red bell pepper, chopped (1 cup)

1 clove garlic, finely chopped

2 packages (9 oz each) frozen chopped spinach, thawed and squeezed to drain

1 package (8 oz) cream cheese, softened

½ cup crumbled feta or Gorgonzola cheese (2 oz)

2 eggs

1 tablespoon chopped fresh or 1 teaspoon dried dill weed

½ teaspoon salt

¼ teaspoon pepper

8 sheets frozen phyllo (18 × 14 inch), thawed

2 tablespoons margarine or butter, melted*

1 Heat oven to 375°F. Grease bottom and side of pie plate, 9 inches, with margarine.

2 Heat oil in 10-inch skillet, over medium-high heat. Cook onion, bell pepper and garlic in oil, stirring frequently, until vegetables are crisp-tender. Remove from heat.

3 Stir in spinach, cream cheese, feta cheese, eggs, dill weed, salt and pepper.

4 Cut stack of phyllo sheets into 12-inch squares; discard extra phyllo. Cover with waxed paper, then with damp towel to prevent phyllo from drying out. Brush each of 4 phyllo squares with melted margarine and layer in pie plate. Gently press into pie plate, allowing corners to drape over edge.

5 Spread spinach mixture evenly over phyllo. Fold ends of phyllo up and over filling so corners overlap on top. Brush with margarine and layer remaining 4 phyllo sheets over pie, allowing corners to drape over edge.

6 Gently tuck phyllo draping over top inside edge of pie plate. Cut through top phyllo layers into 6 wedges using sharp knife or scissors.

7 Bake 35 to 45 minutes or until crust is golden brown and filling is hot. Let stand 10 minutes before serving.

We do not recommend using vegetable oil spreads.

1 Serving: Calories 320 (Calories from Fat 190); Fat 21g (Saturated 11g); Cholesterol 120mg; Sodium 610mg; Carbohydrate 25g (Dietary Fiber 2g); Protein 10g

Impossibly Easy Broccoli 'n' Cheddar Pie

6 servings   Prep Time: 15 minutes   Start to Finish: 50 minutes

It takes only minutes to prepare this cheesy broccoli pie. Quickly thaw the broccoli by removing the outer wrapper from the package and then piercing the package with a knife. Microwave on High 1½ to 2½ minutes or until partially thawed. Break up the broccoli with a fork and drain thoroughly. This pie is terrific served with coleslaw and assorted fruits.

2 packages (10 oz each) frozen chopped broccoli, thawed and drained

2 cups shredded Cheddar cheese (8 oz)

⅔ cup chopped onion

1⅓ cups milk

3 eggs

¾ cup Original Bisquick

½ teaspoon salt

¼ teaspoon pepper

1 Heat oven to 400°F. Grease pie plate, 10 inches.

2 Mix broccoli, 1⅓ cups of the cheese and the onion in pie plate.

3 Stir milk, eggs, Bisquick, salt and pepper with fork until blended. Pour into pie plate.

4 Bake 30 to 35 minutes or until knife inserted in center comes out clean. Sprinkle with remaining cheese. Bake 1 to 2 minutes longer or until cheese is melted. Cool 5 minutes.

1 Serving: Calories 300 (Calories from Fat 160); Fat 18g (Saturated 10g); Cholesterol 150mg; Sodium 720mg; Carbohydrate 19g (Dietary Fiber 3g); Protein 18g

Bean and Cheese Pie

8 servings | Prep Time: 25 minutes | Start to Finish: 50 minutes

Serve this "chili in a pie" with a simple salad to round out the meal—try slices of mandarin oranges and avocado drizzled with your favorite vinaigrette.

¾ cup all-purpose flour

1½ cups shredded Cheddar cheese (6 oz)

1½ teaspoons baking powder

½ teaspoon salt

⅓ cup milk

1 egg, slightly beaten

1 can (15 to 16 oz) garbanzo beans, drained

1 can (15 to 16 oz) kidney beans, drained

1 can (8 oz) tomato sauce

1 small green bell pepper, chopped (½ cup)

1 small onion, chopped (¼ cup)

2 teaspoons chili powder

2 teaspoons chopped fresh or ½ teaspoon dried oregano leaves

¼ teaspoon garlic powder

1 Heat oven to 375°F. Spray pie plate, 10 inches, with cooking spray.

2 Mix flour, ½ cup of the cheese, the baking powder and salt in medium bowl. Stir in milk and egg until blended. Spread over bottom and up side of pie plate.

3 Mix ½ cup of the remaining cheese and the remaining ingredients. Spoon into pie plate. Sprinkle with remaining ½ cup cheese. Bake uncovered about 25 minutes or until edge is puffy and light brown. Let stand 10 minutes before cutting.

1 Serving: Calories 260 (Calories from Fat 90); Fat 10g (Saturated 5g); Cholesterol 50mg; Sodium 840mg; Carbohydrate 34g (Dietary Fiber 6g); Protein 15g

Thin-Crust Pizza

6 servings | Prep Time: 25 minutes | Start to Finish: 40 minutes

If you like a thin, delicate crust, this is the pizza for you. Since this crust is not yeast-risen, it will just take a few moments to put together. If you are looking for a thicker crust, check out the Chicago Deep-Dish Pizza on page 96.

Thin Crust (right)

Sauce (below right)

Meat Toppings (below right)

Vegetable Toppings (below right)

1½ cups shredded mozzarella cheese (6 oz)

1 Move oven rack tp lowest position. Heat oven to 450°F.

2 Make Thin Crust; spread with Sauce. Top with one of the Meat Toppings and desired Vegetable Toppings. Sprinkle with mozzarella cheese. Bake on lowest oven rack 12 to 15 minutes or until crust is brown and cheese is melted and bubbly.

Thin Crust
1½ cups Original Bisquick
⅓ cup very hot water

1 Mix Bisquick and hot water and beat vigorously 20 strokes. Turn dough onto surface generously dusted with Bisquick. Knead until smooth and no longer sticky, about 60 times.

2 Press dough into 13-inch circle on greased cookie sheet or press in greased 12-inch pizza pan with hands dipped in Bisquick. Pinch edge, forming ½-inch rim.

Sauce
1 can (8 oz) tomato sauce
1 teaspoon Italian seasoning
⅛ teaspoon garlic powder

Mix all ingredients.

Meat Toppings
½ to 1 lb ground beef, cooked and drained
½ to 1 lb bulk Italian sausage, cooked and drained
1 package (3½ oz) sliced pepperoni
1 package (6 oz) sliced Canadian-style bacon

Vegetable Toppings
Sliced mushrooms
Chopped green pepper
Sliced green onions or chopped onion
Sliced ripe olives

1 Serving: Calories 295 (Calories from Fat 135); Fat 15g (Saturated 7g); Cholesterol 35mg; Sodium 870mg; Carbohydrate 24g (Dietary Fiber 1g); Protein 17g

Greek Pizza

6 servings   Prep Time: 15 minutes   Start to Finish: 45 minutes

Kasseri cheese is a Greek cheese made from sheep's or goat's milk. It has a sharp, salty flavor and melts beautifully. Plus the cheese is hard, so it is perfect for shredding. Look for this creamy, gold-colored cheese in your grocer's refrigerator case or at speciality cheese shops.

Crust (right)

1 cup shredded Kasseri or mozzarella cheese (4 oz)

1 package (10 oz) frozen chopped spinach, thawed and squeezed to drain

½ lb ground lamb

1 tablespoon chopped fresh oregano leaves or 1 teaspoon dried oregano leaves

1 medium tomato, chopped (¾ cup)

½ cup crumbled feta cheese

½ cup Greek or ripe olives, cut up

1 tablespoon olive oil, if desired

1 Move oven rack to lowest position. Heat oven to 425°F.

2 Make Crust. Sprinkle remaining ingredients evenly over top to within ½ inch of edge. Bake on lowest oven rack 25 to 30 minutes or until crust is golden brown. Drizzle with 1 tablespoon olive oil.

Crust

1 package regular active dry yeast
1 cup warm water (105°F to 115°F)
2½ cups all-purpose flour
2 tablespoons olive or vegetable oil
1 teaspoon sugar
1 teaspoon salt

1 Dissolve yeast in warm water in 2½-quart bowl. Stir in remaining ingredients. Beat vigorously 20 strokes. Let rest 5 minutes.

2 With floured fingers, press dough in greased 12-inch pizza pan or into 11-inch circle on greased cookie sheet.

1 Serving: Calories 415 (Calories from Fat 160); Fat 18g (Saturated 7g); Cholesterol 45mg; Sodium 780mg; Carbohydrate 46g (Dietary Fiber 3g); Protein 20g

COUNTRY COOKING WISDOM

Fantastic Feta

Considered a pickled cheese because it's cured and stored in brine, feta is a white, crumbly, semisoft Greek cheese with a very sharp, salty flavor. Traditionally made of sheep's or goat's milk, feta is commercially produced using cow's milk. Stir feta into salads or on sandwiches.

Chicago Deep-Dish Pizza

8 servings | Prep Time: 45 minutes | Start to Finish: I hour 10 minutes

You'll get cheers when you serve this hearty, thick-crusted pizza. The make-it-your-way style pleases kids and adults alike.

Chicago Deep-Dish Crust (right)

4 cups shredded mozzarella cheese (16 oz)

Meat Toppings (below right)

Vegetable Toppings (below right)

I can (28 oz) plum tomatoes, chopped and well drained

I tablespoon chopped fresh or I to 2 teaspoons dried oregano leaves or Italian herb seasoning

1/4 to 1/2 cup grated Parmesan cheese

1 Move oven rack to lowest position. Heat oven to 425°F. Make Deep-Dish Crust. Sprinkle with mozzarella cheese.

2 Top with one of the Meat Toppings, desired Vegetable Toppings and the tomatoes. Sprinkle with oregano and Parmesan cheese.

3 Bake on lowest oven rack 20 to 25 minutes or until crust is brown and cheese is melted and bubbly.

Chicago Deep-dish Crust

I package regular active dry yeast
3/4 cup warm water (105°F to 115°F)
3 cups Original Bisquick
2 tablespoons olive or vegetable oil

1 Dissolve yeast in warm water in large bowl. Stir in Bisquick and oil; beat vigorously 20 strokes. Turn dough onto surface generously dusted with Bisquick. Knead dough until smooth and no longer sticky, about 60 times. Let rest 5 minutes.

2 Press dough in bottom and up sides of jelly roll pan, 15 × 10 inch, greased with olive oil if desired. Or divide dough into halves and press in bottom and up sides of 2 round pans, 9 inches, greased with olive oil if desired.

Meat Toppings

1/2 to I lb bulk Italian sausage, cooked and drained
I package (3.5 oz) sliced pepperoni

Vegetable Toppings

Sliced mushrooms
Chopped green or red bell pepper
Chopped onion
Sliced ripe olives
Sliced pimiento-stuffed olives
Coarsely chopped sun-dried tomatoes in oil

I **Serving:** Calories 565 (Calories from Fat 305); Fat 24g (Saturated 13g); Cholesterol 60mg; Sodium 1,890mg; Carbohydrate 39g (Dietary Fiber 3g); Protein 29g

Pesto Chicken Pizza

4 servings | Prep Time: 15 minutes | Start to Finish: 15 minutes

For a change of pace, pita breads make a delicious alternative to the Italian bread shells. Or fill 4 pita bread halves with the chicken mixture for a meal on the go.

1 tablespoon olive or vegetable oil

1 medium stalk celery, chopped (1/2 cup)

1 cup cut-up cooked chicken

1/3 cup pesto

1 package (8 oz) Italian pizza crusts (6 inch)

2 tablespoons shredded Parmesan cheese

1/2 cup shredded lettuce

1 Heat oil in 10-inch skillet over medium-high heat. Cook celery in oil 4 to 5 minutes, stirring occasionally, until crisp-tender; reduce heat. Stir in chicken and pesto. Cook, stirring occasionally, until hot.

2 Spoon chicken mixture onto pizza crusts. Mix cheese and lettuce and sprinkle over chicken mixture. Cut each pizza crust in half.

1 Serving: Calories 535 (Calories from Fat 225); Fat 25g (Saturated 6g); Cholesterol 45mg; Sodium 760mg; Carbohydrate 52g (Dietary Fiber 1g); Protein 27g

Italian Sausage Calzone

4 servings | Prep Time: 15 minutes | Start to Finish: 55 minutes

A calzone is a stuffed pizza and looks like a large turnover. While this is made with a sausage filling, other fillings may include vegetables, cheese and other meats.

1/2 lb bulk Italian sausage

1 small onion chopped (1/4 cup)

1/3 cup pizza sauce

1 can (2 oz) mushroom pieces and stems, drained

2 cups Original Bisquick

1/3 cup hot water

1 tablespoon vegetable oil

1 cup shredded mozzarella cheese (4 oz)

1/4 cup grated Parmesan cheese

1 egg white

1 Heat oven to 450°F.

2 Cook sausage, stirring frequently, until brown; drain. Stir in onion, pizza sauce and mushrooms. Reserve mixture.

3 Mix Bisquick, hot water and oil until dough forms. Roll into 12-inch circle on cloth-covered surface dusted with Bisquick. Transfer circle to ungreased cookie sheet.

4 Top half of the circle with mozzarella cheese, sausage mixture and Parmesan cheese to within 1 inch of edge. Fold dough over filling and press edge with fork to seal. Brush with egg white. Bake 15 to 20 minutes or until golden brown. Cool 5 minutes; cut into wedges.

1 Serving: Calories 515 (Calories from Fat 260); Fat 29g (Saturated 10g); Cholesterol 50mg; Sodium 1,620mg; Carbohydrate 41g (Dietary Fiber 2g); Protein 24g

Whole Wheat Vegetable Calzone

6 servings   Prep Time: 25 minutes   Start to Finish: 55 minutes

The whole wheat dough adds a nice nutty flavor and denser texture to this calzone. Warmed tomato sauce makes a good accompaniment for dipping.

Whole Wheat Calzone Dough (right)

1 package (10 oz) frozen chopped broccoli

⅓ cup creamy Italian dressing

½ teaspoon salt

1 package (3 oz) cream cheese, softened

1 cup sliced mushrooms, or 1 jar (4.5 oz) sliced mushrooms, drained

2 medium carrots, shredded (1 cup)

1 medium tomato, chopped (³/₄ cup)

½ small green pepper, chopped (½ cup)

1 egg, beaten

Coarse salt, if desired

1 Heat oven to 375°F.

2 Make Whole Wheat Calzone Dough. Divide into 6 equal pieces. Pat each into 7-inch circle on lightly floured surface, turning dough over occasionally to coat with flour.

3 Rinse frozen broccoli in cold water to separate; drain. Mix dressing, salt and cream cheese until well blended (mixture will appear curdled). Stir in broccoli and remaining vegetables.

4 Top half of each circle with ⅔ cup vegetable mixture to within 1 inch of edge. Fold dough over filling; fold edge up and pinch securely to seal. Place on greased cookie sheet; brush with egg. Sprinkle with coarse salt. Bake 25 to 30 minutes or until golden brown.

Whole Wheat Calzone Dough

1 package regular active dry yeast
1 cup warm water (105°F to 115°F)
1 tablespoon sugar
2 tablespoons vegetable oil
1 teaspoon salt
2½ to 3 cups whole wheat flour

1 Dissolve yeast in warm water in large bowl. Stir in sugar, oil, salt and 1 cup of the flour. Beat until smooth. Mix in enough remaining flour to make dough easy to handle.

2 Turn dough onto lightly floured surface. Knead about 5 minutes until smooth and elastic. Cover with bowl and let rest 5 minutes.

1 Serving: Calories 350 (Calories from Fat 155); Fat 17g (Saturated 5g); Cholesterol 50mg; Sodium 770mg; Carbohydrate 47g (Dietary Fiber 9g); Protein 11g

CHAPTER THREE

Down-Home Poultry and Fish

SIT DOWN TO DINNER WITH THESE DELIGHTFUL POULTRY AND FISH MEALS. SAVORY AND SATISFYING, THE POULTRY

dishes are perfect for any night of the week. Quick, casual stir-fries and sautés make weeknight meals fast and flavorful. Hearty rich chilies and casseroles are perfect for weekends as aromas fill your home and pique the appetite. The delectable flavors of the sea will have your family clamoring for more. Whether grilled, sautéed or tossed with pasta, each fish dish is sure to please.

Wilted Spinach Salad (*bottom left*, page 229); Fried Chicken (*middle*);
Garlic Smashed Potatoes (*top*, page 201)

Fried Chicken

6 servings   Prep Time: 25 minutes   Start to Finish: I hour

Fried chicken used to be the Sunday dinner of choice for many Southern families. Most cooks swear by a heavy cast-iron skillet for frying chicken, to make it crisp on the outside, moist and tender on the inside. If you don't have a cast-iron skillet, a heavy enameled Dutch oven will do well, too.

¹/₂ cup all-purpose flour

I teaspoon salt

I teaspoon paprika

¹/₄ teaspoon pepper

2¹/₂- to 3-lb cut-up broiler-fryer chicken

Vegetable oil

Creamy Gravy (below right)

1 Mix flour, salt, paprika and pepper. Coat chicken with flour mixture.

2 Heat oil (¼ inch) in 12-inch skillet over medium-high heat until hot. Cook chicken in oil about 10 minutes or until light brown on all sides; reduce heat. Cover tightly and simmer, turning once or twice, until juice of chicken is clear when thickest piece is cut to bone (170°F for breasts; 180°F for thighs and drumsticks). If skillet cannot be covered tightly, add 1 to 2 tablespoons water.

3 Remove cover during the last 5 minutes of cooking to crisp chicken. Remove chicken; keep warm. Make Creamy Gravy; serve with chicken.

Creamy Gravy

I tablespoons all-purpose flour
¹/₂ cup chicken broth or water
¹/₂ cup milk
   Salt and pepper

1 Pour drippings from skillet into bowl, leaving brown particles in skillet. Return 2 tablespoons drippings to skillet. Stir in flour.

2 Cook over low heat, stirring constantly, until smooth and bubbly; remove from heat. Stir in broth and milk. Heat to boiling, stirring constantly. Boil and stir 1 minute. Stir in a few drops browning sauce, if desired. Stir in salt and pepper.

I Serving: Calories 310 (Calories from Fat 170); Fat 19g (Saturated 4g); Cholesterol 70mg; Sodium 710mg; Carbohydrate 10g (Dietary Fiber 0g); Protein 25g

Baked Chicken and Rice

6 servings   Prep Time: 10 minutes   Start to Finish: 1 hour 10 minutes

This hearty favorite is based on a traditional Spanish recipe, Arroz con Pollo, "chicken with rice." A specialty of Mexico and Puerto Rico, this classic dish is especially popular in the Southwest.

2¹/₂- to 3-lb cut-up broiler-fryer chicken

³/₄ teaspoon salt

¹/₄ to ¹/₂ teaspoon paprika

¹/₄ teaspoon pepper

2¹/₂ cups chicken broth

1 cup uncooked regular long grain rice

1 medium onion, chopped (¹/₂ cup)

1 clove garlic, finely chopped

¹/₂ teaspoon salt

1¹/₂ teaspoons chopped fresh or ¹/₂ teaspoon dried oregano leaves

¹/₈ teaspoon ground turmeric

1 dried bay leaf

2 cups shelled fresh green peas*

Pimiento strips

Pitted ripe olives

1 Heat oven to 350°F.

2 Place chicken, skin sides up, in ungreased rectangular baking dish, 13 × 9 inches. Sprinkle with salt, paprika and pepper. Bake uncovered 30 minutes.

3 Heat broth to boiling. Remove chicken and drain fat from dish. Mix broth, rice, onion, garlic, salt, oregano, turmeric, bay leaf and peas in baking dish. Top with chicken. Cover with foil and bake about 30 minutes or until rice is done, liquid is absorbed and juice of chicken is clear when thickest piece is cut to bone (170°F for breasts; 180°F for thighs and drumsticks). Remove bay leaf. Top with pimiento strips and olives.

*1 package (10 oz) frozen green peas, thawed and drained, can be substituted for the fresh green peas.

1 Serving: Calories 355 (Calories from Fat 110); Fat 12g (Saturated 6g); Cholesterol 70mg; Sodium 1,030mg; Carbohydrate 36g (Dietary Fiber 3g); Protein 29g

COUNTRY KITCHEN WISDOM

Purchasing Poultry

Everyone loves chicken. Choosing fresh poultry is easier if you follow these tips:

- Check the sell-by date on the label. This shows the last day the product should be sold. The product will be fresh if cooked and eaten within 2 days of this date.

- Package trays and bags should have very little or no liquid in the bottom.

- Avoid packages that are stacked too high in the refrigerator case. They may not be cold enough, which shortens shelf life.

- Frozen poultry should be hard to the touch and free of freezer burn and tears in the packaging.

- Check for a fresh odor (you can usually smell off odors through plastic). If you smell anything unusual, the product isn't fresh.

Baked Barbecued Chicken

6 servings   Prep Time: 5 minutes   Start to Finish: 1 hour 5 minutes

Barbecued chicken is a year-round favorite. Serve with a side of mashed potatoes, coleslaw or corn bread to make this best-loved recipe a best-loved meal.

1/4 cup margarine or butter

2 1/2- to 3-lb cut-up broiler-fryer chicken

1 cup ketchup

1/2 cup water

1/4 cup lemon juice

1 tablespoon Worcestershire sauce

2 teaspoons paprika

1/2 teaspoon salt

1 medium onion, finely chopped (1/2 cup)

1 clove garlic, finely chopped

1 Heat oven to 375°F.

2 Heat margarine in rectangular pan, 13 × 9 inches, in oven. Place chicken in margarine, turning to coat. Arrange skin side down in pan. Bake uncovered 30 minutes.

3 Mix remaining ingredients in 1-quart saucepan. Heat to boiling; remove from heat. Drain fat from chicken; turn skin side up. Spoon sauce over chicken. Bake uncovered about 30 minutes longer or until juice of chicken is clear when thickest piece is cut to bone (170°F for breasts; 180°F for thighs and drumsticks).

1 Serving: Calories 315 (Calories from Fat 170); Fat 19g (Saturated 4g); Cholesterol 70mg; Sodium 710mg; Carbohydrate 10g (Dietary Fiber 1g); Protein 23g

Grilled Lemon Chicken

6 servings   Prep Time: 5 minutes   Start to Finish: 4 hours 5 minutes

Lemon and chicken go together so well. The lemon adds a nice flavor to the chicken and keeps the meat juicy and tender.

2 1/2- to 3-lb broiler-fryer chicken, cut up

1/2 cup dry white wine

1/4 cup lemon juice

2 tablespoons vegetable oil

1 teaspoon paprika

2 lemons, thinly sliced

1 clove garlic, crushed

Paprika

Celery leaves, if desired

1 Place chicken in glass or plastic bowl. Mix remaining ingredients except slices from 1 of the lemons and paprika; pour over chicken. Cover and refrigerate at least 3 hours.

2 Remove chicken and discard lemon slices; reserve marinade. Cover and grill chicken, bone sides down, 5 to 6 inches from medium heat 15 to 20 minutes; turn chicken. Cover and grill, turning and brushing 2 or 3 times with marinade, 20 to 40 minutes longer or until juice of chicken is clear when thickest piece is cut to bone (170°F for breasts; 180°F for thighs and drumsticks).

3 Roll edges of remaining lemon slices in paprika; arrange around chicken. Garnish with celery leaves.

1 Serving: Calories 240 (Calories from Fat 145); Fat 16g (Saturated 4g); Cholesterol 70mg; Sodium 70mg; Carbohydrate 2g (Dietary Fiber 0g); Protein 22g

Chicken and Dumplings

4 to 6 servings | Prep Time: 35 minutes | Start to Finish: 2 hours 35 minutes

Who can resist the classic chicken and dumplings? This is a good meal to make when the wind is blowing and you need dinner to warm your body and soul.

3- to $3\frac{1}{2}$-lb stewing chicken, cut up
4 celery stalk tops
I medium carrot, sliced ($\frac{1}{2}$ cup)
I small onion, sliced
2 sprigs parsley, chopped
I teaspoon salt
$\frac{1}{8}$ teaspoon pepper
5 cups water
$2\frac{1}{2}$ cups Original Bisquick
$\frac{2}{3}$ cup milk

1 Remove any excess fat from chicken. Place chicken, giblets (except liver), neck, celery, carrot, onion, parsley, salt, pepper and water in Dutch oven. Cover and heat to boiling; reduce heat to low. Cook over low heat about 2 hours or until juice of chicken is clear when thickest piece is cut to bone (170°F for breasts; 180°F for thighs and drumsticks).

2 Remove chicken and vegetables from Dutch oven. Skim $\frac{1}{2}$ cup fat from broth; reserve. Remove broth; reserve 4 cups and refrigerate the rest for another use.

3 Heat reserved fat in Dutch oven over low heat. Stir in $\frac{1}{2}$ cup of the Bisquick. Cook, stirring constantly, until mixture is smooth and bubbly; remove from heat. Stir in reserved broth. Heat to boiling, stirring constantly. Boil and stir 1 minute. Return chicken and vegetables to Dutch oven; heat until hot.

4 Mix remaining 2 cups Bisquick and the milk until soft dough forms. Drop dough by spoonfuls onto hot chicken mixture (do not drop directly into liquid). Cook uncovered over low heat 10 minutes. Cover and cook 10 minutes longer.

I Serving: Calories 645 (Calories from Fat 260); Fat 29g (Saturated 8g); Cholesterol 130mg; Sodium 1,750mg; Carbohydrate 51g (Dietary Fiber 2g); Protein 47g

COUNTRY KITCHEN WISDOM

Dumplings

Drop the dough by spoonfuls onto the meat or vegetables in the stew, not into the gravy or liquid. If the dough is dropped right into the liquid, the simmering action may break up the dumplings.

Chicken in Cream

Sophisticated yet easy to make, this recipe is perfect when you want a romantic dinner for two. Just double the recipe if serving four.

2 lb bone-in chicken pieces (thighs, legs, breast)

1 can (10.5 oz) condensed cream of chicken soup

$^1\!/_2$ cup apple cider

1 tablespoon plus 2 teaspoon Worcestershire sauce

$^3\!/_4$ teaspoon salt

$^1\!/_3$ cup chopped onion

1 clove garlic, finely chopped

1 can (3 oz) sliced mushrooms, drained

Paprika

1 Heat oven to 350°F.

2 Place chicken in ungreased baking pan, 9 × 9 inches. Mix all ingredients except paprika and pour on chicken.

3 Bake uncovered 1 hour, spooning off excess fat and basting once with sauce. Sprinkle with paprika and bake about 30 minutes or until juice of chicken is clear when thickest piece is cut to bone (170°F for breasts; 180°F for thighs and drumsticks).

1 Serving: Calories 560 (Calories from Fat 290); Fat 32g (Saturated 9g); Cholesterol 175mg; Sodium 1,429mg; Carbohydrate 14g (Dietary Fiber 1g); Protein 55g

Country Captain

6 servings   Prep Time: 15 minutes   Start to Finish: 1 hour 20 minutes

An American classic, this recipe is said to have gotten its name from a British officer who brought the recipe home from India. It is a mixture of chicken and vegetables, seasoned with curry and other spices, cooked over low heat, then garnished with almonds and served over rice.

$\frac{1}{2}$ cup all-purpose flour

1$\frac{1}{4}$ teaspoons salt

$\frac{1}{4}$ teaspoon pepper

2$\frac{1}{2}$- to 3-lb cut-up broiler-fryer chicken

$\frac{1}{4}$ cup vegetable oil

1$\frac{1}{2}$ teaspoons curry powder

1$\frac{1}{2}$ teaspoons chopped fresh or $\frac{1}{2}$ teaspoon dried thyme leaves

1 large onion, chopped (1 cup)

1 large green bell pepper, chopped (1$\frac{1}{2}$ cups)

1 clove garlic, finely chopped, or $\frac{1}{8}$ teaspoon garlic powder

1 can (16 oz) whole tomatoes, undrained

$\frac{1}{4}$ cup currants or raisins

$\frac{1}{3}$ cup slivered almonds, toasted

3 cups hot cooked rice

Grated fresh coconut and chutney, if desired

1   Heat oven to 350°F.

2   Mix flour, 1 teaspoon of the salt and the pepper. Coat chicken with flour mixture. Heat oil in 10-inch skillet until hot. Cook chicken in oil over medium heat 15 to 20 minutes or until light brown. Place chicken in ungreased 2$\frac{1}{2}$-quart casserole. Drain oil from skillet.

3   Add curry powder, thyme, the remaining $\frac{1}{4}$ teaspoon salt, the onion, bell pepper, garlic and tomatoes to skillet. Heat to boiling, stirring frequently to loosen brown particles from skillet. Pour over chicken. Cover and bake about 40 minutes or until juice of chicken is clear when thickest piece is cut to bone (170°F for breasts; 180°F for thighs and drumsticks). Skim fat from liquid if necessary. Add currants and bake uncovered 5 minutes. Sprinkle with almonds. Serve with rice and, if desired, grated fresh coconut and chutney.

1 Serving: Calories 490 (Calories from Fat 215); Fat 12g (Saturated 5g); Cholesterol 70mg; Sodium 670mg; Carbohydrate 44g (Dietary Fiber 3g); Protein 28g

COUNTRY KITCHEN WISDOM

A Couple of Currants

There are actually two very different fruits that are called currants. The first, used in this recipe, is similar to a raisin only smaller. It is the dried form of the zante grape. The second type of currant is a tiny berry in either black, red or white. The red and white ones are typically eaten out of hand or used in baking. The black ones are used for syrups, preserves and liqueurs such as cassis.

Chicken Cacciatore

6 servings   Prep Time: 15 minutes   Start to Finish: 1 hour 15 minutes

Slash time from the preparation of this dish by using 2 cups of your favorite prepared tomato pasta sauce for the whole tomatoes, tomato sauce, oregano, basil and salt.

3- to 3½-lb cut-up broiler-fryer chicken
½ cup all-purpose flour
¼ cup vegetable oil
1 medium green bell pepper
2 medium onions
2 cloves garlic, crushed
1 can (16 oz) whole tomatoes, drained
1 can (8 oz) tomato sauce
1 cup sliced mushrooms (3 oz)*
1½ teaspoons chopped fresh or ½ teaspoon dried oregano leaves
1 teaspoon chopped fresh or ¼ teaspoon dried basil leaves
½ teaspoon salt
Grated Parmesan cheese

1 Coat chicken with flour.

2 Heat oil in 12-inch skillet over medium-high heat. Cook chicken in oil 15 to 20 minutes or until brown on all sides; drain.

3 Cut bell pepper and onions crosswise in half; cut each half into fourths. Stir bell pepper, onions and remaining ingredients except cheese into chicken in skillet, breaking up tomatoes. Heat to boiling; reduce heat. Cover and simmer 30 to 40 minutes or until juice of chicken is clear when thickest piece is cut to bone (170°F for breasts; 180°F for thighs and drumsticks). Serve with cheese.

*1 can (4 oz) sliced mushrooms, drained, can be substituted for the fresh mushrooms.

1 Serving: Calories 330 (Calories from Fat 145); Fat 16g (Saturated 4g); Cholesterol 75mg; Sodium 730mg; Carbohydrate 19g (Dietary Fiber 3g); Protein 30g

COUNTRY KITCHEN WISDOM

Call It Cacciatore

Cacciatore is Italian for "hunter," and the name refers to foods prepared with mushrooms, onions, tomatoes, and herbs or "hunter-style." Cacciatore can be prepared with chicken, meat or game although chicken is the most common.

Cornmeal Chicken with Casera Sauce

7 servings | **Prep Time: 15 minutes** | **Start to Finish: 1 hour 15 minutes**

If you eat a lot of chicken, this recipe offers a nice change. Casera sauce is a mixture of tomato and spicy peppers that gives the chicken a little kick.

2¹/₂- to 3-lb broiler-fryer chicken

2 tablespoons yellow cornmeal

¹/₈ teaspoon salt

¹/₂ teaspoon chili powder

¹/₄ teaspoon dried oregano leaves

2 tablespoons margarine or butter

2 tablespoons vegetable oil

Casera Sauce (below right)

1 Heat oven to 375°F.

2 Cut chicken into pieces; cut each breast half into halves and remove skin. Mix cornmeal, salt, chili powder and oregano. Coat chicken with cornmeal mixture.

3 Heat margarine and oil in rectangular pan, 13 × 9 inches, in oven until margarine is melted. Place chicken, meaty sides down, in pan. Bake uncovered 30 minutes; turn chicken. Cook 20 to 30 minutes longer or until juice of chicken is clear when thickest piece is cut to bone (170°F for breasts; 180°F for thighs and drumsticks).

4 Prepare Casera Sauce; serve with chicken.

Casera Sauce

1 medium tomato, finely chopped

1 small onion, chopped (¹/₄ cup)

1 small clove garlic, crushed

1 canned green chile or jalapeño pepper, seeded and finely chopped

2 teaspoons finely chopped cilantro or parsley

2 teaspoons lemon juice

¹/₄ teaspoon dried oregano leaves

Mix all ingredients in large bowl.

1 Serving: Calories 200 (Calories from Fat 110); Fat 12g (Saturated 2g); Cholesterol 55mg; Sodium 160mg; Carbohydrate 5g (Dietary Fiber 1g); Protein 19g

COUNTRY KITCHEN WISDOM

Sublime Sangria

Nothing cools down a spicy meal like sweet sangria. Here's a quick recipe for this delectable beverage. Combine ²/₃ cup lemon juice, ¹/₃ cup orange juice and ¹/₄ cup sugar in a half-gallon pitcher. Stir until the sugar is dissolved. Stir in 1 bottle (750 milliliters) dry red or white wine. Add ice, if desired. Add orange and lemon slices to the pitcher. Delicious!

Cornmeal Chicken with Casera Sauce (*left*)
and Spanish Rice (*right*, page 213)

Stuffed Chicken Breasts

4 servings   Prep Time: 20 minutes   Start to Finish: 1 hour 15 minutes

Stuffing chicken breasts is a beautiful way to dress up chicken. Not only does the stuffing add color, it's delicious as well!

4 chicken breast halves
  (about 1¼ lb)

Apple-Hazelnut Stuffing
(below right)

½ teaspoon salt

¼ teaspoon pepper

2 teaspoons margarine or
  butter, melted

1 Heat oven to 375°F. Grease square pan, 9 × 9 inches, with shortening.

2 Remove bones from chicken breasts. Loosen, but do not remove, skin from chicken breasts.

3 Make stuffing.

4 Spread one-fourth of the stuffing evenly between meat and skin of each chicken breast. Smooth skin over breasts, tucking under loose areas. Place chicken, skin sides up, in pan. Sprinkle with salt and pepper. Drizzle with margarine.

5 Bake uncovered 45 to 55 minutes or until thickest pieces are fork-tender and juices run clear.

Apple-Hazelnut Stuffing

¼ cup chopped hazelnuts (filberts)
1 medium apple, chopped (1 cup)
1 package (3 oz) cream cheese, softened

Mix all ingredients in medium bowl.

1 Serving: Calories 330 (Calories from Fat 190); Fat 21g (Saturated 7g); Cholesterol 95mg; Sodium 440mg; Carbohydrate 7g (Dietary Fiber 1g); Protein 29g

Chicken in Red Wine Vinegar

6 servings | Prep Time: 15 minutes | Start to Finish: 35 minutes

Simmering in red wine vinegar keeps the chicken moist and juicy and lends a sophisticated flavor to the dish. Even better, this can be done in about 30 minutes. Serve it with rice and a nice green salad on the side.

- 2 tablespoons margarine or butter
- 2 cloves garlic, crushed
- 3 shallots, chopped
- 6 boneless, skinless chicken breast halves (about 1³/₄ lb)
- ¹/₂ cup red wine vinegar
- 2 medium tomatoes, finely chopped (1¹/₂ cups)
- 2 teaspoons chopped fresh or ¹/₂ teaspoon dried thyme leaves
- ¹/₂ teaspoon salt
- ¹/₄ teaspoon pepper

1 Melt margarine in 10-inch skillet. Add garlic, shallots and chicken. Cook over medium-high heat 12 to 15 minutes, turning after 6 minutes, until chicken is no longer pink. Reduce heat to low. Add vinegar, cover and cook 5 minutes.

2 Stir in remaining ingredients, turn chicken. Cook over low heat 10 to 12 minutes until juice of chicken is clear when center of thickest part is cut (170°F).

1 Serving: Calories 195 (Calories from Fat 70); Fat 8g (Saturated 2g); Cholesterol 75mg; Sodium 320mg; Carbohydrate 5g (Dietary Fiber 1g); Protein 27g

Savory Chicken and Rice

4 servings | Prep Time: 10 minutes | Start to Finish: 25 minutes

This same recipe can easily tranform beef and pork into a savory meal. Just use 1 lb of beef boneless sirloin steak or pork tenderloin, cut into 1-inch pieces, in place of the chicken. Cook the meat in oil about 5 minutes or until beef is of desired doneness or pork is no longer pink in center.

- 1 lb boneless, skinless chicken breast halves
- 1¹/₂ cups sliced mushrooms (4 oz)
- 1 cup baby-cut carrots
- 1¹/₂ cups water
- 1 package (4.1 oz) long grain and wild rice mix with chicken and herbs

1 Trim fat from chicken. Cut chicken into 1-inch pieces.

2 Spray 10-inch nonstick skillet with cooking spray. Heat over medium heat. Cook chicken in skillet about 5 minutes, stirring occasionally, until fork-tender and juices run clear.

3 Stir in remaining ingredients. Heat to boiling; reduce heat. Cover and simmer 15 minutes, stirring occasionally. Uncover and simmer about 3 minutes longer, stirring occasionally, until carrots are tender.

1 Serving: Calories 255 (Calories from Fat 45); Fat 5g (Saturated 2g); Cholesterol 70mg; Sodium 280mg; Carbohydrate 25g (Dietary Fiber 1g); Protein 29g

Cheesy Chicken Tortellini

5 servings   Prep Time: 10 minutes   Start to Finish: 30 minutes

To turn this into an interesting meatless meal, omit the chicken and add an additional cup chopped red or yellow bell peppers. Serve with warm crusty bread to dip into the cheesy sauce and, for dessert, slices of cut-up fresh melon.

1 package (7 oz) dried cheese-filled tortellini

1 tablespoon vegetable oil

1 lb boneless, skinless chicken breast halves, cut into thin slices

1/4 cup margarine or butter

1 small green bell pepper, chopped (1/2 cup)

2 shallots, finely chopped

1 clove garlic, finely chopped

1/4 cup all-purpose flour

1/4 teaspoon pepper

1 3/4 cups milk

1/2 cup shredded mozzarella cheese (2 oz)

1/2 cup shredded Swiss cheese (2 oz)

1/4 cup grated Parmesan or Romano cheese

1 Cook and drain tortellini as directed on package.

2 While tortellini is cooking, heat oil in 3-quart saucepan over medium-high heat. Cook chicken in oil, stirring frequently, until fork-tender and juices run clear. Remove from saucepan; keep warm.

3 Melt margarine in saucepan over medium-high heat. Cook bell pepper, shallots and garlic in margarine, stirring frequently, until bell pepper is crisp-tender. Stir in flour and pepper. Cook over medium heat, stirring constantly, until mixture is bubbly, remove from heat. Stir in milk. Heat to boiling, stirring constantly. Boil and stir 1 minute; remove from heat.

4 Stir in mozzarella and Swiss cheeses until melted. Stir in tortellini and chicken until coated. Sprinkle with Parmesan cheese.

1 Serving: Calories 430 (Calories from Fat 225); Fat 25g (Saturated 9g); Cholesterol 110mg; Sodium 400mg; Carbohydrate 18g (Dietary Fiber 1g); Protein 34g

Chicken and Pepper Stir-Fry

4 servings | Prep Time: 25 minutes | Start to Finish: 25 minutes

Here's the answer for those hectic days when you feel like time is not on your side. Mix up the marinade when you get home and let it sit 15 minutes while you change into comfortable clothes. If you prepare quick-cooking rice, a satisfying dinner will be on the table in no time flat!

2 tablespoons soy sauce

2 tablespoons ketchup

$^1/_2$ teaspoon ground ginger

2 cloves garlic, finely chopped

$^3/_4$ lb boneless, skinless chicken breast halves, thinly sliced

3 tablespoons vegetable oil

6 medium green onions, cut into 1-inch pieces

2 medium bell peppers, thinly sliced

4 cups hot cooked rice

1 Mix soy sauce, ketchup, ginger and garlic in large resealable food-storage plastic bag. Add chicken; seal bag. Let stand 15 minutes.

2 Heat 1 tablespoon oil in 10-inch skillet or wok over medium-high heat. Add onions and bell peppers; stir-fry until crisp-tender. Remove mixture from skillet.

3 Heat remaining 2 tablespoons oil in same skillet. Add chicken; stir-fry until fork-tender and juices run clear. Stir in pepper mixture. Serve over rice.

1 Serving: Calories 415 (Calories from Fat 115); Fat 13g (Saturated 3g); Cholesterol 45mg; Sodium 650mg; Carbohydrate 52g (Dietary Fiber 2g); Protein 24g

COUNTRY KITCHEN WISDOM

Cooking with Cheese

Be creative when cooking with cheese. Use cheeses with similar flavor and texture interchangeably. Here are some tips that will come in handy:

- To prevent cheese from becoming tough and stringy, keep cooking temps low and cooking times short.
- Cheese melts and blends better with other ingredients if you shred it or cut it into small pieces.
- Place cheese in the freezer for 30 minutes for easier slicing and shredding.
- To shred very soft cheese, use a grater with large holes, or finely chop it.
- Keep in mind that lower-fat cheeses don't melt well. They also become rubbery, and the flavor may change.
- Add a cheese topping to casseroles during the last 5 to 10 minutes of baking for perfect melting.
- When broiling cheese-topped dishes, keep a close eye on them—the cheese melts fast.
- Cheese microwaves well, but use lower power settings.

Chinese Chicken Stir-Fry

4 servings   Prep Time: 15 minutes   Start to Finish: 15 minutes

No need for take-out when this recipe can be ready before you even find the menu! Put the rice on to cook first as it takes 5 minutes longer than the stir-fry.

1 tablespoon vegetable oil

1 lb cut-up chicken breast for stir-fry

1/2 cup teriyaki baste and glaze (from 12-oz bottle)

3 tablespoons lemon juice

1 package (16 oz) frozen broccoli, carrots, water chestnuts and red peppers

Hot cooked rice, couscous or noodles, if desired

1 Heat wok or 12-inch skillet over high heat. Add oil; rotate wok to coat side. Add chicken; stir-fry 3 to 4 minutes or until chicken is fork-tender and juices run clear.

2 Stir in remaining ingredients except rice. Heat to boiling, stirring constantly; reduce heat to low. Cover and simmer about 6 minutes or until vegetables are crisp-tender. Serve with rice.

1 Serving: Calories 245 (Calories from Fat 45); Fat 7g (Saturated 1g); Cholesterol 66mg; Sodium 1,312mg; Carbohydrate 19g (Dietary Fiber 2g); Protein 29g

Chicken with Spaghetti Sauce

6 servings | Prep Time: 5 minutes | Start to Finish: 1 hour 5 minutes

Looking for a tasty way to use up leftover chicken? This dish fits the bill—and it is popular with the younger set, too, so it is sure to please the entire family!

1 cup water

1 teaspoon salt

1 teaspoon sugar

1 tablespoon chopped fresh or 1 teaspoon dried oregano leaves

2 teaspoons chopped fresh or ³/₄ teaspoon dried basil leaves

1 teaspoon chopped fresh or ¹/₂ teaspoon dried marjoram leaves

¹/₂ teaspoon chopped fresh or ¹/₄ teaspoon dried rosemary leaves, if desired

1 large onion, chopped (¹/₂ cup)

1 clove garlic, crushed

1 dried bay leaf

1 can (8 oz) tomato sauce

1 can (6 oz) tomato paste

1¹/₂ cups cut-up cooked chicken

Hot cooked spaghetti

Grated Parmesan cheese, if desired

1 Heat all ingredients except chicken, spaghetti and cheese to boiling in 10-inch skillet; reduce heat. Cover and simmer 30 minutes, stirring occasionally.

2 Stir in chicken. Cover and simmer 30 minutes, stirring occasionally. Remove bay leaf. Serve sauce over spaghetti. Sprinkle with Parmesan cheese.

1 Serving: Calories 125 (Calories from Fat 45); Fat 5g (Saturated 1g); Cholesterol 30mg; Sodium 870mg; Carbohydrate 12g (Dietary Fiber 3g); Protein 11g

Chicken Pot Pie

6 servings | Prep Time: 20 minutes | Start to Finish: 55 minutes

Traditionally, whenever fried chicken was made (whether for Sunday dinner, a picnic or a potluck supper), the pan drippings were saved. The next day, the drippings were made into gravy and combined with leftover chicken and vegetables for chicken pot pie. Many cooks liked to personalize their pot pies, some preferring a lattice top and others using small cookie cutters to cut openings for the steam.

$1/3$ cup margarine or butter

$1/3$ cup all-purpose flour

$1/3$ cup chopped onion

$1/2$ teaspoon salt

$1/4$ teaspoon pepper

$1 3/4$ cups chicken or turkey broth

$2/3$ cup milk

$2 1/2$ to 3 cups cut-up cooked chicken or turkey

1 cup shelled fresh green peas*

2 medium carrots, diced (1 cup)*

Standard Pastry for Two-Crust 9-inch Pie (page 297)

1 Heat margarine in 2-quart saucepan over low heat until melted. Stir in flour, onion, salt and pepper. Cook, stirring constantly, until mixture is bubbly; remove from heat.

2 Stir in broth and milk. Heat to boiling, stirring constantly. Boil and stir 1 minute. Stir in chicken, peas and carrots.

3 Heat oven to 425°F.

4 Prepare Pastry. Roll two-thirds of the pastry into 13-inch square; ease into ungreased square pan, 9 × 9 inches. Pour chicken mixture into pastry-lined pan. Roll remaining pastry into 11-inch square. Fold pastry in half and cut slits near center so steam can escape. Place square over filling; turn edges under the flute. Bake until golden brown, about 35 minutes.

1 package (10 oz) frozen peas and carrots can be substituted for the fresh peas and carrots. Rinse with cold water to separate; drain.

1 Serving: Calories 655 (Calories from Fat 385); Fat 43g (Saturated 14g); Cholesterol 65mg; Sodium 1,120mg; Carbohydrate 45g (Dietary Fiber 3g); Protein 25g

COUNTRY KITCHEN WISDOM

Keeping It Cool

Having a last minute gathering? You picked up the drinks, but they came right off the shelf. Here's how to chill them quickly. Completely submerge bottles and cans in a bucket or large pot filled half with ice and half water for about 20 minutes. This also works well for carbonated beverages that will be added at the last minute to a punch or used to mix with other ingredients.

Roast Turkey with Stuffing

10 servings   Prep Time: 40 minutes   Start to Finish: 5 hours 10 minutes

This holiday classic is delicious whether you stuff it with our Chestnut Stuffing (page 216), Corn Bread Stuffing (page 217), Rice Stuffing (page 215), or a favorite tried-and-true stuffing recipe of your own.

Stuffing (pages 215–217)
10- to 12-lb turkey
Margarine or butter, melted

1 Make stuffing. Fill wishbone area with stuffing. Fasten neck skin to back with skewer. Fold wings across back with tips touching. Fill body cavity lightly with stuffing. (Do not pack—stuffing will expand.) Tuck drumsticks under band of skin at tail or skewer to tail.

2 Heat oven to 325°F. Place turkey, breast side up, on rack in shallow roasting pan. Brush with margarine. If using a meat thermometer, insert meat thermometer so tip is in thickest part of inside thigh muscle or thickest part of breast meat and does not touch bone. (Tip of thermometer can be inserted in center of stuffing.) Do not add water. Do not cover. Place a tent of foil loosely over turkey when it begins to turn golden. When two-thirds done, cut band or remove skewer holding legs.

3 Roast 3 hours 30 minutes to 4 hours 30 minutes or until thermometer reads 180°F and drumsticks move easily when lifted or twisted. Thermometer inserted in center of stuffing should read 165°F.

4 Let stand about 20 minutes before carving. As soon as possible after serving, remove all stuffing from turkey. Promptly refrigerate stuffing and turkey separately; use within 2 days.

1 Serving (without stuffing): Calories 436 (Calories from Fat 132); Fat 15g (Saturated 4g); Cholesterol 257mg; Sodium 197mg; Carbohydrate 0g (Dietary Fiber 0g); Protein 71g

COUNTRY KITCHEN WISDOM

Stuffing Lore

What's a Thanksgiving meal without stuffing? The *Plimouth Plantation Cookbook* (note the original spelling of Plymouth, Massachusetts) shows us that the Pilgrims fancied spicy, sweet stuffings instead of savory, often sage-flavored stuffings so popular today.

Savory Southern Turkey Barbecue

8 servings   Prep Time: 30 minutes   Start to Finish: 30 minutes

Tangy and spicy, this is a nice change from Sloppy Joes or burgers. Classic Crunchy Coleslaw (page 224) and a fruit salad would be perfect accompaniments. Trim the fat even more by choosing ground turkey breast.

2 tablespoons water

1 small onion, diced ($1/4$ cup)

$1/4$ cup diced green bell pepper

1 lb ground turkey

$1/4$ cup cider vinegar

2 tablespoons packed brown sugar

1 teaspoon ground mustard

1 teaspoon chili powder

1 teaspoon paprika

1 teaspoon Worcestershire sauce

$1/4$ teaspoon pepper

1 can (8 oz) tomato sauce

8 kaiser rolls, split

1 Heat water in 10-inch skillet over medium heat. Cook onion and bell pepper in water about 2 minutes, stirring occasionally, until crisp-tender. Stir in turkey. Cook 4 to 5 minutes, stirring occasionally, until no longer pink.

2 Stir in remaining ingredients except rolls; reduce heat. Cover and simmer about 20 minutes, stirring occasionally, until hot. Fill rolls with turkey mixture.

1 Serving: Calories 265 (Calories from Fat 70); Fat 8g (Saturated 2g); Cholesterol 40mg; Sodium 490mg; Carbohydrate 33g (Dietary Fiber 2g); Protein 17g

Wild Rice and Turkey Casserole

6 servings   Prep Time: 5 minutes   Start to Finish: 1 hour 10 minutes

This wonderful casserole can be put together in a snap. Are you a mushroom lover? Then, stir in a can (4 oz) sliced mushrooms, drained, in step 2. Complete the meal by serving steamed broccoli on the side.

2 cups cut-up cooked turkey

$2 1/4$ cups boiling water

$1/3$ cup milk

1 small onion, chopped ($1/4$ cup)

1 can (10.75 oz) condensed cream of mushroom soup

1 package (6 oz) seasoned long grain and wild rice

1 Heat oven to 350°F.

2 Mix all ingredients, including seasoning packet from rice mix, in ungreased 2-quart casserole.

3 Cover and bake 45 to 50 minutes or until rice is tender. Uncover and bake 10 to 15 minutes longer or until liquid is absorbed.

1 Serving: Calories 155 (Calories from Fat 45); Fat 5g (Saturated 2g); Cholesterol 40mg; Sodium 500mg; Carbohydrate 12g (Dietary Fiber 0g); Protein 16g

Turkey Divan

Don't wait until you have Thanksgiving leftovers to make this recipe! Use 6 large slices of turkey (about 1/4 inch thick) from the deli. This is also wonderful with fresh asparagus spears in place of the broccoli.

1½ lb broccoli*

¼ cup margarine or butter

¼ cup all-purpose flour

⅛ teaspoon ground nutmeg

1½ cups chicken broth

1 cup grated Parmesan cheese

2 tablespoons dry white wine or chicken broth

½ cup whipping cream

6 large slices cooked turkey breast, ¼ inch thick (¾ lb)

1 Heat water to boiling in medium saucepan; add broccoli. Cook about 10 minutes or until stems are crisp-tender; drain.

2 Melt margarine in 1-quart saucepan over medium heat. Stir in flour and nutmeg. Cook, stirring constantly, until smooth and bubbly; remove from heat. Stir in broth. Heat to boiling, stirring constantly. Boil and stir 1 minute; remove from heat. Stir in ½ cup of the cheese and the wine.

3 Beat whipping cream in chilled small bowl with electric mixer on high speed until stiff. Fold cheese sauce into whipped cream.

4 Place hot broccoli in ungreased rectangular baking dish, 11 × 7 inches. Top with turkey. Pour cheese sauce over turkey. Sprinkle with remaining ½ cup cheese.

5 Set oven control to broil.

6 Broil with top 3 to 5 inches from heat, about 3 minutes, or until cheese is bubbly and light brown.

*2 packages (10 oz each) frozen broccoli spears, cooked and drained, can be substituted for the fresh broccoli.

1 Serving: Calories 325 (Calories from Fat 190); Fat 21g (Saturated 9g); Cholesterol 75mg; Sodium 600mg; Carbohydrate 9g (Dietary Fiber 2g); Protein 27g

COUNTRY KITCHEN WISDOM

Succulent Substitutions

This dish turns leftovers into a delicious meal. You can vary the ingredients for a different dish each time. For any of these variations, chicken or pork roast can replace the turkey. Try one of the following:

- Substitute asparagus for the broccoli and Gouda for the parmesan.
- Try broccoli rabe in place of the broccoli and Asiago for the parmesan.
- Replace the broccoli with fennel and use Jarlsburg in place of the parmesan.

Turkey Tetrazzini

6 servings | Prep Time: 15 minutes | Start to Finish: 45 minutes

Here's a tasty way to get only 13 grams fat and 390 calories per serving and keep the flavor and creaminess of the dish. Use 2 teaspoons chicken bouillon granules and 4 cups evaporated skimmed milk for the chicken broth and half-and-half. Then decrease the flour to ¼ cup, the margarine to 2 tablespoons and the almonds to ¼ cup. Top with reduced-fat Cheddar cheese. Yum!

1 package (7 oz) spaghetti
2 cups chicken or turkey broth
2 cups half-and-half or milk
½ cup all-purpose flour
¼ cup margarine or butter
½ teaspoon salt
¼ teaspoon pepper
2 cups cut-up cooked turkey or chicken
1 cup sliced ripe olives
½ cup slivered almonds
1 cup shredded Cheddar cheese (4 oz)

1 Heat oven to 350°F. Cook and drain spaghetti as directed on package.

2 Mix broth, half-and-half, flour, margarine, salt and pepper in 3-quart saucepan. Heat to boiling over medium heat, stirring constantly. Boil and stir 1 minute.

3 Stir in spaghetti, turkey, olives and almonds. Spread in ungreased 2-quart casserole. Sprinkle with cheese.

4 Bake uncovered 25 to 30 minutes or until hot and bubbly.

1 Serving: Calories 590 (Calories from Fat 315); Fat 35g (Saturated 13g); Cholesterol 85mg; Sodium 1,030mg; Carbohydrate 42g (Dietary Fiber 3g); Protein 30g

Black-and-White Turkey Chili

6 servings | Prep Time: 20 minutes | Start to Finish: 50 minutes

Cannellini beans are large, white Italian kidney beans that are quite delicious. Top your chili with some sliced avocado, chopped fresh cilantro or a dollop of sour cream to add a creamy texture and kick of flavor to this chili.

1 tablespoon vegetable oil

1½ lb turkey breast tenderloins, cut into ½-inch cubes

1 medium onion, chopped (1 cup)

½ cup chopped Anaheim or poblano chiles

1 clove garlic, finely chopped

3 cups chicken broth

1 tablespoon chili powder

1 large tomato, chopped (1 cup)

1 can (15 oz) black beans, drained

1 can (15 to 16 oz) cannellini beans, rinsed and drained

1 Heat oil in 3-quart saucepan over medium-high heat. Cook turkey, onion, chiles and garlic in oil, stirring occasionally, until turkey is no longer pink and onion is tender.

2 Stir in remaining ingredients. Heat to boiling; reduce heat. Cover and simmer 30 minutes, stirring occasionally.

1 Serving: Calories 350 (Calories from Fat 65); Fat 7g (Saturated 2g); Cholesterol 65mg; Sodium 770mg; Carbohydrate 39g (Dietary Fiber 9g); Protein 42g

Broiled Salmon with Hazelnut Butter

4 servings   Prep Time: 10 minutes   Start to Finish: 25 minutes

Salmon and hazelnuts are both native to—and favorites of—the Pacific Northwest. Fresh king salmon, the largest of the Pacific salmon, and silver salmon, with its deep coral color, are especially prized. You'll find the delicate Hazelnut Butter a wonderful topping for not only fish but also vegetables and poultry.

Hazelnut Butter (below right)

4 salmon fillets (1 to 1½ lb)

½ teaspoon salt

⅛ teaspoon pepper

1 Make Hazelnut Butter.

2 Set oven control to broil. Grease shallow roasting pan or jelly roll pan, 15 × 10 inches.

3 Sprinkle both sides of fish with salt and pepper. Place in pan. Broil fish with tops 4 to 6 inches from heat 4 minutes. Turn and spread each fillet with about 1 tablespoon Hazelnut Butter. Broil until fish flakes easily with fork, 4 to 8 minutes.

Hazelnut Butter

2 tablespoons finely chopped hazelnuts (filberts)
3 tablespoons margarine or butter, softened
1 tablespoon chopped fresh parsley
1 teaspoon lemon juice

Heat oven to 350°F. Spread hazelnuts on ungreased cookie sheet. Bake 4 to 6 minutes, stirring occasionally, until golden brown; cool. Mix with remaining ingredients.

1 Serving: Calories 245 (Calories from Fat 160); Fat 18g (Saturated 3g); Cholesterol 55mg; Sodium 450mg; Carbohydrate 1g (Dietary Fiber 0g); Protein 20g

Wild Rice–Stuffed Pike

Summer in any lake region of North America is highlighted with an abundance of fresh fish. Whether you caught the fish yourself or selected them from your fishmonger, this dressed fish, stuffed with wild rice, mushrooms, celery and almonds, is delectable.

Wild Rice Stuffing (below right)

2½- to 3-lb northern pike, cleaned, or any mild-flavored dressed fish, such as walleyed pike, lake trout or bass

Lemon juice

Salt

Vegetable oil

¼ cup margarine or butter, melted

2 tablespoons lemon juice

Lemon wedges

1 Make Wild Rice Stuffing. Heat oven to 350°F.

2 Pat pike dry inside and out. Rub cavity with lemon juice; sprinkle with salt.

3 Loosely stuff with Wild Rice Stuffing. Close opening with skewers and lace with string. (Spoon any remaining stuffing into buttered baking dish; cover and refrigerate. Place in oven with pike 30 minutes before fish is done.) Brush pike with oil; place in shallow roasting pan.

4 Mix margarine and 2 tablespoons lemon juice.

5 Bake pike uncovered 50 to 60 minutes, brushing occasionally with margarine mixture, until pike flakes easily with fork. Serve with lemon wedges.

Wild Rice Stuffing

¾ cup uncooked wild rice

2 cups water

1½ teaspoons chicken bouillon granules

1 medium stalk celery (with leaves), thinly sliced (½ cup)

1 medium onion, chopped (½ cup)

¼ cup slivered almonds

¼ cup margarine or butter

1 package (8 oz) mushrooms, sliced (3 cups)

1 Heat rice, water, and bouillon granules to boiling, stirring once or twice; reduce heat. Cover and simmer until tender, 40 to 50 minutes. After cooking rice 30 minutes, check to see that rice is not sticking to pan. Add 2 to 3 tablespoons water if necessary.

2 Cook and stir celery, onion and almonds in margarine in 10-inch skillet over medium heat until vegetables are tender and almonds are light brown. Add mushrooms; cook until tender, about 5 minutes longer. Stir in wild rice.

1 Serving: Calories 350 (Calories from Fat 177); Fat 20g (Saturated 4g); Cholesterol 37mg; Sodium 275mg; Carbohydrate 20g (Dietary Fiber 3g); Protein 24g

Broiled Trout

4 servings | Prep Time: 10 minutes | Start to Finish: 10 minutes

Fresh fish never tasted so good! Lemon and parsley are all the flavors needed to enhance fresh fish. This simple recipe comes together in minutes and is sure to please.

4 rainbow trout or other small fish (6 to 8 oz each), cleaned, boned and butterflied

¼ cup margarine or butter, melted

2 tablespoons lemon juice

1 tablespoon chopped fresh parsley

Salt

Paprika

1 Set oven control to broil. Grease broiler pan. Place fish in pan, skin sides down.

2 Mix margarine, lemon juice and parsley; brush on fish. Sprinkle lightly with salt and paprika.

3 Broil fish with tops 4 inches from heat 5 to 6 minutes or until fish flakes easily with fork.

1 Serving: Calories 265 (Calories from Fat 158); Fat 18g (Saturated 4g); Cholesterol 69mg; Sodium 247mg; Carbohydrate 1g (Dietary Fiber 0g); Protein 25g

Southern Fried Catfish

6 servings | Prep Time: 10 minutes | Start to Finish: 50 minutes

Pan-fried catfish used to be a southern secret, but it seems the rest of the country has caught on. Dipped in seasoned cornmeal and quickly fried, catfish served with hush puppies and coleslaw steals the show at fish fries in the South. Found naturally in the Mississippi River and Southern inland waterways, catfish are also farmed in several states of the Mississippi Delta.

Vegetable oil

1¼ cup cornmeal

1 teaspoon salt

½ teaspoon ground red pepper (cayenne)

¼ teaspoon pepper

6 small catfish (about ½ lb each), skinned and pan-dressed

½ cup all-purpose flour

2 eggs, slightly beaten

Lemon wedges, if desired

1 Heat oven to 275°F.

2 Heat oil (½ inch) in 12-inch skillet over medium-high heat until hot. Mix cornmeal, salt, red pepper and pepper; set aside.

3 Coat catfish with flour; dip into eggs. Coat with cornmeal mixture. Fry catfish, 2 at a time, about 6 minutes on each side until golden brown. Keep warm in oven while frying remaining catfish. Garnish with lemon wedges.

1 Serving: Calories 340 (Calories from Fat 45); Fat 5g (Saturated 1g); Cholesterol 175mg; Sodium 450mg; Carbohydrate 28g (Dietary Fiber 2g); Protein 48g

Grilled Tuna with Salsa

6 servings | Prep Time: 10 minutes | Start to Finish: 2 hours 10 minutes

To seed tomatoes, cut in half crosswise and squeeze gently—the seeds will slide right out.

³/₄ cup finely chopped fresh parsley

¹/₄ cup finely chopped onion (¹/₄ cup)

¹/₃ cup lemon juice

2 tablespoons vegetable oil

¹/₄ teaspoon salt

2 medium tomatoes, seeded and chopped

1 clove garlic, crushed

1 can (4.25 oz) chopped black olives, drained

6 tuna or shark steaks (about 5 oz each)

1 Combine all ingredients except tuna in glass bowl. Cover tightly and refrigerate salsa 2 to 4 hours to blend flavors.

2 Place tuna on oiled grill over medium-heat and cook 3 minutes. Turn steaks and cook 4 to 5 minutes or until tuna turns opaque in center. Remove from grill; keep warm.

3 Serve with salsa.

To broil: Set oven control to broil. Arrange steaks on oiled rack in broiler pan. Broil with steaks about 4 inches from heat 10 to 15 minutes, turning after 6 minutes, until fish flakes easily with fork. Continue as directed.

1 Serving: Calories 280 (Calories from Fat 125); Fat 14g (Saturated 3g); Cholesterol 55mg; Sodium 320mg; Carbohydrate 5g (Dietary Fiber 1g); Protein 34g

COUNTRY KITCHEN WISDOM

How Much to Buy?

Whether you catch your own or shop at a fish market, use this easy serving guide to determine how much fish to you'll need:

- Whole fish: About 1 lb per serving
- Drawn fish: About ³/₄ lb per serving
- Pan-dressed fish: About ¹/₂ lb per serving
- Fish steaks: About ¹/₄ to ¹/₃ lb per serving
- Fish fillets: About ¹/₄ to ¹/₃ lb per serving

Impossibly Easy Tuna and Cheddar Pie

6 to 8 servings | Prep Time: 20 minutes | Start to Finish: 1 hour

This recipe is a hit with adults and kids alike. A big plus is that it uses ingredients you usually have on hand, making it a snap to put together.

- 2 large onions, chopped (2 cups)
- ¼ cup margarine or butter
- 2 cans (6 oz each) tuna, drained
- 2 cups shredded Cheddar cheese (8 oz)
- 3 eggs
- 1¼ cups milk
- 1 cup Original Bisquick
- ⅛ teaspoon pepper
- 2 tomatoes, thinly sliced

1 Heat oven to 400°F. Grease glass pie plate, 10 inches, or square baking dish, 8 × 8 inches, or six 10-oz custard cups.

2 Cook onions in margarine in 10-inch skillet over low heat, stirring occasionally, until onions are light brown. Sprinkle tuna, 1 cup of the cheese and the onions in pie plate.

3 Stir eggs, milk, Bisquick and pepper with fork until blended. Pour into pie plate.

4 Bake pie plate or square dish 25 to 30 minutes or custard cups, 20 to 25 minutes, or until knife inserted in center comes out clean. Top with tomato slices and remaining 1 cup cheese. Bake 3 to 5 minutes longer or until cheese is melted. Cool 5 minutes.

1 Serving: Calories 445 (Calories from Fat 245); Fat 27g (Saturated 12g); Cholesterol 165mg; Sodium 850mg; Carbohydrate 22g (Dietary Fiber 1g); Protein 30g

Tuna Noodles Romanoff

6 servings | Prep Time: 15 minutes | Start to Finish: 55 minutes

You can use crushed croutons or seasoned crackers if you run short on seasoned bread crumbs.

- 4 cups uncooked egg noodles (8 oz)
- 2 cans (6 oz each) tuna, drained
- 1 cup sliced mushrooms (3 oz)
- 2 tablespoons capers
- 1½ cups sour cream
- ¾ cup milk
- 1 teaspoon salt
- ¼ teaspoon pepper
- ¼ cup seasoned dry bread crumbs
- ¼ cup grated Romano or Parmesan cheese
- 2 tablespoons margarine or butter, melted

1 Heat oven to 350°F.

2 Cook and drain noodles as directed on package. Mix noodles, tuna, mushrooms, capers, sour cream, milk, salt and pepper in ungreased 2-quart casserole or square baking dish, 8 × 8 inches.

3 Mix bread crumbs, cheese and margarine; sprinkle over tuna mixture. Bake uncovered 35 to 40 minutes or until hot and bubbly.

1 Serving: Calories 350 (Calories from Fat 175); Fat 19g (Saturated 10g); Cholesterol 90mg; Sodium 957mg; Carbohydrate 25g (Dietary Fiber 1g); Protein 23g

Spaghetti with White Clam Sauce

4 servings | Prep Time: 15 minutes | Start to Finish: 15 minutes

For a flavor twist, add some chopped fresh basil with the parsley.

1 package (7 oz) spaghetti

1/4 cup margarine or butter

2 cloves garlic, finely chopped

2 tablespoons chopped fresh parsley

2 cans (6.5 oz each) minced clams, undrained

Chopped fresh parsley

1/2 cup grated Parmesan cheese

1 Cook spaghetti as directed on package.

2 While spaghetti is cooking, melt margarine in 1½-quart saucepan over medium heat. Cook garlic in margarine about 3 minutes, stirring occasionally, until light golden. Stir in 2 tablespoons parsley and the clams. Heat to boiling; reduce heat to low. Simmer uncovered 3 to 5 minutes.

3 Drain spaghetti. Pour sauce over spaghetti; toss. Sprinkle with parsley and cheese.

1 Serving: Calories 400 (Calories from Fat 145); Fat 16g (Saturated 5g); Cholesterol 35mg; Sodium 370mg; Carbohydrate 43g (Dietary Fiber 1g); Protein 22g

Angel Hair Pasta with Shrimp

4 servings | Prep Time: 15 minutes | Start to Finish: 15 minutes

This is a great meal to make when you want something a bit fancy but don't have a lot of time. Of course, any long pasta will do—fettuccini, spaghetti or angel hair.

1 package (16 oz) capellini (angel hair) pasta

1/4 cup olive or vegetable oil

2 tablespoons chopped fresh parsley

2 cloves garlic, finely chopped

1 small red chile, seeded and finely chopped

1/3 cup dry white wine or vegetable broth

1/2 teaspoon freshly grated nutmeg

3/4 lb uncooked peeled deveined small shrimp, thawed if frozen

1 Cook and drain pasta as directed on package.

2 While pasta is cooking, heat oil in Dutch oven or 12-inch skillet over medium-high heat. Cook parsley, garlic and chile in oil 1 minute, stirring occasionally. Stir in wine, nutmeg and shrimp; reduce heat. Cover and simmer about 5 minutes or until shrimp are pink and firm.

3 Add pasta to shrimp mixture and cook over medium heat 2 minutes, stirring occasionally.

1 Serving: Calories 565 (Calories from Fat 170); Fat 19g (Saturated 3g); Cholesterol 215mg; Sodium 160mg; Carbohydrate 75g (Dietary Fiber 3g); Protein 27g

Linguine with Red Clam Sauce

6 servings | Prep Time: 15 minutes | Start to Finish: 30 minutes

No fresh clams? Then use 2 cans (6.5 oz each) minced clams, drained and liquid reserved, for the fresh clams in this recipe. Serve this pasta dish with a Caesar salad, garlic bread and dry red wine for a special meal.

12 oz uncooked linguine

1/4 cup olive or vegetable oil

3 cloves garlic, finely chopped

1 can (28 oz) whole Italian-style tomatoes, drained and chopped

1 small red chile, seeded and finely chopped

1 pint shucked fresh small clams, drained and liquid reserved

1 tablespoon chopped fresh parsley

1 teaspoon salt

1 Cook and drain linguine as directed on package.

2 While linguine is cooking, heat oil in 3-quart saucepan over medium-high heat. Cook garlic in oil, stirring frequently, until golden. Stir in tomatoes and chile. Cook 3 minutes, stirring frequently.

3 Stir in clam liquid. Heat to boiling; reduce heat. Simmer uncovered 10 minutes.

4 Chop clams. Stir clams, parsley and salt into tomato mixture. Cover and simmer about 15 minutes, stirring occasionally, until clams are tender. Serve over linguine.

1 Serving: Calories 320 (Calories from Fat 100); Fat 11g (Saturated 1g); Cholesterol 15mg; Sodium 600mg; Carbohydrate 44g (Dietary Fiber 3g); Protein 14g

Scallop Stir-Fry

4 servings | Prep Time: 15 minutes | Start to Finish: 15 minutes

The different between bay scallops and sea scallops is their size: Bay scallops are smaller. If you are using whole bay scallops, you can skip cutting them into smaller pieces.

1 package (3 oz) Oriental flavor ramen noodles

1 tablespoon olive oil or vegetable oil

3/4 lb asparagus, cut into 1-inch pieces

1 large red bell pepper, cut into thin strips

1 small onion, chopped (1/4 cup)

2 cloves garlic, finely chopped

3/4 lb sea scallops, cut into 1-inch pieces

1 tablespoon soy sauce

2 tablespoons lemon juice

1 teaspoon sesame oil

1/4 teaspoon red pepper sauce

1 Reserve seasoning packet from noodles. Cook and drain noodles as directed on package.

2 While noodles are cooking, heat olive oil in 12-inch skillet over high heat. Add asparagus, bell pepper, onion and garlic. Stir-fry 2 to 3 minutes or until vegetables are crisp-tender. Add scallops; stir-fry until white.

3 Mix contents of reserved seasoning packet, the soy sauce, lemon juice, sesame oil and pepper sauce. Stir into scallop mixture. Stir in noodles; heat through.

1 Serving: Calories 185 (Calories from Fat 65); Fat 7g (Saturated 1g); Cholesterol 25mg; Sodium 580mg; Carbohydrate 12g (Dietary Fiber 2g); Protein 21g

Linguine with Red Clam Sauce

Marinated Ginger Shrimp

6 servings   Prep Time: 10 minutes   Start to Finish: 1 hour 10 minutes

Fresh ginger adds a wonderful flavor kick to these easy-to-make shrimp. It is all the tastes of summer wrapped into one bite.

1½ lb uncooked fresh or frozen large shrimp, peeled and deveined

1 tablespoon soy sauce

1 tablespoon lemon juice

1 teaspoon vegetable oil

1 teaspoon finely chopped fresh gingerroot

1 Place shrimp in glass baking dish. Mix remaining ingredients and pour over shrimp. Cover and refrigerate at least 30 minutes.

2 Set oven control to broil. Drain shrimp; arrange on rack in broiler pan. Broil 4 inches from heat 5 to 8 minutes, turning once, until shrimp turn pink. Refrigerate shrimp at least 30 minutes until cold.

1 Serving: Calories 60 (Calories from Fat 10); Fat 1g (Saturated 0g); Cholesterol 0mg; Sodium 270mg; Carbohydrate 1g (Dietary Fiber 0g); Protein 12g

COUNTRY KITCHEN WISDOM

Go for Gingerroot

Gingerroot is a gnarled, brown root. Side branches have a milder tangy ginger flavor than the main root, which can have a hot "bite." Grate unpeeled gingerroot, or peel and chop or slice it, to add flavor to foods such as stir-fries, sauces and baked goods. The easiest way to peel gingerroot is to scrape off the skin with the edge of a spoon. Slice the gingerroot and stack the slices to chop or mince.

Seafood à la Newburg

6 servings   Prep Time: 15 minutes   Start to Finish: 15 minutes

You can enjoy this rich, creamy dish by using imitation crab and lobster pieces if fresh seafood isn't readily available. You may want to try an updated version served over spinach fettuccine or ladled into flaky pastry shells instead of the traditional biscuits or toast points.

2 egg yolks

¼ cup margarine or butter

¼ cup all-purpose flour

½ teaspoon salt

¼ teaspoon pepper

2 cups milk

1 tablespoon dry sherry or lemon juice

2 cups cut-up cooked seafood

Baking Powder Biscuits (page 254) or toast points

1 Beat egg yolks with fork in small bowl.

2 Melt margarine in 2-quart saucepan over low heat. Stir in flour, salt and pepper. Cook over medium heat, stirring constantly, until smooth and bubbly; remove from heat. Gradually stir in milk. Heat to boiling, stirring constantly. Boil and stir 1 minute.

3 Immediately stir at least half of the hot mixture into egg yolks; stir back into hot mixture in saucepan. Boil and stir 1 minute; remove from heat. Stir in sherry and seafood. Heat until seafood is hot.

4 Serve over hot biscuits.

1 Serving: Calories 220 (Calories from Fat 110); Fat 12g (Saturated 3g); Cholesterol 135mg; Sodium 490mg; Carbohydrate 10g (Dietary Fiber 0g); Protein 18g

Shrimp Fajitas

4 servings (2 fajitas each)   Prep Time: 20 minutes   Start to Finish: 20 minutes

Try these fajitas for fun and variety. They're easy to assemble and delicious to consume! After you peel the shrimp, rub your hands with cut lemon and then wash as usual. The lemon leaves your hands fresh-smelling and odor-free.

1 lb uncooked medium shrimp in shells

8 flour tortillas (7 or 8 inch)

1 tablespoon vegetable oil

1 tablespoon lime juice

1½ teaspoons chopped fresh or ½ teaspoon dried oregano leaves

¼ teaspoon ground cumin

1 clove garlic, finely chopped

1 cup salsa

1 cup guacamole

1 Peel shrimp. (If shrimp are frozen, do not thaw; peel in cold water.) Make a shallow cut lengthwise down back of each shrimp; wash out vein.

2 Heat oven to 250°F.

3 Wrap tortillas in foil, or place on heatproof serving plate and cover with foil. Heat in oven about 15 minutes or until warm.

4 Heat oil in 10-inch skillet over medium heat. Cook shrimp, lime juice, oregano, cumin and garlic in oil about 5 minutes, stirring constantly, until shrimp are pink and firm.

5 Divide shrimp evenly among tortillas. Top with salsa and guacamole. Fold one end of each tortilla up about 1 inch over shrimp mixture. Fold right and left sides over folded end, overlapping. Fold down remaining end. Serve fajitas with additional salsa and guacamole if desired.

1 Serving: Calories 475 (Calories from Fat 160); Fat 18g (Saturated 3g); Cholesterol 160mg; Sodium 1,060mg; Carbohydrate 58g (Dietary Fiber 7g); Protein 27g

COUNTRY KITCHEN WISDOM

Fabulous Fajitas

Hailing from Northern Mexico, the term *fajita* means "girdle," referring to the part of the steer where the meat used in beef fajitas comes from. Americans call this cut a skirt steak. But we're no longer limited to beef—chicken, fish and seafood also make delicious fajitas.

Savory Seafood Gumbo

8 servings   Prep Time: 30 minutes   Start to Finish: 1 hour 45 minutes

Gumbo is a perfect example of why America is "the great melting pot." Back in the eighteenth century, French Canadians who settled in the bayou country, southwest of New Orleans, became known as Cajuns. They made a hearty soup-like stew. Creoles, locals of Spanish and/or French descent, added hot red pepper to the stew. And the African Americans contributed okra, a native African vegetable, to thicken it.

1 large onion, chopped (1 cup)

1 medium green bell pepper, chopped (1 cup)

2 medium stalks celery, chopped (1 cup)

1½ lb fresh okra, cut into ½-inch pieces

2 cloves garlic, crushed

¼ cup plus 2 tablespoons margarine or butter

½ cup all-purpose flour

1 can (16 oz) whole tomatoes, undrained

5 cups chicken broth, clam juice or water

2 teaspoons salt

½ teaspoon white pepper

½ teaspoon black pepper

½ teaspoon ground red pepper (cayenne)

2 dried bay leaves

1 lb uncooked fresh or frozen medium shrimp, peeled and deveined

¾ lb cooked lump crabmeat

3 cups hot cooked rice

1 Mix onion, bell pepper, celery, okra and garlic; reserve.

2 Heat margarine in 6- to 8-quart Dutch oven over medium heat until hot. Gradually stir in flour. Cook, stirring constantly, until caramel colored, about 7 minutes.

3 Add half of reserved onion mixture. Cook, stirring constantly, about 1 minute. Stir in remaining onion mixture. Cook until celery is crisp-tender, about 4 minutes. Stir in and break up tomatoes. Stir in chicken broth, salt, white pepper, black pepper, red pepper and bay leaves. Heat to boiling; reduce heat. Simmer uncovered, stirring occasionally, 1 hour.

4 Add shrimp and crabmeat to Dutch oven. Heat to boiling. Boil uncovered 1½ minutes; remove from heat. Cover and let stand 15 minutes. Stir and remove bay leaves. Serve over rice.

1 Serving: Calories 345 (Calories from Fat 0); Fat 11g (Saturated 0g); Cholesterol 95mg; Sodium 1,690mg; Carbohydrate 40g (Dietary Fiber 0g); Protein 22g

Shrimp Creole

4 servings   Prep Time: 10 minutes   Start to Finish: 20 minutes

Overcooking shrimp makes them tough, so cook shrimp just until pink and firm. Hot corn bread muffins served with honey would taste great with this spicy dish.

2 cups frozen stir-fry bell peppers and onions (from 16-oz package)

1 lb uncooked peeled deveined medium shrimp, thawed if frozen

1 can (14.5 oz) chunky tomatoes with crushed red pepper, undrained

1 teaspoon chopped fresh or $1/4$ teaspoon dried thyme leaves

$1/8$ teaspoon garlic powder

Hot cooked rice, if desired

1 Spray 12-inch nonstick skillet with cooking spray. Heat over medium-high heat. Cook frozen vegetables in skillet about 3 minutes, stirring occasionally, until crisp-tender.

2 Stir in remaining ingredients, except rice. Heat to boiling; reduce heat. Cover and simmer 8 to 10 minutes, stirring occasionally, until shrimp are pink and firm. Serve with rice.

1 Serving: Calories 110 (Calories from Fat 10); Fat 1g (Saturated 0g); Cholesterol 160mg; Sodium 350mg; Carbohydrate 8g (Dietary Fiber 2g); Protein 19g

Maryland Crab Cakes

4 servings   Prep Time: 15 minutes   Start to Finish: 1 hour 45 minutes

You don't need to go to Maryland to enjoy these savory cakes. For an irresistible meal, serve hot crab cakes with fresh lemon slices or top each with a dollop of tangy tartar sauce.

1 lb lump crabmeat, cooked, cartilage removed, and flaked ($2^1/2$ to 3 cups)

$1^1/2$ cups soft white bread crumbs (without crusts)

2 tablespoons margarine or butter, melted

1 teaspoon dry mustard

$1/2$ teaspoon salt

$1/8$ teaspoon pepper

2 egg yolks, beaten

Vegetable oil

1 Mix all ingredients except oil. Shape into 4 patties, each about $3^1/2$ inches in diameter. Refrigerate until firm, about 1 hour 30 minutes.

2 Heat oil (1 inch) to 375°F. Fry patties 4 to 5 minutes or until golden brown on both sides; drain.

1 Serving: Calories 315 (Calories from Fat 180); Fat 21g (Saturated 4g); Cholesterol 165mg; Sodium 889mg; Carbohydrate 9g (Dietary Fiber 1g); Protein 24g

CHAPTER FOUR

Country Meats and Mainstays

GATHERING AROUND THE TABLE IS A GREAT TIME FOR YOUR FAMILY TO SHARE THE DAY OVER A HOME-COOKED DINNER.

Roasted, grilled, baked, broiled or fried—whatever you might want to satisfy any craving. You'll find succulent and marvelously seasoned beef, pork and lamb dishes ranging from savory pot roast and meat loaf to hearty casseroles and stews to tender ribs and lamb chops.

Western Meat Loaf

8 servings   Prep Time: 20 minutes   Start to Finish: 1 hour 45 minutes

Rustle up this loaf when you're hankering for something a little different. The horseradish adds a nice little kick.

1 can (8 oz) tomato sauce

1½ lb ground beef

½ lb ground pork

2 cups soft bread crumbs (about 3 slices bread)

2 to 4 tablespoons prepared horseradish

1¼ teaspoons ground mustard

½ teaspoon salt

¼ teaspoon pepper

1 medium onion, finely chopped (½ cup)

2 eggs, slightly beaten

1 tablespoon packed brown sugar

1 Heat oven to 350°F.

2 Reserve ¼ cup of the tomato sauce. Mix the remaining tomato sauce and remaining ingredients except ¼ teaspoon of the mustard and brown sugar.

3 Pack in ungreased loaf pan, 8 × 4 or 9 × 5 inches, or shape mixture into loaf in ungreased rectangular pan, 13 × 9 inches. Mix reserved tomato sauce, ¼ teaspoon dry mustard and brown sugar and spread over loaf.

4 Bake uncovered until done, 1 hour to 1 hour 15 minutes or until meat thermometer inserted in center of loaf reads 160°F. Cover loosely with foil; let stand 10 minutes. Remove from pan.

1 Serving: Calories 370 (Calories from Fat 170); Fat 19g (Saturated 7g); Cholesterol 120mg; Sodium 625mg; Carbohydrate 25g (Dietary Fiber 1g); Protein 26g

Old-Fashioned Meat Loaf

6 servings | Prep Time: 15 minutes | Start to Finish: 1 hour 30 minutes

Rolled oats are a cook's secret ingredient of the perfect meat loaf, because they bind the meat mixture into a loaf of wonderful texture and juiciness. Tomatoes, tomato sauce and ketchup are often added to contribute moisture as well as flavor. Some cooks also believe that using only beef makes a drier meat loaf, so this recipe uses a combination of ground pork and beef.

1 can (16 oz) whole tomatoes
1¼ lb ground beef
¼ lb ground pork
¾ cup old-fashioned oats
⅓ cup chopped onion
1 egg
1 teaspoon salt
¼ teaspoon pepper

1 Heat oven to 375°F.

2 Drain tomatoes, reserving ¼ cup liquid. Cut tomatoes up with fork. Mix reserved liquid, the tomatoes and remaining ingredients thoroughly.

3 Pack in ungreased loaf pan, 8 × 4 inches. Bake uncovered until done, 1 hour to 1 hour 15 minutes or until meat thermometer inserted in center of loaf reads 160°F. Cover loosely with foil; let stand 10 minutes. Remove from pan.

1 Serving: Calories 435 (Calories from Fat 250); Fat 28g (Saturated 11g); Cholesterol 150mg; Sodium 600mg; Carbohydrate 11g (Dietary Fiber 2g); Protein 37g

Impossibly Easy Cheeseburger Pie

6 servings | Prep Time: 15 minutes | Start to Finish: 40 minutes

We've made mealtime truly easy! This main-dish pie makes its own crust with the help of Bisquick baking mix. Serve this family favorite with green beans and whole wheat rolls for a super supper!

1 lb ground beef
1 large onion, chopped (1 cup)
¼ teaspoon pepper
1½ cups milk
3 eggs
¾ cup Original Bisquick
2 medium tomatoes, sliced
4 slices (1 oz each) Cheddar or American cheese, cut in half

1 Heat oven to 400°F. Grease pie plate, 10 inches, or square baking dish, 8 × 8 inches, or six 10-oz custard cups.

2 Cook beef and onion in 10-inch skillet over medium heat 8 to 10 minutes, stirring occasionally, until beef is brown; drain. Stir in pepper. Spread in pie plate.

3 Stir milk, eggs and Bisquick with fork until blended. Pour into pie plate.

4 Bake 25 minutes. Top with tomatoes and cheese. Bake 5 to 8 minutes longer or until knife inserted in center comes out clean. Cool 5 minutes.

1 Serving: Calories 270 (Calories from Fat 135); Fat 15g (Saturated 8g); Cholesterol 145mg; Sodium 570mg; Carbohydrate 18g (Dietary Fiber 1g); Protein 16g

Corn Bread Beef Bake

Sloppy Joes with Potatoes and Onion

4 servings | Prep Time: 10 minutes | Start to Finish: 40 minutes

This version of sloppy joes uses potatoes and onions instead of buns, so it's not quite as sloppy but still a favorite of kids. Round out the meal with Traditional Corn Bread (page 245) and Avocado-Citrus Salad (page 226).

1 lb lean ground beef

Salt and pepper

1 medium onion, sliced and separated into rings

2 medium potatoes, thinly sliced

1 can (15.5 oz) sloppy joe sauce

1 Crumble ground beef into 10-inch skillet. Sprinkle with salt and pepper. Layer onion and potatoes on beef; pour sauce over top.

2 Cover and cook over low heat about 30 minutes or until beef is done and potatoes are tender.

1 Serving: Calories 410 (Calories from Fat 180); Fat 20g (Saturated 7g); Cholesterol 65mg; Sodium 890mg; Carbohydrate 37g (Dietary Fiber 3g); Protein 24g

Corn Bread Beef Bake

6 servings | Prep Time: 20 minutes | Start to Finish: 1 hour

A cast-iron skillet works well for this casserole. For a Spanish twist, leave out the corn and add ½ cup pitted green olives, ¼ cup raisins and ¼ cup slivered almonds.

1 lb ground beef

1 can (14.5 oz) Mexican-style stewed tomatoes, undrained

1 can (15 oz) black beans, rinsed and drained

1 can (8 oz) tomato sauce

½ cup frozen whole kernel corn

2 teaspoons chili powder

1 can (11.5 oz) refrigerated corn bread twists

1 Heat oven to 350°F.

2 Cook beef in 10-inch ovenproof skillet over medium heat 8 to 10 minutes, stirring occasionally, until beef is brown; drain. Stir in tomatoes, beans, tomato sauce, corn and chili powder; heat to boiling.

3 Immediately top with corn bread twists left in round shape (do not unwind), pressing down gently.

4 Bake uncovered 35 to 40 minutes or until corn bread is golden brown.

1 Serving: Calories 450 (Calories from Fat 170); Fat 19g (Saturated 7g); Cholesterol 45mg; Sodium 1,050mg; Carbohydrate 51g (Dietary Fiber 6g); Protein 25g

Salisbury Steak

4 servings   Prep Time: 20 minutes   Start to Finish: 30 minutes

This classic dish was named after Dr. J. H. Salisbury who recommended his patients eat plenty of beef for a wide variety of ailments.

1 lb ground beef

1/3 cup dry bread crumbs

1/2 teaspoon salt

1/4 teaspoon pepper

1 egg

1 large onion, sliced and separated into rings

1 can (10.5 oz) condensed beef broth

8 oz mushrooms, sliced (about 3 cups)*

2 tablespoons cold water

2 teaspoons cornstarch

1 Mix ground beef, bread crumbs, salt, pepper and egg; shape into 4 oval patties, each about ¾ inch thick.

2 Cook patties in 10-inch skillet over medium heat about 10 minutes, turning occasionally, until brown; drain. Add onion, broth and mushrooms. Heat to boiling; reduce heat. Cover and simmer about 10 minutes or until patties are done.

3 Remove patties; keep warm. Heat onion mixture to boiling. Mix water and cornstarch; stir into onion mixture. Boil and stir 1 minute. Serve over patties.

*1 can (4 oz) mushroom pieces and stems, drained, can be substituted for the fresh mushrooms.

1 Serving: Calories 325 (Calories from Fat 162); Fat 18g (Saturated 7g); Cholesterol 115mg; Sodium 830mg; Carbohydrate 15g (Dietary Fiber 2g); Protein 28g

Chili

4 servings | Prep Time: 15 minutes | Start to Finish: 1 hour 35 minutes

Cocoa in chili? Yes, indeed. It lends a deep, rich flavor to the chili and will leave your guests wondering what the secret ingredient may be.

1 lb ground beef

1 large onion, chopped (1 cup)

2 cloves garlic, crushed

1 tablespoon chili powder

1/2 teaspoon salt

1 teaspoon ground cumin

1 teaspoon dried oregano leaves

1 teaspoon baking cocoa

1/2 teaspoon red pepper sauce

1 can (16 oz) whole tomatoes, undrained

1 can (15 to 16 oz) red kidney beans, undrained

1 Cook beef, onion and garlic in 3-quart saucepan over medium heat 8 to 10 minutes, stirring occasionally, until beef is brown; drain.

2 Stir in remaining ingredients except beans, breaking up tomatoes. Heat to boiling; reduce heat to low. Cover and simmer 1 hour, stirring occasionally.

3 Stir in beans. Heat to boiling; reduce heat to low. Simmer uncovered about 20 minutes, stirring occasionally, until desired thickness.

1 Serving: Calories 340 (Calories from Fat 155); Fat 17g (Saturated 7g); Cholesterol 65mg; Sodium 890mg; Carbohydrate 27g (Dietary Fiber 9g); Protein 29g

Meatball Porcupines

2 servings | Prep Time: 20 minutes | Start to Finish: 1 hour 5 minutes

Don't worry—these porcupines won't prick you! The combination of rice and ground beef gives these meatballs the appearance of little porcupines.

¹/₂ lb ground beef

¹/₄ cup uncooked rice

¹/₄ cup milk or water

2 tablespoons chopped onion

¹/₂ teaspoon salt

¹/₄ teaspoon celery salt

¹/₈ teaspoon garlic salt

Dash of pepper

1 tablespoon shortening

1 can (8 oz) tomato sauce

¹/₂ cup water

1¹/₂ teaspoons Worcestershire sauce

1 Mix beef, rice, milk, onion, salt, celery salt, garlic salt and pepper. Form into 4 medium balls.

2 Fry in melted shortening, turning frequently, until light brown (but not crusty) on all sides. Add tomato sauce, water and Worcestershire sauce. Mix well.

3 Cover; simmer 45 minutes over low heat. Add a small amount of additional water if liquid cooks down too much.

1 Serving: Calories 440 (Calories from Fat 215); Fat 24g (Saturated 8g); Cholesterol 65mg; Sodium 1,630mg; Carbohydrate 32g (Dietary Fiber 2g); Protein 26g

Barbecued Beef and Beans

6 servings | Prep Time: 20 minutes | Start to Finish: 30 minutes

This meaty, cheesy meal, complete with savory beans, is made even better with Traditional Corn Bread (page 245) served alongside for sopping up any extra sauce.

I lb ground beef

I teaspoon chili powder

I teaspoon garlic salt

I can (16 oz) barbecue beans

I can (10.75 oz) condensed tomato soup

I can (4 oz) chopped green chiles

I cup shredded American or Monterey Jack cheese (4 oz)

1 Mix ground beef, chili powder and garlic salt. Shape into 6 patties, each about $1/2$ inch thick.

2 Cook in 10-inch skillet over medium heat, turning frequently, until brown. Remove patties from skillet; drain drippings from skillet.

3 Stir beans, soup and chiles into skillet until well mixed; place patties on top. Heat to boiling; reduce heat. Cover and simmer about 5 minutes or until patties are of desired doneness.

4 Sprinkle with cheese; cover and let stand about 2 minutes or until cheese is melted. Serve over corn bread or toasted hamburger buns if desired.

I Serving: Calories 320 (Calories from Fat 160); Fat 18g (Saturated 8g); Cholesterol 60mg; Sodium 1,200mg; Carbohydrate 21g (Dietary Fiber 4g); Protein 23g

Family-Favorite Tacos

6 servings   Prep Time: 25 minutes   Start to Finish: 25 minutes

Tacos are always family favorites since you get to fix them the way you like them. Don't forget to offer salsa to top off everyone's creation—and for those who like a little heat, sliced jalapeños are the perfect trick.

1 lb ground beef

1 large onion, chopped (1 cup)

1 envelope (about 1.25 oz) taco seasoning mix

1 cup water

1 package (12 oz) tortilla chips

1/2 head lettuce, shredded

2 medium tomatoes, chopped (1 1/2 cups)

1 can (2.25 oz) sliced ripe olives, drained

1 cup shredded Cheddar or Monterey Jack cheese (4 oz)

2/3 cup dairy sour cream

1 Cook beef and onion in 10-inch skillet over medium heat 8 to 10 minutes, stirring occasionally, until beef is brown; drain. Stir in seasoning mix (dry) and water.

2 Heat to boiling; reduce heat. Simmer uncovered 10 minutes, stirring occasionally. Spoon beef mixture onto chips. Top with remaining ingredients.

1 Serving: Calories 575 (Calories from Fat 315); Fat 35g (Saturated 13g); Cholesterol 80mg; Sodium 950mg; Carbohydrate 46g (Dietary Fiber 6g); Protein 25g

Beef Goulash

6 servings   Prep Time: 15 minutes   Start to Finish: 55 minutes

Any collection of favorite recipes has to include goulash. The mixture of macaroni and ground meat is always a family favorite—and it's easy to make. Add a nice tossed salad to round out the meal.

1 1/2 lb ground beef

1 medium onion, chopped (1/2 cup)

1 medium stalk celery, sliced (1/2 cup)

1 can (16 oz) stewed tomatoes

1 tomato can (2 cups) water

1 package (7 oz) uncooked elbow macaroni (2 cups)

1 can (6 oz) tomato paste

1 tablespoon Worcestershire sauce

1 teaspoon salt

1/2 teaspoon pepper

1 Heat oven to 350°F.

2 Cook beef, onion and celery in 4-quart ovenproof Dutch oven about 10 minutes, stirring occasionally, until beef is brown; drain. Stir in remaining ingredients.

3 Cover and bake about 40 minutes or until liquid is absorbed and goulash is hot; stir.

1 Serving: Calories 405 (Calories from Fat 155); Fat 17g (Saturated 7g); Cholesterol 65mg; Sodium 910mg; Carbohydrate 39g (Dietary Fiber 3g); Protein 27g

Fiesta Taco Casserole

6 servings | Prep Time: 15 minutes | Start to Finish: 45 minutes

Olé! Create your own fiesta when you serve this popular dish. This is a great way to use up the broken tortilla chips.

1 lb ground beef

1 can (15 to 16 oz) spicy chili beans, undrained

1 cup salsa

2 cups coarsely broken tortilla chips

1/2 cup sour cream

4 medium green onions, sliced (1/2 cup)

1 medium tomato, chopped (3/4 cup)

1 cup shredded Cheddar or Monterey Jack cheese (4 oz)

Tortilla chips, if desired

Shredded lettuce, if desired

Salsa, if desired

1 Heat oven to 350°F.

2 Cook beef in 10-inch skillet over medium heat 8 to 10 minutes, stirring occasionally, until brown; drain. Stir in beans and 1 cup salsa. Heat to boiling, stirring occasionally.

3 Place broken tortilla chips in ungreased 2-quart casserole. Top with beef mixture. Spread with sour cream. Sprinkle with green onions, tomato and cheese.

4 Bake uncovered 20 to 30 minutes or until hot and bubbly. Arrange tortilla chips around edge of casserole and serve with lettuce and salsa.

1 **Serving:** Calories 360 (Calories from Fat 205); Fat 23g (Saturated 11g); Cholesterol 75mg; Sodium 590mg; Carbohydrate 19g (Dietary Fiber 4g); Protein 23g

COUNTRY KITCHEN WISDOM

Cinco de Mayo Celebration

Cinco de Mayo (May 5), the celebration of Mexican unity and national pride, is observed with parades, fireworks, mariachi music, *folklórico* dancing and, of course, delicious food. Gather friends and family and have yourself a fantastic fiesta! ¡Viva Mexico! Here are a few ways to make the gathering a success:

- Use margarita glasses for the lemonade as well as for the margaritas. Purchase disposable glasses from party stores. Rub the rims of the glasses with the cut side of a lemon or lime wedge, then dip the rim into a shallow dish of coarse salt. (This can be done ahead of time.) Garnish the drinks with fresh strawberries.

- Cut Chili-Cheese Corn Bread (page 245) into triangles or other shapes, and pile in a large basket lined with colorful napkins. Arrange the napkins with the points up for a fun, spiky look.

- Place an assortment of fresh chiles in a bowl as a festive centerpiece.

Beef Enchiladas

When you chop the chilies, be sure to wear plastic gloves to prevent the oil in the chili from getting on your hands or even under your nails. The gloves give you a disposable protective layer, so later you don't have to worry about skin or eye irritation caused by the oil.

1 lb lean ground beef

1 medium onion, chopped (1/2 cup)

1/2 cup sour cream

1 cup shredded Cheddar cheese (4 oz)

2 tablespoons chopped fresh parsley

1/4 teaspoon pepper

1/3 cup chopped green bell pepper

2/3 cup water

1 tablespoon chili powder

1 1/2 teaspoons chopped fresh or 1/2 teaspoon dried oregano leaves

1/4 teaspoon ground cumin

2 whole green chiles, chopped, if desired

1 clove garlic, finely chopped

1 can (15 oz) tomato sauce

8 corn tortillas (6 inch)

Shredded cheese, sour cream and chopped onions, if desired

1 Heat oven to 350°F.

2 Cook beef in 10-inch skillet over medium heat 8 to 10 minutes, stirring occasionally, until brown, drain. Stir in onion, sour cream, 1 cup cheese, the parsley and pepper. Cover and set aside.

3 Heat bell pepper, water, chili powder, oregano, cumin, chiles, garlic and tomato sauce to boiling, stirring occasionally; reduce heat to low. Simmer uncovered 5 minutes. Pour sauce into ungreased pie plate, 9 inches.

4 Dip each tortilla into sauce to coat both sides. Spoon about 1/4 cup beef mixture onto each tortilla; roll tortilla around filling. Place in ungreased rectangular baking dish, 11 × 7 inches. Pour remaining sauce over enchiladas.

5 Bake uncovered about 20 minutes or until bubbly. Garnish with shredded cheese, sour cream and chopped onions.

1 Serving: Calories 560 (Calories from Fat 295); Fat 33g (Saturated 16g); Cholesterol 115mg; Sodium 980mg; Carbohydrate 37g (Dietary Fiber 5g); Protein 34g

Pepperoni Pizza–Hamburger Pie

6 servings   Prep Time: 15 minutes   Start to Finish: 50 minutes

We've added a new twist to this family favorite! This pie has the flavors of traditional pizza—but instead of ground beef sprinkled on top, it has a ground beef crust!

1 lb lean ground beef

¹/₃ cup dry bread crumbs

1 egg

1¹/₂ teaspoons chopped fresh or ¹/₂ teaspoon dried oregano leaves

¹/₄ teaspoon salt

¹/₂ cup sliced mushrooms

1 small green bell pepper

¹/₃ cup chopped pepperoni (2 oz)

¹/₄ cup sliced ripe olives

1 cup spaghetti sauce

1 cup shredded mozzarella cheese (4 oz)

1 Heat oven to 400°F.

2 Mix beef, bread crumbs, egg, oregano and salt. Press evenly against bottom and side of ungreased pie plate, 9 inches.

3 Sprinkle mushrooms, bell pepper, pepperoni and olives into meat-lined plate. Pour spaghetti sauce over toppings.

4 Bake uncovered 25 minutes or until beef is thoroughly cooked and no longer pink in center; carefully drain. Sprinkle with cheese. Bake about 5 minutes longer or until cheese is light brown. Let pie stand 5 minutes before cutting.

1 Serving: Calories 310 (Calories from Fat 180); Fat 20g (Saturated 8g); Cholesterol 95mg; Sodium 740mg; Carbohydrate 10g (Dietary Fiber 1g); Protein 23g

Mexican Beef-and-Bean Casserole

4 servings   Prep Time: 20 minutes   Start to Finish: 1 hour 5 minutes

If you like Mexican food topped with gooey cheese and a spicy kick, try using Monterey Jack cheese with jalapeño peppers.

1 lb lean ground beef

2 cans (15 to 16 oz each) pinto beans, drained

1 can (8 oz) tomato sauce

¹/₂ cup mild chunky salsa

1 teaspoon chili powder

1 cup shredded Monterey Jack cheese (4 oz)

1 Heat oven to 375°F.

2 Cook beef in 10-inch skillet over medium heat 8 to 10 minutes, stirring occasionally, until brown; drain.

3 Mix beef, beans, tomato sauce, salsa and chili powder in ungreased 2-quart casserole.

4 Cover and bake 40 to 45 minutes, stirring once or twice, until hot and bubbly. Sprinkle with cheese. Bake uncovered about 5 minutes or until cheese is melted.

1 Serving: Calories 565 (Calories from Fat 235; Fat 26g (Saturated 12g); Cholesterol 90mg; Sodium 1,230mg; Carbohydrate 54g (Dietary Fiber 15g); Protein 44g

Overnight Lasagna

6 servings   Prep Time: 35 minutes   Start to Finish: 14 hours

Lasagna is an American favorite, always perfect for family meals, casual get-togethers and potluck suppers. Even better, you can put this lasagna together the night before and bake it the following day.

1 lb ground beef

1 medium onion, chopped (1/2 cup)

1 clove garlic, crushed

1/3 cup chopped fresh or 2 tablespoons dried parsley leaves

1 tablespoon sugar

2 tablespoons chopped fresh or 1 1/2 teaspoons dried basil leaves

1 teaspoon seasoned salt

1 can (16 oz) whole tomatoes, undrained

1 can (10.75 oz) condensed tomato soup

1 can (6 oz) tomato paste

2 1/2 cups water

12 uncooked lasagna noodles (about 12 oz)

1 container (12 oz) creamed cottage cheese

2 cups shredded mozzarella cheese (8 oz)

1/4 cup grated Parmesan cheese

1 Cook and stir ground beef, onion and garlic in Dutch oven over medium heat 8 to 10 minutes, stirring occasionally, until beef is brown; drain. Stir in parsley, sugar, basil, seasoned salt, tomatoes, tomato soup, tomato paste and water; break up tomatoes.

2 Heat to boiling, stirring occasionally; reduce heat. Simmer uncovered 20 minutes.

3 Spread 2 cups of the sauce mixture in ungreased rectangular baking dish, 13 × 9 inches. Top with 4 noodles. Spread half of the cottage cheese over noodles; top with 2 cups of the sauce mixture. Sprinkle with 1 cup of the mozzarella cheese. Repeat with 4 noodles, the remaining cottage cheese, 2 cups of the sauce mixture and the remaining mozzarella cheese. Top with the remaining noodles and sauce mixture; sprinkle with Parmesan cheese. Cover and refrigerate up to 12 hours.

4 Heat oven to 350°F. Bake covered 30 minutes. Uncover and bake 30 to 40 minutes longer or until hot and bubbly. Let stand 15 minutes before cutting.

1 Serving: Calories 425 (Calories from Fat 155); Fat 17g (Saturated 8g); Cholesterol 55mg; Sodium 1,160mg; Carbohydrate 41g (Dietary Fiber 3g); Protein 30g

Savory Spaghetti

6 servings | Prep Time: 25 minutes | Start to Finish: 1 hour 20 minutes

This delicious, moist spaghetti dish is really simple to do. The best part is that you don't have to boil the spaghetti separately. The noodles and sauce all cook up in one skillet. Now that's easy!

- 1/2 lb ground beef
- 1/4 lb ground pork
- 1 small onion, chopped (1/4 cup)
- 1 small green pepper, sliced
- 1/2 cup sliced ripe olives
- 1 can (2 oz) mushrooms, drained
- 1 can (8 oz) tomato sauce
- 2 1/2 cups tomatoes (1 lb 4 oz)
- 2 cups water
- 2 teaspoons salt
- 1/4 teaspoon pepper
- 1 teaspoon Worcestershire sauce
- 6 drops red pepper sauce
- 4 oz uncooked long spaghetti or noodles

1 Cook beef and pork in large skillet over medium heat 8 to 10 minutes, stirring occasionally, until brown. Add onion and green pepper and cook 5 minutes. Add olives, mushrooms and tomato sauce and mix lightly. Stir tomatoes, water, salt, pepper, Worcestershire sauce and red pepper sauce into meat mixture.

2 Add spaghetti and bring to boil. Cover tightly, reduce heat to low and simmer about 40 minutes, stirring occasionally. Uncover and simmer 15 minutes longer.

1 Serving: Calories 275 (Calories from Fat 115); Fat 13g (Saturated 4g); Cholesterol 45mg; Sodium 1,230mg; Carbohydrate 25g (Dietary Fiber 3g); Protein 18g

Meat Management

For the freshest, safest meat every time, follow these simple steps once you've purchased your meats:

Tips for Handling Raw Meat

- Wash your hands in hot, soapy water before and after handling meat.
- Wash all surfaces and utensils in hot, soapy water after contact with raw meat.
- Use disposable paper towels when working with raw meat or cleaning up afterward. If you use a dishcloth, throw it in the washer with hot water and detergent before using it again.
- Never carry raw meat to the grill and then serve the cooked meat on the same unwashed platter. The same goes for knives and cutting boards.

Tips for Storing Meat

- If meat is wrapped in white butcher paper, unwrap it and repackage tightly in moisture- and vapor-resistant materials such as plastic wrap, foil or plastic freezer bags.
- You don't need to rewrap meat packaged in clear plastic wrap, but you may want to put it in a plastic bag in case the original packaging leaks.
- Store meat immediately in the meat compartment or coldest part of your refrigerator, or freeze it as soon as possible. Ground meat is more perishable than other cuts, so use it within 2 days.
- Cook or freeze meat within 2 days of the sell-by date.

Tips for Thawing Frozen Meat

- Don't thaw meat on the countertop because bacteria thrive at room temperature.
- If the meat was refrigerated several days before freezing, use it the same day you thaw it.
- Meat can be thawed quickly in the microwave following the manufacturer's directions.
- To thaw meat in the fridge, place the wrapped meat in a dish, baking pan with sides or plastic bag to catch any drips during thawing.

Chicken Fried Steak

This fried steak and gravy dish, popular in Texas and throughout the Southwest, was invented out of necessity on cattle drives. To feed hungry cowboys, trail cooks would slice beef off a hind quarter, tenderize it by pounding with a meat cleaver, roll it in seasoned coating and fry it in hot sizzling oil like chicken—hence its name. If you'd like to save a bit of time, substitute tenderized cubed steaks for the round steaks.

1½ lb boneless beef round steak, about ½ inch thick

1 tablespoon water

1 egg

1 cup soda cracker crumbs (28 squares)

¼ teaspoon pepper

¼ cup vegetable oil

Milk Gravy (below right)

1 Cut beef into 6 serving pieces. Pound each piece until ¼ inch thick to tenderize.

2 Beat water and egg; reserve. Mix cracker crumbs and pepper. Dip beef into egg mixture, then coat with cracker crumbs.

3 Heat oil in 12-inch skillet over medium-high heat until hot. Cook beef in oil 6 to 7 minutes, turning once, until brown. Remove beef from skillet; keep warm.

4 Reserve drippings. Make Milk Gravy; serve with steak.

Milk Gravy

¼ cup all-purpose flour
½ teaspoon salt
2 cups milk

Measure reserved drippings (from step 4). Add enough vegetable oil to drippings, if necessary, to measure ¼ cup. Return drippings to skillet. Stir in flour and salt. Cook over low heat, stirring constantly to loosen brown particles from skillet, until smooth and bubbly; remove from heat. Slowly pour milk into skillet, stirring constantly. Heat to boiling over low heat, stirring constantly. Boil and stir 1 minute.

1 Serving: Calories 325 (Calories from Fat 155); Fat 17g (Saturated 4g); Cholesterol 100mg; Sodium 410mg; Carbohydrate 15g (Dietary Fiber 0g); Protein 28g

COUNTRY COOKING WISDOM

Getting the Grade

Beef is graded for quality by the U.S. Department of Agriculture (USDA). This grading, unlike meat inspection, is optional. The grade of meat indicates its tenderness, flavor and overall quality. Although there are eight USDA grades in all, the following are the most common:

- *Choice* and *Select* are the grades we typically find in the supermarket. These are the second- and third-highest grades.

- *Prime* is the highest grade and is usually reserved for restaurant use but can be found in some meat stores and supermarkets.

Fajitas

6 servings   Prep Time: 35 minutes   Start to Finish: 8 hours 35 minutes

You'll flip for these fajitas. Remember to allow some time for the meat to marinate—just pop it in before going to work in the morning and it will be ready to cook when you get home!

Fajita Marinade (below right)

1½ lb boneless beef top sirloin steak, 1½ inches thick

12 flour tortillas (10 inch)

2 tablespoons vegetable oil

2 large onions, sliced

2 medium green or red bell peppers, cut into ¼-inch strips

1 jar (8 oz) picante sauce (1 cup)

1 cup shredded Cheddar or Monterey Jack cheese (4 oz)

1½ cups prepared guacamole

¾ cup sour cream

1 Mix Fajita Marinade ingredients in ungreased, square glass baking dish, 8 × 8 inches. Set aside.

2 Trim excess fat from beef. Pierce beef with fork in several places. Place beef in marinade, turning to coat both sides. Cover and refrigerate at least 8 hours but no longer than 24 hours, turning beef occasionally.

3 Heat oven to 325°F. Wrap tortillas in foil. Heat in oven about 15 minutes or until warm. Remove tortillas from oven; keep wrapped.

4 Set oven control to broil. Remove beef from marinade; reserve marinade. Place beef on rack in broiler pan. (For easy cleanup, line broker pan with foil before placing beef on rack.) Broil beef with top about 3 inches from heat about 8 minutes or until brown. Turn; brush beef with marinade. Broil 7 to 8 minutes longer for medium-rare to medium doneness. Discard any remaining marinade.

5 While beef is broiling, heat oil in 10-inch skillet over medium-high heat. Cook onions and bell peppers in oil 6 to 8 minutes, stirring frequently, until crisp-tender.

6 Cut beef across grain into very thin slices.

7 For each fajita, place a few slices of beef, some of the onion mixture, 1 heaping tablespoonful each picante sauce and cheese, about 2 table-spoons guacamole and 1 tablespoon sour cream in center of tortilla. Fold 1 end of tortilla up about 1 inch over filling; fold right and left sides over folded end, overlapping. Fold remaining end down.

Fajita Marinade

¼ cup vegetable oil	1 teaspoon chili powder
¼ cup red wine vinegar	½ teaspoon garlic powder
1 teaspoon sugar	½ teaspoon salt
1 teaspoon dried oregano leaves	¼ teaspoon pepper

1 Serving: Calories 690 (Calories from Fat 325); Fat 36g (Saturated 12g); Cholesterol 90mg; Sodium 1,110mg; Carbohydrate 64g (Dietary Fiber 7g); Protein 35g

Beefy Baked Chili

6 servings | Prep Time: 10 minutes | Start to Finish: 4 hours 10 minutes

Here's the perfect chili for entertaining—just pop it in the oven and let it cook slowly until it's savory and full of flavor.

1½ cups dried pinto beans

6 cups water

1½ lb boneless beef chuck, tip or round steak, cut into 1-inch pieces

1 teaspoon chili powder

1 tablespoon cumin seed

1½ teaspoons salt

1½ teaspoons ground red pepper (cayenne)

3 medium onions, chopped (1½ cups)

3 cloves garlic, finely chopped

3 cans (8 oz each) tomato sauce

1 Heat oven to 325°F.

2 Heat beans and water to boiling in 4-quart ovenproof Dutch oven. Boil 2 minutes.

3 Stir remaining ingredients into bean mixture. Cover and bake about 4 hours until beef and beans are tender. Garnish with sour cream, chopped onion and shredded Cheddar cheese, if desired.

1 Serving: Calories 315 (Calories from Fat 125); Fat 14g (Saturated 5g); Cholesterol 70mg; Sodium 1,340mg; Carbohydrate 25g (Dietary Fiber 7g); Protein 29g

Classic Beef Stroganoff

8 servings | Prep Time: 20 minutes | Start to Finish: 40 minutes

This elegant entree, named after 19th-century Russian diplomat Count Stroganov, combines a sour cream sauce with tender beef, onions and mushrooms. Don't let the sauce boil once you've added the sour cream or it will curdle.

2 lb beef sirloin steak, ½ inch thick

8 oz mushrooms, sliced

2 medium onions, thinly sliced

1 clove garlic, finely chopped

¼ cup margarine or butter

1½ cups beef broth

1 teaspoon salt

1 teaspoon Worcestershire sauce

¼ cup all-purpose flour

1½ cups sour cream

4 cups hot cooked egg noodles

1 Cut beef across grain into strips, 1½ × ½ inches.

2 Cook mushrooms, onions and garlic in margarine in 10-inch skillet, stirring occasionally, until onions are tender; remove from skillet. Cook beef in same skillet until brown. Stir in 1 cup of the broth, the salt and the Worcestershire sauce. Heat to boiling; reduce heat. Cover and simmer 15 minutes.

3 Stir remaining ½ cup broth into flour; stir into beef mixture. Add onion mixture; heat to boiling, stirring constantly. Boil and stir 1 minute. Stir in sour cream; heat until hot (do not boil). Serve over noodles.

1 Serving: Calories 385 (Calories from Fat 170); Fat 19g (Saturated 10g); Cholesterol 125mg; Sodium 300mg; Carbohydrate 28g (Dietary Fiber 2g); Protein 27g

Zesty T-Bone Steaks (*bottom*) and
Bountiful Twice-Baked Potatoes (*top*, page 199)

Zesty T-Bone Steaks

4 servings   Prep Time: 10 minutes   Start to Finish: 1 hour 30 minutes

A rub of fresh garlic and crushed black peppercorns takes grilled steak to new flavor heights! While one T-bone may have served one person in bygone days, we suggest feeding two people per T-bone.

- 2 beef T-bone steaks, 1½ inches thick (about 1½ lb each)
- 1 clove garlic, cut in half
- 2 teaspoons black peppercorns, crushed
- ¼ cup margarine or butter, softened
- 1 tablespoons Dijon mustard
- ½ teaspoon Worcestershire sauce
- ¼ teaspoon lime juice

1 Trim fat on beef steaks to ¼-inch thickness. Rub beef with garlic. Press pepper into steaks. Cover and refrigerate 1 hour.

2 Mix margarine, mustard, Worcestershire sauce and lime juice; reserve.

3 Cover and grill beef 4 to 5 inches from medium heat, about 16 to 18 minutes for medium doneness, turning halfway through cooking. Season after cooking, if desired.

4 Place beef on warm platter; remove bone. Cut beef at slanted angle into thin slices; serve with reserved margarine mixture.

To broil: Follow steps 1 and 2. Set oven control to broil. Place beef on rack in broiler pan. Broil beef with tops 3 to 5 inches from heat, until brown, about 35 minutes for medium doneness, turning halfway through cooking. Continue as directed.

1 Serving: Calories 608 (Calories from Fat 417); Fat 46g (Saturated 16g); Cholesterol 130mg; Sodium 391mg; Carbohydrate 1g (Dietary Fiber 0g); Protein 44g

COUNTRY COOKING WISDOM

Texas T-bones

In 1854 *Harper's Weekly* reported that the most common meal in America, bar none, was steak. Texas became a prime beef producer, with its vast plains and plentiful buffalo grass to nourish sturdy Texas longhorns. Cooking steaks on an open fire was a common practice on Texas cattle drives, one that carried over to our traditional backyard barbecues.

Beef Brisket Barbecue

12 servings | Prep Time: 10 minutes | Start to Finish: 3 hours 10 minutes

The slow-cooking brisket emerges as a tender and succulent piece of meat. Any leftovers can be transformed into delicious sandwiches the next day. Or you can shred the brisket and stir in enough warm barbecue sauce to moisten it. It is delicious as a sandwich or spooned over hot mashed potatoes or rice.

4 to 5 lb well-trimmed fresh boneless beef brisket (not corned)

1 teaspoon salt

1/2 cup ketchup

1/4 cup white vinegar

1 tablespoon Worcestershire sauce

1 1/2 teaspoons liquid smoke

1/4 teaspoon pepper

1 medium onion, finely chopped (1/2 cup)

1 dried bay leaf

1 Heat oven to 325°F.

2 Rub surface of beef with salt. Place in ungreased rectangular pan, 18 × 9 inches. Mix remaining ingredients and pour over beef.

3 Cover and bake about 3 hours or until beef is tender.

4 Cut thin diagonal slices across grain at an angle from 2 or 3 "faces" of beef. Spoon any remaining pan juices over sliced beef, if desired. Remove bay leaf.

1 Serving: Calories 245 (Calories from Fat 100); Fat 11g (Saturated 4g); Cholesterol 85mg; Sodium 390mg; Carbohydrate 4g (Dietary Fiber 0g); Protein 33g

COUNTRY COOKING WISDOM

Smokey Seasoning

Liquid smoke is a seasoning ingredient used to mimic the flavor of foods cooked over an open wood fire. It's made by burning hardwood chips (typically hickory) and condensing the smoke into liquid form. It's then filtered to remove any impurities. Look for liquid smoke in your supermarket aisle along with the barbecue sauces and marinades.

Beef Brisket Barbecue (*left*)
and Country Potato Salad (*right*, page 219)

Pot Roast

A whole jar of horseradish might sound overpowering to you, but we assure you that it adds a nice, savory flavor to this dish without overwhelming your tastebuds. The meat and vegetables simmer away in the juices and emerge from the oven tender and tasty. This roast also makes a great gravy.

4 lb beef arm, blade or cross rib pot roast*

1 to 2 teaspoons salt

1 teaspoon pepper

1 jar (8 oz) prepared horseradish

1 cup water

8 small potatoes, cut in half

8 medium carrots, cut into fourths

8 small onions

Pot Roast Gravy (right)

1   Cook beef in Dutch oven over medium heat until brown on all sides; reduce heat to low.

2   Sprinkle beef with salt and pepper. Spread horseradish over all sides of beef. Add water to Dutch oven. Heat to boiling; reduce heat to low. Cover and simmer 2 hours 30 minutes.

3   Add potatoes, carrots and onions. Cover and simmer about 1 hour or until beef and vegetables are tender.

4   Remove beef and vegetables to warm platter; keep warm. Make Pot Roast Gravy. Serve with beef and vegetables.

Pot Roast Gravy

Water
$\frac{1}{2}$ cup cold water
$\frac{1}{4}$ cup all-purpose flour

Skim excess fat from broth in Dutch oven. Add enough water to broth to measure 2 cups. Shake $\frac{1}{2}$ cup cold water and the flour in tightly covered container; gradually stir into broth. Heat to boiling, stirring constantly. Boil and stir 1 minute.

*3 lb beef bottom round, rolled rump, tip or chuck eye roast can be substituted; decrease salt to $\frac{3}{4}$ teaspoon.

1 Serving: Calories 365 (Calories from Fat 100); Fat 11g (Saturated 4g); Cholesterol 85mg; Sodium 400mg; Carbohydrate 38g (Dietary Fiber 6g); Protein 35g

Yankee Pot Roast

12 servings   Prep Time: 30 minutes   Start to Finish: 3 hours 30 minutes

Nothing says "home cooking" like slow-simmered pot roast with vegetables. It's a classic.

- 1/4 cup all-purpose flour
- 2 teaspoons salt
- 1/2 teaspoon pepper
- 4- to 5-lb boneless beef shoulder pot roast
- 1 tablespoon shortening
- 1/2 cup water
- 4 medium stalks celery, cut into fourths
- 4 medium carrots, cut into fourths
- 3 medium potatoes, cut into 1 1/2-inch pieces
- 2 medium rutabagas or yellow turnips, cut into 1 1/2-inch pieces
- 1 large onion, chopped (1 cup)

1   Mix flour, salt and pepper; rub over pot roast. Heat shortening in 12-inch skillet or Dutch oven until melted and brown beef on all sides. Drain fat from skillet; add water. Heat to boiling; reduce heat. Cover tightly and simmer on top of range or cook in 325°F oven 2 hours.

2   Arrange remaining ingredients around beef. Add 1/4 cup water, if necessary. Cover and simmer 45 minutes to 1 hour, stirring vegetables occasionally, until beef and vegetables are tender. Remove beef and vegetables from skillet. Skim fat from broth; serve broth with beef.

1 Serving: Calories 444 (Calories from Fat 263); Fat 29g (Saturated 12g); Cholesterol 103mg; Sodium 525mg; Carbohydrate 13g (Dietary Fiber 4g); Protein 31g

New England Boiled Dinner

6 servings   Prep Time: 5 minutes   Start to Finish: 2 hours 25 minutes

One pot is all you'll need to prepare this hearty and comforting meal. Typical of New England cooking, the meat and vegetables simmer for hours in a flavorful broth.

- 2- lb well-trimmed corned beef boneless brisket or round
- 7 small onions
- 1 clove garlic, crushed
- 6 medium carrots
- 3 potatoes, cut in half
- 3 turnips, cut into fourths
- 1 small head green cabbage, cut into 6 wedges

1   Pour enough cold water on corned beef in Dutch oven just to cover. Add 1 small onion, cut into fourths, and the garlic. Heat to boiling; reduce heat. Cover and simmer about 1 hour 40 minutes or until beef is almost tender.

2   Skim fat from broth. Add remaining onions, the carrots, potatoes and turnips. Cover and simmer 20 minutes.

3   Remove beef; keep warm. Add cabbage. Heat to boiling; reduce heat. Simmer uncovered about 15 minutes or until vegetables are tender.

1 Serving: Calories 448 (Calories from Fat 205); Fat 23g (Saturated 7g); Cholesterol 82mg; Sodium 1,972mg; Carbohydrate 33g (Dietary Fiber 10g); Protein 28g

Tender Beef Stew with Dumplings

6 servings | Prep Time: 30 minutes | Start to Finish: 3 hours 30 minutes

What's better on a cold winter evening than hearty beef stew and fluffy dumplings? Want some company in the kitchen? Recruit family members to help you chop the vegetables!

- 1 tablespoon vegetable oil or shortening
- 1 lb boneless beef chuck, tip or round roast, cut into 1-inch cubes
- 3 cups hot water
- 1½ teaspoons salt
- ⅛ teaspoon pepper
- 2 medium carrots, cut into 1-inch pieces (1 cup)
- 1 large potato, cut into 1½-inch pieces (1¼ cups)
- 1 medium turnip, cut into 1-inch pieces (1 cup)
- 1 medium green bell pepper, cut into 1-inch pieces (1 cup)
- 1 medium stalk celery, cut into 1-inch pieces (½ cup)
- 1 small onion, chopped (¼ cup)
- ½ teaspoon browning sauce, if desired
- 1 dried bay leaf
  Dumplings (right), if desired
- ½ cup cold water
- 2 tablespoons all-purpose flour

1 Heat oil in 12-inch skillet or Dutch oven. Cook beef in oil about 15 minutes, stirring occasionally, until beef is brown. Add hot water, ½ teaspoon salt and the pepper. Heat to boiling; reduce heat to low. Cover and simmer 2 hours to 2 hours 30 minutes or until beef is almost tender.

2 Stir in remaining ingredients except Dumplings, cold water and flour. Cover and simmer about 30 minutes or until vegetables are tender. Remove bay leaf.

3 Make Dumplings.

4 Shake cold water and flour in tightly covered container; gradually stir into beef mixture. Heat to boiling, stirring constantly. Boil and stir 1 minute; reduce heat to low.

5 Drop 10 to 12 spoonfuls dumpling dough onto hot stew (do not drop directly into liquid). Cook uncovered 10 minutes. Cover and cook 10 minutes longer.

Dumplings

- 3 tablespoons shortening
- 1½ cups all-purpose flour
- 1 tablespoon dried parsley flakes, if desired
- 2 teaspoons baking powder
- ½ teaspoon salt
- ¾ cup milk

Cut shortening into flour, parsley, baking powder and salt in medium bowl, using pastry blender or crisscrossing 2 knives, until mixture looks like fine crumbs. Stir in milk.

1 Serving: Calories 250 (Calories from Fat 145); Fat 16g (Saturated 6g); Cholesterol 45mg; Sodium 590mg; Carbohydrate 14g (Dietary Fiber 2g); Protein 14g

Beef Burgundy Stew

8 servings | Prep Time: 25 minutes | Start to Finish: 2 hours 30 minutes

This is a great dish to make when you are having a crowd over. It feeds a lot of people without much work for you! Grab several loaves of good French bread—this stew makes a wonderfully rich Burgundy sauce which is oh-so-good sopped up with crusty bread.

2 tablespoons margarine or butter

5 medium onions, sliced

1 lb sliced mushrooms (6 cups)

3 lb beef stew meat, cut into 1-inch cubes

2 cloves garlic, finely chopped

2 teaspoons salt

1 teaspoon chopped fresh or $^1/_2$ teaspoon dried marjoram leaves

1 teaspoon chopped fresh or $^1/_2$ teaspoon dried thyme leaves

$^1/_4$ teaspoon pepper

3 cups beef broth

3 tablespoons all-purpose flour

$3^1/_2$ cups red Burgundy

French bread, if desired

1 Melt margarine in Dutch oven or 3-quart saucepan over medium heat. Cook onions and mushrooms in margarine about 10 minutes, stirring occasionally, until onions are tender. Remove vegetables from Dutch oven; drain and reserve.

2 Cook beef and garlic in Dutch oven over medium heat, stirring occasionally, until beef is brown; drain. Sprinkle with salt, marjoram, thyme and pepper.

3 Mix broth and flour; pour over beef. Heat to boiling, stirring constantly. Boil and stir 1 minute.

4 Stir in Burgundy. Cover and simmer 1 hour 30 minutes to 2 hours, stirring in onions and mushrooms 5 minutes before end of simmer time. Serve in bowls with bread for dipping into sauce.

1 Serving: Calories 550 (Calories from Fat 315); Fat 35g (Saturated 14g); Cholesterol 100mg; Sodium 890mg; Carbohydrate 13g (Dietary Fiber 2g); Protein 33g

COUNTRY COOKING WISDOM

Make-Ahead Magic

The flavors of stews and soups tend to develop and mellow with age, so making them ahead of time is ideal. Here are some storage guidelines to help you plan and prepare easy do-ahead meals:

- Cover and refrigerate stews and soups for up to 3 days.

- For stews and soups made with fish or shellfish, refrigerate no longer than 1 day.

- Heat broth-based soups over medium heat, stirring occasionally, until hot; or reheat in the microwave.

- Reheat thick purees or soups containing milk, cream, eggs or cheese over low heat, stirring frequently. Boiling may cause ingredients to separate.

Texas Chili

These chunks of tender steak in a rich tomato sauce are delicious served on slices of corn bread and with a green salad.

3 lb boneless beef round steak, cut into 1/2-inch cubes

3 tablespoons vegetable oil

1/2 cup chopped fresh parsley

4 cups water

3 tablespoons chopped fresh or 1 tablespoon dried oregano leaves

1 tablespoon paprika

2 teaspoons ground cumin

1 1/2 teaspoons salt

1 to 2 teaspoons crushed red pepper

3/4 teaspoon ground coriander

1 large dried bay leaf

3 large cloves garlic, crushed

1 large onion, chopped (1 cup)

1 can (8 oz) tomato sauce

1 cup shredded Cheddar or Monterey Jack cheese (4 oz)

1 cup sour cream

1 medium avocado, chopped

1   Cook half of the beef at a time in oil in Dutch oven over medium heat, stirring frequently, until light brown.

2   Stir in parsley, water, seasonings, garlic, onion and tomato sauce. Heat to boiling; reduce heat. Cover and simmer 1 hour, stirring occasionally. Uncover and simmer about 1 hour 30 minutes longer, stirring occasionally, until mixture thickens.

3   Remove bay leaf. Serve with cheese, sour cream and avocado.

1 Serving: Calories 454 (Calories from Fat 230); Fat 26g (Saturated 10g); Cholesterol 78mg; Sodium 793mg; Carbohydrate 9g (Dietary Fiber 3g); Protein 45g

Texas Chili with Beans: Substitute 3 lb ground beef for the beef steak. Omit oil. Cook ground beef, stirring frequently, until brown; drain. Continue as directed. After removing bay leaf, stir in 3 cans (15 oz each) pinto beans, undrained; heat to boiling.

Venison Stew

Cooked in red wine, along with bacon, potatoes, carrots and pearl onions, venison is delicious and tender in this hearty stew.

4 slices bacon, cut into $1/2$-inch pieces

I lb boneless venison, cut into 1-inch cubes

2 cups water

I cup dry red wine or beef broth

$3/4$ teaspoon chopped fresh or $1/4$ teaspoon dried thyme leaves

$3/4$ teaspoon chopped fresh or $1/4$ teaspoon dried marjoram leaves

$1/2$ teaspoon salt

$1/4$ teaspoon pepper

4 oz tiny pearl onions (about I cup)

2 medium carrots, cut into 1-inch pieces

I large potato, cut into 1-inch pieces

$1/2$ cup cold water

3 tablespoons all-purpose flour

$1/2$ teaspoon browning sauce, if desired

2 tablespoons chopped fresh parsley

1 Cook bacon in Dutch oven, stirring occasionally, until crisp. Remove bacon with slotted spoon; reserve.

2 Cook venison in bacon fat, stirring frequently, about 7 minutes or until brown. Add 2 cups water, the wine, thyme, marjoram, salt and pepper. Heat to boiling; reduce heat. Cover and simmer until venison is almost tender, about 2 hours.

3 Stir in onions, carrots and potato. Heat to boiling; reduce heat. Cover and simmer until vegetables are tender, about 30 minutes.

4 Shake $1/2$ cup cold water and the flour in tightly covered container; gradually stir into stew. Stir in browning sauce. Heat to boiling, stirring constantly. Boil and stir 1 minute. Sprinkle with bacon and parsley.

I Serving: Calories 250 (Calories from Fat 50); Fat 5g (Saturated 2g); Cholesterol 69mg; Sodium 323mg; Carbohydrate 22g (Dietary Fiber 2g); Protein 21g

Beef Stew: Substitute 1 lb beef for the venison.

COUNTRY COOKING WISDOM

Venison Variations

Venison isn't a type of animal—it's a term used for deer, elk, moose, antelope, reindeer and caribou. Farm-raised venison, whether fresh or frozen, is available in cuts similar to beef or pork. Look for it at specialty stores, meat markets that carry game, game farms and venison farms.

Venison is very lean meat with a rich, full-bodied flavor. Like most game, it will become tough if over-cooked. Before cooking, remove the silvery membrane from the meat, and trim as much fat as possible, because the fat has a concentration of gamy flavor, congeals quickly and is unpleasant to eat. Game fat can become rancid quickly. To tenderize fresh venison, marinate it in the refrigerator overnight.

Country-Style Ribs

6 servings | Prep Time: 10 minutes | Start to Finish: 2 hours 40 minutes

These mighty meaty ribs come both bone-in and boneless, so check in the meat department or with your butcher. You'll need about 2 lb if you prefer boneless. To save cleanup time and elbow grease, we like to line the pan with heavy-duty foil.

3 lb pork country-style ribs

²/₃ cup chili sauce

½ cup grape jelly

1 tablespoon dry red wine

1 teaspoon Dijon mustard

1 Heat oven to 325°F.

2 Cut ribs into serving pieces if necessary. Place ribs, meaty sides up, in ungreased rectangular pan, 13 × 9 inches.

3 Cover and bake about 2 hours or until tender; drain.

4 Heat remaining ingredients, stirring occasionally, until jelly is melted. Pour over ribs.

5 Bake uncovered 30 minutes, spooning sauce over ribs occasionally.

1 Serving: Calories 340 (Calories from Fat 135); Fat 15g (Saturated 5g); Cholesterol 80mg; Sodium 400mg; Carbohydrate 24g (Dietary Fiber 0g); Protein 27g

Wine-Marinated Country-Style Ribs

6 servings | Prep Time: 15 minutes | Start to Finish: 5 hours 25 minutes

Ribs can sometimes be messy, but they're oh-so-good. Have lots of napkins or wet towelettes handy when serving these!

2 tablespoons vegetable oil

1 tablespoon chopped fresh or 1 teaspoon dried rosemary leaves, crushed

1 clove garlic, finely chopped

½ cup dry red wine or grape juice

1 teaspoon sugar

½ teaspoon salt

¼ teaspoon pepper

3 lb pork country-style ribs, cut into serving pieces

1 Heat oil in 1½-quart saucepan over medium heat. Cook rosemary and garlic in oil, stirring frequently, until garlic is golden; remove from heat. Stir in wine, sugar, salt and pepper.

2 Place pork in glass dish. Pour wine mixture over pork; turn to coat. Cover and refrigerate 4 hours, turning pork occasionally.

3 If using charcoal grill, arrange charcoal around edge of firebox and place drip pan under grilling area.

4 Remove pork from marinade; reserve marinade. Cover and grill pork over drip pan and 4 to 5 inches from medium heat 1 hour 10 minutes, turning occasionally and brushing with marinade, until pork is tender and no longer pink next to bones. Discard remaining marinade.

1 Serving: Calories 280 (Calories from Fat 170); Fat 19g (Saturated 6g); Cholesterol 80mg; Sodium 230mg; Carbohydrate 1g (Dietary Fiber 0g); Protein 26g

Baked Spareribs with Spicy Barbecue Sauce
(*bottom*) and Sweet-Sour Coleslaw
(*top*, page 224)

Baked Spareribs with Spicy Barbecue Sauce

8 servings   Prep Time: 5 minutes   Start to Finish: 2 hours 20 minutes

Since you don't need a grill, these ribs are great to make in the winter when you want the flavor of summer in your dinner. Serve these with Sweet-Sour Coleslaw (page 224) and Buttermilk Biscuits (page 254).

4½ lb rack fresh pork loin back ribs, cut into serving pieces

Spicy Barbecue Sauce (below right)

1 Heat oven to 325°F. Place pork ribs, meaty sides up, on rack in shallow roasting pan. Roast uncovered 1 hour 30 minutes.

2 Prepare Spicy Barbecue Sauce. Brush onto ribs. Roast, turning and brushing frequently with sauce, about 45 minutes longer or until tender and no longer pink next to bone. Serve with remaining sauce.

Spicy Barbecue Sauce

⅓ cup margarine or butter
2 tablespoons vinegar
2 tablespoons water
1 teaspoon sugar
½ teaspoon garlic powder
½ teaspoon onion powder
½ teaspoon pepper
Dash of ground red pepper

Heat all ingredients, stirring frequently, until margarine is melted.

1 Serving: Calories 550 (Calories from Fat 405); Fat 45g (Saturated 15g); Cholesterol 150mg; Sodium 220mg; Carbohydrate 1g (Dietary Fiber 0g); Protein 36g

COUNTRY COOKING WISDOM

Call It Barbecue

Definitions vary—for some, *barbecue* is interchanged with *grilling*, whereas others use the term to describe the entertaining event of outdoor cooking. And in the South, the word refers to the long, hot-smoke cooking of large, seasoned meat cuts over low heat that yields fall-off-the-bone tender meat. Styles vary from a sweet, spicy tomato sauce to an oil and vinegar marinade, each offering a mouthwatering meal.

Stuffed Pork Chops

4 servings   Prep Time: 30 minutes   Start to Finish: 1 hour 30 minutes

This is a must-have for pork lovers—tender, juicy chops filled with savory stuffing.

1/3 cup chopped celery (with leaves)

3 tablespoons finely chopped onion

1/4 cup margarine or butter

2 1/4 cups soft bread cubes (about 4 slices bread)

1/2 teaspoon salt

1/4 teaspoon rubbed sage

3/4 teaspoon chopped fresh or 1/4 teaspoon dried thyme leaves

1/8 teaspoon pepper

4 pork loin chops, 1 inch thick

2 tablespoons vegetable oil

1/4 cup apple cider or juice

1 Cook celery and onion in margarine in 2-quart saucepan over medium heat, stirring frequently, until celery is tender; remove from heat. Stir in bread cubes, salt, sage, thyme and pepper.

2 Cut a deep pocket in each pork chop on the meatiest side of the bone. Stuff each pocket with about 1/3 cup of the bread mixture. Secure openings with toothpicks.

3 Fry in oil in 10-inch skillet over medium heat about 15 minutes or until brown on both sides; drain. Add apple cider; reduce heat. Cover and simmer about 1 hour or until pork is no longer pink near bone on stuffed sides of pork. Remove toothpicks before serving.

1 Serving: Calories 395 (Calories from Fat 245); Fat 28g (Saturated 6g); Cholesterol 60mg; Sodium 580mg; Carbohydrate 16g (Dietary Fiber 1g); Protein 20g

Grilled Honey-Mustard Pork Chops

4 servings   Prep Time: 15 minutes   Start to Finish: 15 minutes

Orange juice sweetens up this nice spicy mustard glaze. This is a great dinner to throw on the grill when you want lots of flavor. Add some slices of fresh pineapple on the grill for the perfect accompaniment to these pork chops.

1/4 cup honey

2 tablespoons Dijon mustard

1 tablespoon orange juice

1 teaspoon chopped fresh or 1/4 teaspoon dried tarragon leaves

1 teaspoon cider vinegar

1/2 teaspoon white wine or regular Worcestershire sauce

Dash of onion powder

4 boneless pork loin chops, 1/2 inch thick (about 1 lb)

1 Mix all ingredients except pork.

2 Cover and grill pork 4 to 5 inches from medium heat 10 to 12 minutes, brushing occasionally with honey mixture and turning once, until pork is tender and no longer pink in center. Discard any remaining honey mixture.

1 Serving: Calories 285 (Calories from Fat 115); Fat 13g (Saturated 5g); Cholesterol 70mg; Sodium 140mg; Carbohydrate 19g (Dietary Fiber 0g); Protein 23g

Pork Chop and New Potato Skillet

6 servings | Prep Time: 15 minutes | Start to Finish: 55 minutes

New potatoes are young potatoes of any variety. If you can't find any new potatoes, use round red or round white instead. If they are large, you might have to cut them into sixths instead of fourths.

6 pork loin or rib chops, ½ inch thick (about 1½ lb)

1 can (10.75 oz) condensed cream of mushroom soup

1 can (4 oz) mushroom pieces and stems, undrained

¼ cup water

2 tablespoons dry white wine or apple juice

¾ teaspoon chopped fresh or ¼ teaspoon dried thyme leaves

½ teaspoon garlic powder

½ teaspoon Worcestershire sauce

6 medium new potatoes (about 1½ lb), cut into fourths

1 tablespoon chopped pimiento

1 package (10 oz) frozen green peas, rinsed and drained

1 Spray 10-inch nonstick skillet with nonstick cooking spray. Heat skillet over medium-high heat. Cook pork in skillet until brown on both sides.

2 Mix soup, mushrooms, water, wine, thyme, garlic powder and Worcestershire sauce; pour over pork. Heat to boiling, stirring occasionally; reduce heat. Cover and simmer 15 minutes.

3 Add potatoes. Cover and simmer 15 minutes. Stir in pimiento and peas. Cover and simmer about 10 minutes, stirring occasionally, until pork is tender and no longer pink in center and peas are tender.

1 Serving: Calories 385 (Calories from Fat 155); Fat 17g (Saturated 6g); Cholesterol 70mg; Sodium 580mg; Carbohydrate 34g (Dietary Fiber 5g); Protein 29g

COUNTRY COOKING WISDOM

Seasoning Cast-Iron Skillets

Cast iron gives steady, even heat. If properly seasoned, cast iron is as good as nonstick surfaces. To season a skillet, thoroughly wash and dry it. Generously brush the interior with vegetable oil. Place in a heated 300°F oven for 1 hour. Cool and wipe with a paper towel. Be sure to season a new skillet before using and periodically as needed.

Wild Rice– and Almond-Stuffed Pork Chops

4 servings   Prep Time: 20 minutes   Start to Finish: I hour 5 minutes

Quick-cooking wild rice is faster to prepare than regular wild rice and is equally delicious. If you can't find wild rice, try a wild rice blend or brown rice instead.

Wild Rice and Almond
Stuffing (below right)

4 pork loin chops, I inch thick

$1/3$ cup apricot preserves

I tablespoon dry white wine
or apple juice

$1/8$ teaspoon ground cinnamon

1 Make Wild Rice and Almond Stuffing.

2 Cut a deep pocket in each pork chop on the meatiest side of the bone. Press about $1/3$ cup stuffing mixture into each pocket. Secure openings with toothpicks. Mix apricot preserves, wine and cinnamon.

3 Cover and grill pork 4 to 5 inches from medium-low coals 40 to 45 minutes, brushing occasionally with apricot mixture and turning 2 or 3 times, until pork is no longer pink near bone on the stuffed sides of chops. Remove toothpicks.

Wild Rice and Almond Stuffing

$1/3$ cup finely chopped celery
I medium green onion, finely chopped (I tablespoon)
I teaspoon margarine or butter
I cup cooked wild rice
I tablespoon sliced almonds
$1/4$ teaspoon salt
$1/8$ teaspoon pepper

Cook celery and onion in margarine in 8-inch skillet over medium heat, stirring frequently, until celery is crisp-tender. Stir in remaining ingredients.

I Serving: Calories 440 (Calories from Fat 0); Fat 20g (Saturated 0g); Cholesterol 115mg; Sodium 380mg; Carbohydrate 29g (Dietary Fiber 0g); Protein 36g

COUNTRY COOKING WISDOM

Rice Recognition

Wild rice is not actually a rice but the seed of a grass that grows in marshes and rivers. Very dark greenish brown in color, it has a distinctive nutlike flavor and chewy texture. It's often found in rice mixtures with white or brown rice.

Wild Rice– and Almond-Stuffed Pork Chops *(left)*
and Pacific Green Beans *(right*, page 194)

Pecan-Breaded Pork Chops

6 servings | Prep Time: 25 minutes | Start to Finish: 25 minutes

Add a little sweetness to these savory chops by using a honey Dijon mustard. Serve rice on the side to sop up all the nice pan juices.

1 egg white, slightly beaten

1 tablespoon Dijon mustard

3/4 cup soft bread crumbs (1 1/2 slices)

1/2 cup finely chopped pecans

1 clove garlic, finely chopped

6 pork loin chops, about 3/4 inch thick (about 2 lb)

2 tablespoons vegetable oil

1/2 cup dry white wine or chicken broth

1 tablespoon chopped fresh parsley

1 teaspoon Dijon mustard

1 Mix egg white and 1 tablespoon mustard. Mix bread crumbs, pecans and garlic. Dip pork into mustard mixture, then coat with pecan mixture.

2 Heat oil in 10-inch skillet over low heat. Cook pork in oil about 10 minutes on each side or until coating is golden brown and pork is tender and no longer pink and meat thermometer inserted in center reads 160°F. Remove pork from skillet.

3 Stir wine, parsley and 1 teaspoon mustard into skillet. Heat to boiling over high heat. Cook 3 to 4 minutes, stirring constantly, until sauce is reduced by half. Pour sauce over pork.

1 Serving: Calories 345 (Calories from Fat 225); Fat 25g (Saturated 6g); Cholesterol 70mg; Sodium 130mg; Carbohydrate 6g (Dietary Fiber 1g); Protein 25g

Zesty Pork Tenderloin

6 servings | Prep Time: 5 minutes | Start to Finish: 1 hour 35 minutes

The tenderloin is considered the choicest of pork cuts. It may be a little higher in price per pound than loin roast, but tenderloin is a good value because it is lean and has no waste.

1/4 cup ketchup

1 tablespoon sugar

1 tablespoon dry white wine or water

1 tablespoon hoisin sauce

1/2 teaspoon salt

1 clove garlic, finely chopped

2 pork tenderloins (about 3/4 lb each)

1 Mix all ingredients except pork in shallow glass or plastic dish. Add pork; turn to coat with marinade. Cover and refrigerate at least 1 hour but no longer than 24 hours.

2 Heat oven to 425°F. Place pork on rack in shallow roasting pan. Insert meat thermometer horizontally so tip is in thickest part of pork. Roast uncovered 27 to 29 minutes until pork has slight blush of pink in center and meat thermometer inserted in center reads 160°F (medium doneness).

1 Serving: Calories 155 (Calories from Fat 35); Fat 4g (Saturated 2g); Cholesterol 70mg; Sodium 340mg; Carbohydrate 6g (Dietary Fiber 0g); Protein 24g

Parmesan-Breaded Pork Chops

4 servings | Prep Time: 15 minutes | Start to Finish: 25 minutes

Bread crumbs seasoned with parmesan coat boneless pork chops, which are delicious bathed in a zesty tomato sauce.

⅓ cup Italian-style dry bread crumbs

2 tablespoons grated Parmesan cheese

4 pork boneless butterfly lion chops, ½ inch thick (about 1¼ lb)

1 egg, beaten

1 can (14.5 oz) chunky tomatoes with olive oil, garlic and spices, undrained

1 can (8 oz) tomato sauce

1 small green bell pepper, chopped (½ cup)

1 Mix bread crumbs and cheese.

2 Dip pork in egg, then coat with crumb mixture.

3 Spray 12-inch nonstick skillet with cooking spray; heat over medium heat. Cook pork in skillet about 5 minutes, turning once, until brown.

4 Stir in remaining ingredients. Heat to boiling, then reduce heat to low. Cover and simmer 10 to 12 minutes, stirring occasionally, until pork is no longer pink in center.

1 Serving: Calories 233 (Calories from Fat 70); Fat 8g (Saturated 3g); Cholesterol 102mg; Sodium 793mg; Carbohydrate 15g (Dietary Fiber 2g); Protein 24g

Apricot-Glazed Pork

4 servings | Prep Time: 10 minutes | Start to Finish: 10 minutes

Keep these ingredients on hand for a last-minute dinner. Serve over hot steamed rice or hot linguine for a change of pace.

1 tablespoon chili oil or vegetable oil

1 lb pork tenderloin, cut into ½-inch slices

1 package (16 oz) frozen broccoli, cauliflower and carrots

3 tablespoons apricot preserves

1 tablespoon oyster sauce or hoisin sauce

Hot cooked rice or noodles, if desired

1 Heat wok or 12-inch skillet over high heat. Add oil; rotate wok to coat side.

2 Add pork and stir-fry 4 to 5 minutes or until no longer pink in center. Add vegetables and stir-fry 2 minutes. Stir in preserves and oyster sauce. Cook and stir about 30 seconds or until hot. Serve with rice.

1 Serving: Calories 235 (Calories from Fat 67); Fat 8g (Saturated 2g); Cholesterol 74mg; Sodium 118mg; Carbohydrate 16g (Dietary Fiber 3g); Protein 26g

Stuffed Crown Roast of Pork

14 servings   Prep Time: 20 minutes   Start to Finish: 4 hours

This lovely recipe is a delicious choice for special-occasion dinner parties. The hearty apple, walnut and bread stuffing and rich Pan Gravy perfectly complement this wonderful roast.

- 8 lb pork crown roast
- 2 teaspoons seasoned salt
- 1/2 teaspoon pepper
- 1/2 teaspoon ground mustard
- 1 medium stalk celery, chopped (1/2 cup)
- 1 medium onion, finely chopped (1/2 cup)
- 1/2 cup chopped walnuts
- 1/4 cup plus 2 tablespoons margarine or butter
- 2 cups chopped peeled or unpeeled cooking apples
- 2 tablespoons sugar
- 3 cups soft bread cubes (about 4 1/2 slices bread)
- 1/4 cup chopped fresh parsley
- 1/2 teaspoon ground sage
- 2 teaspoons chopped fresh or 1/2 teaspoon dried thyme leaves
- 1/4 teaspoon ground nutmeg
- Spiced crab apples or paper frills, if desired
- Pan Gravy (right)

1 Heat oven to 325°F. Place pork roast, bone ends up, on rack in shallow roasting pan. Mix seasoned salt, pepper and mustard and sprinkle over pork. Wrap bone ends in foil to prevent excessive browning. Insert meat thermometer so tip is in center of thickest part of pork and does not touch bone or rest in fat. Roast uncovered 1 hour 30 minutes.

2 Cook celery, onion and walnuts in margarine in Dutch oven or 12-inch skillet, stirring frequently, until onion is tender. Stir in apples and sugar. Cook 3 to 5 minutes, until apples soften; remove from heat. Stir in bread cubes, parsley, sage, thyme and nutmeg.

3 Fill center of pork roast with stuffing mixture. Roast uncovered about 2 hours longer or until meat thermometer reads 155°F. (Allow 20 to 25 minutes per lb total cooking time.) Cover with foil if top becomes too brown. Remove from heat; cover with foil and let stand 15 minutes until thermometer reads 160°F. Remove roast to serving platter; keep warm. Prepare Pan Gravy. Just before serving, cover bone ends with spiced crabapples or paper frills, if desired.

Pan Gravy

Water or chicken broth
1/4 cup all-purpose flour

Strain pork drippings into bowl. Let fat rise to top of drippings. Skim off fat, reserving 1/4 cup. Add enough water to drippings to measure 2 cups; reserve. Stir flour into reserved 1/4 cup fat in 2-quart saucepan. Cook over medium heat, stirring constantly, until smooth and bubbly; remove from heat. Stir in reserved drippings. Heat to boiling, stirring constantly. Boil and stir 1 minute. Serve gravy with roast.

1 Serving: Calories 405 (Calories from Fat 177); Fat 20g (Saturated 5g); Cholesterol 102mg; Sodium 576mg; Carbohydrate 12g (Dietary Fiber 1g); Protein 43g

Fruit-Stuffed Pork Roast

12 servings | Prep Time: 20 minutes | Start to Finish: 1 hour 50 minutes

Perfect for Sunday dinner, this lovely roast boasts sweet fruit and savory beef. Yum!

1/2 teaspoon ground cinnamon

1/4 teaspoon ground cloves

15 dried apricot halves (3 oz)

9 pitted prunes (3 oz)

4- lb boneless pork double loin roast

3/4 teaspoon salt

1/4 teaspoon pepper

1 1/4 cups apple cider or juice

1 tablespoon cornstarch

1 tablespoon cold water

1 Sprinkle cinnamon and cloves over apricots and prunes; toss to coat. Stuff fruit lengthwise between the 2 pieces of pork roast, forming a ribbon of the mixture about 2 inches wide (work from both ends of roast). Tie roast. Sprinkle with salt and pepper.

2 Heat oven to 325°F. Place pork, fat side up, on rack in shallow roasting pan. Insert meat thermometer so tip is in center of thickest part of pork and does not rest in fat or fruit mixture. Roast uncovered about 1 hour 30 minutes or until meat thermometer reads 155°F. After 45 minutes, brush occasionally with 1/4 cup of apple cider.

3 Remove pork and rack from pan; cover with foil and let stand 10 minutes until thermometer reads 160°F. Pour remaining 1 cup cider into roasting pan; stir to loosen brown particles. Mix cornstarch and water; stir into cider mixture. Heat to boiling, stirring constantly. Boil and stir 1 minute. Serve with pork.

1 Serving: Calories 265 (Calories from Fat 70); Fat 8g (Saturated 3g); Cholesterol 95mg; Sodium 250mg; Carbohydrate 13g (Dietary Fiber 0g); Protein 34g

COUNTRY COOKING WISDOM

Ham Hints

Ham—cured meat from the hind legs of hogs—should be firm, plump, fine-grained, rosy pink and without excess moisture. Any fat should be firm and white. Curing gives ham its salty flavor; wood smoke or smoke-flavored liquids give ham its smoky flavor. Curing and smoking may darken the color of the meat. You may notice a rainbow-like appearance on the surface of ham—don't worry, it's perfectly safe. It's called iridescence and is caused by the refraction of light on the cut ends of the muscle fibers.

Fully cooked, brine-cured and spiral-cut ham, the most popular kind of ham, is ready to eat without cooking. To warm, heat to 140°F. Hams labeled "cook before eating" must be cooked to 160°F. If you aren't sure what kind of ham you've bought, cook it to be safe.

Country or country-style hams have been dry-cured and smoked and are often quite salty, the opposite of wet-cured hams, or "city hams" as some people call the ham that's most familiar to us. To serve country or country-style hams hot, heat to 140°F.

Ham and Scalloped Potatoes

6 servings   Prep Time: 25 minutes   Start to Finish: 1 hour 55 minutes

You might want to make this recipe using unpeeled potatoes for some added nutrition and flavor. The few extra minutes it takes to scrub the potatoes will be worth it!

6 medium boiling or baking potatoes (2 lb), peeled

4 tablespoons margarine or butter

1 small onion, finely chopped (¼ cup)

3 tablespoons all-purpose flour

1 teaspoon salt

¼ teaspoon pepper

2½ cups milk

1½ cups diced fully cooked ham

1 Heat oven to 350°F. Grease 2-quart casserole.

2 Cut potatoes into enough thin slices to measure about 4 cups.

3 Melt 3 tablespoons margarine in 2-quart saucepan over medium heat. Cook onion in margarine about 2 minutes, stirring occasionally, until tender. Stir in flour, salt and pepper. Cook, stirring constantly, until smooth and bubbly; remove from heat.

4 Stir milk into sauce. Heat to boiling, stirring constantly. Boil and stir 1 minute. Stir in ham.

5 Spread potatoes in casserole. Pour sauce over potatoes. Dot with 1 tablespoon margarine.

6 Cover and bake 30 minutes. Uncover and bake 1 hour to 1 hour 10 minutes longer or until potatoes are tender. Let stand 5 to 10 minutes before serving.

1 Serving: Calories 295 (Calories from Fat 115); Fat 13g (Saturated 4g); Cholesterol 25mg; Sodium 1,040mg; Carbohydrate 33g (Dietary Fiber 2g); Protein 13g

Honey-Mustard Ham

4 servings   Prep Time: 30 minutes   Start to Finish: 30 minutes

Dinner doesn't get much easier! This satisfying skillet meal, with smokey ham in a creamy sauce, will be on the table in under 30 minutes. Breadsticks and a tossed salad complete the meal without adding much extra time.

¼ cup water

2 tablespoons honey

1 tablespoon Dijon mustard

1 lb fully cooked smoked ham sliced (about 1 inch thick)

½ cup sour cream

1 green onion, sliced

1 Mix water, honey and mustard in 10-inch skillet. Cut ham into 4 serving pieces and add to skillet. Cover and heat to boiling; reduce heat to low. Simmer about 15 minutes, turning once, until ham is heated through. Remove ham from skillet; keep warm.

2 Stir sour cream into mixture in skillet; heat 1 minute. Pour over ham. Sprinkle with onion.

1 Serving: Calories 345 (Calories from Fat 205); Fat 23g (Saturated 9g); Cholesterol 90mg; Sodium 1,130mg; Carbohydrate 11g (Dietary Fiber 0g); Protein 24g

Glazed Baked Ham (*left*) and Candied Sweet Potatoes (*right*, page 208)

Glazed Baked Ham

10 servings   Prep Time: 25 minutes   Start to Finish: 3 hours 10 minutes

Perfect for any gathering, glazed baked ham is a welcomed centerpiece of a holiday feast, elegant brunch or birthday dinner.

$1/4$ cup packed brown sugar

$1/4$ teaspoon ground cloves

$1/4$ teaspoon ground cinnamon

1 can (6 oz) frozen orange juice concentrate, thawed

5- to 7-lb fully cooked smoked ham

Whole cloves, if desired

Orange slices, if desired

Cranberry Sauce or Raisin Sauce (below right)

1   Heat oven to 325°F.

2   Mix brown sugar, cloves, cinnamon and orange juice concentrate.

3   Place ham, fat side up, on rack in shallow roasting pan. Roast uncovered 1 hour 30 minutes to 2 hours or until thoroughly heated.

4   About 30 minutes before ham is done, remove from oven; pour drippings from pan. Cut fat surface of ham in uniform diamond pattern $1/4$ inch deep. Insert whole clove in each diamond, if desired. Spoon or spread remaining juice mixture on ham. Continue baking 30 minutes. Remove from oven. Cover and let stand 10 minutes.

5   Garnish with orange slices. Serve with Cranberry Sauce or Raisin Sauce.

Cranberry Sauce

1 can (16 oz) whole berry cranberry sauce
1 teaspoon grated orange peel
$1/2$ teaspoon ground ginger
$1/4$ teaspoon ground allspice

Heat all ingredients until hot, stirring occasionally. Serve warm.

Raisin Sauce

2 cups apple cider or juice
3 tablespoons cornstarch
1 cup raisins
2 tablespoons margarine or butter

Gradually stir apple cider into cornstarch in 1-quart saucepan. Add raisins and margarine. Heat over medium heat, stirring constantly, until mixture thickens and boils. Boil and stir 1 minute. Serve warm.

1 Serving (including Cranberry Sauce): Calories 390 (Calories from Fat 50); Fat 6g (Saturated 2g); Cholesterol 50mg; Sodium 2,054mg; Carbohydrate 45g (Dietary Fiber 1g); Protein 41g

Sausage Pie

6 servings | Prep Time: 30 minutes | Start to Finish: 1 hour

Want to make this delicious pie in no time flat? Pick up the ready-made rolled-out pastries available in the refrigerated section of the supermarket. Check out the store's variety of sausages—from spicy hot or mild to savory herbs mixed in—while you're there.

1½ lb bulk pork sausage

1 medium onion, chopped (about ½ cup)

1 tablespoon sugar

1½ teaspoons salt

1 medium head green cabbage (1¾ lb), cut into large chunks and cored

1 can (16 oz) whole tomatoes, undrained

Standard Pastry for Baked Pie Crust (see page 297)

2 tablespoons all-purpose flour

¼ cup cold water

1 Cook sausage and onion in Dutch oven, stirring occasionally, until sausage is no longer pink; drain. Stir in sugar, salt, cabbage and tomatoes. Heat to boiling; reduce heat. Cover and simmer 10 minutes.

2 Heat oven to 400°F.

3 Make Pastry for Baked Pie Crust on page 297 through step 2. Roll to fit top of 2-quart casserole. Fold into fourths; cut slits so steam can escape.

4 Mix flour and water and stir into hot sausage mixture. Pour into ungreased casserole. Place pastry over top and unfold. Seal pastry to edge of casserole. Bake 25 to 30 minutes or until crust is brown.

1 Serving: Calories 260 (Calories from Fat 155); Fat 17g (Saturated 6g); Cholesterol 45mg; Sodium 1,420mg; Carbohydrate 18g (Dietary Fiber 5g); Protein 4g

Three-Bean Casserole

8 servings | Prep Time: 20 minutes | Start to Finish: 1 hour 5 minutes

Popular at potlucks and other gatherings, this dish conveniently stays hot for a good while, thanks to the added insulation from the mixture of sausage and beans in a savory tomato sauce.

- 1 lb bulk pork sausage
- 2 medium stalks celery, sliced (1 cup)
- 1 medium onion, chopped (½ cup)
- 1 large clove garlic, crushed
- 2 cans (21 oz each) baked beans in tomato sauce
- 1 can (15 to 16 oz) lima beans, drained
- 1 can (15 to 16 oz) kidney beans, drained
- 1 can (8 oz) tomato sauce
- 1 tablespoon ground mustard (dry)
- 2 tablespoons honey
- 1 tablespoon white vinegar
- ¼ teaspoon red pepper sauce

1 Heat oven to 400°F.

2 Cook sausage, celery, onion and garlic in 10-inch skillet over medium heat about 10 minutes, stirring occasionally, until sausage is no longer pink; drain.

3 Mix sausage mixture and remaining ingredients in ungreased 3-quart casserole. Bake uncovered about 45 minutes, stirring once, until hot and bubbly.

1 Serving: Calories 340 (Calories from Fat 90); Fat 10g (Saturated 3g); Cholesterol 20mg; Sodium 1,670mg; Carbohydrate 54g (Dietary Fiber 14g); Protein 22g

CHAPTER FIVE

Fresh from the Garden

TURN THROUGH THE PAGES FOR THE MARKET'S FRESHEST OFFERINGS FOR VEGETABLES AND OTHER SIDE DISHES.

There are scrumptious recipes for every occasion—from tender vegetables and savory salads to spicy rice and side dishes. We've included a complement for every meal you make.

Broccoli with Pine Nuts

4 servings | Prep Time: 5 minutes | Start to Finish: 15 minutes

Broccoli is chock-full of vitamins and antioxidants. This dish tastes as good as it is for you because the pine nuts, little teardrop-shaped nuts, add a toasted, buttery flavor to the broccoli.

1 cup water

1½ lb fresh broccoli, cut into spears

2 tablespoons margarine or butter

¼ cup pine nuts

1 Heat water to boiling in medium saucepan and add broccoli. Cook about 10 minutes until stems are crisp-tender; drain.

2 Melt margarine in 8-inch skillet; add pine nuts. Cook over medium heat 5 minutes, stirring frequently, until nuts are golden brown. Sprinkle nuts over broccoli.

1 Serving: Calories 135 (Calories from Fat 100); Fat 11g (Saturated 2g); Cholesterol 0mg; Sodium 110mg; Carbohydrate 7g (Dietary Fiber 4g); Protein 4g

COUNTRY COOKING WISDOM

Name That Nut

Also know as pignoli, pine nuts are small, creamy, teardrop-shaped kernels that are the seeds of a pinecone. They have a sweet flavor and an oily consistency.

Vegetables with Lemon Butter

12 servings | Prep Time: 5 minutes | Start to Finish: 15 minutes

The tart lemon butter adds just the right zip to the vegetables. Serve this colorful, tasty side with some broiled fresh fish.

3 packages (10 oz each) frozen whole green beans

1½ lb Brussels sprouts, cut into halves

1 bag (16 oz) carrots, peeled and cut into julienne strips

½ cup margarine or butter, melted

1 tablespoon grated lemon peel

1 tablespoon lemon juice

1 Cook green beans according to package directions; keep warm.

2 Heat 1 inch water to boiling in large saucepan. Add Brussels sprouts. Cover and heat to boiling; reduce heat. Cook 8 to 10 minutes or until stems are tender; keep warm.

3 Heat 1 inch water to boiling in large saucepan. Add carrots. Cover and heat to boiling; reduce heat. Cook 6 to 8 minutes or until tender; keep warm.

4 Combine margarine, lemon peel and lemon juice. Arrange cooked vegetables on platter; pour margarine mixture over vegetables.

1 Serving: Calories 110 (Calories from Fat 70); Fat 8g (Saturated 1g); Cholesterol 0mg; Sodium 130mg; Carbohydrate 12g (Dietary Fiber 5g); Protein 3g

Spinach Gourmet

4 servings | Prep Time: 5 minutes | Start to Finish: 30 minutes

Impress your guests when you serve this creamy side. Swiss chard—with tender leaves and firm, crisp stalks—can also be used in place of spinach. This succulent side goes perfectly with slices of steak.

- 1 bag (16 oz) fresh spinach* or other fresh greens
- 1 can (4 oz) button mushrooms, drained
- 1 teaspoon instant minced onion
- 1 small clove garlic, crushed
- ½ teaspoon salt
- ⅓ cup sour cream
- 1 tablespoon half-and-half or milk

1 Remove imperfect spinach leaves and root ends. Wash greens several times in water, lifting out of water each time so sand sinks to bottom; drain.

2 Place greens with just the water that clings to leaves in saucepan. Cover and cook 3 to 10 minutes for spinach; 5 to 15 minutes for beet tops; 15 to 20 minutes for chicory, escarole and lettuce; 10 to 15 minutes for collards; 15 to 20 minutes for Swiss chard and mustard greens; 15 to 25 minutes for turnip greens and kale. Drain thoroughly and chop.

3 Stir together greens, mushrooms and seasonings in saucepan. Blend sour cream and half-and-half and pour over spinach mixture. Heat just to boiling.

With frozen spinach: Use 1 package (10 oz) frozen chopped spinach, cooked and drained; add 2 tablespoons butter to ingredients in saucepan.

1 Serving: Calories 75 (Calories from Fat 45); Fat 5g (Saturated 3g); Cholesterol 15mg; Sodium 490mg; Carbohydrate 6g (Dietary Fiber 3g); Protein 4g

COUNTRY COOKING WISDOM

Great Greens

All of the varieties of greens—beet, chicory, collards, escarole, kale, mustard, spinach, Swiss chard and turnip—have a strong, biting flavor and a rich green color. Young greens are milder and more tender and can be tossed in salads; older greens become bitter and should be cooked for the best flavor.

- When buying greens, choose tender, young, unblemished leaves with a bright green color.
- When preparing, remove root ends and imperfect leaves. Wash several times in water, lifting out each time; drain.
- When cooking greens, except spinach, cover and cook with just the water that clings to leaves over medium-high heat 8 to 10 minutes or until tender. For spinach, cover and cook with just the water that clings to the leaves over medium-high heat 3 to 5 minutes or until tender.

Stuffed Zucchini

8 servings | Prep Time: 15 minutes | Start to Finish: 1 hour

Trying to figure out how to use up the pounds of zucchini that grew in your garden? This tasty side dish can help with that—but if you didn't have a garden, head to the store and buy some zucchini. This goes well with any chicken recipe.

4 medium zucchini (2 lb)

1 medium onion, chopped (1/2 cup)

1/4 cup margarine or butter

1 can (4 oz) chopped green chilies, drained

1 jar (2 oz) diced pimientos, drained

1 1/2 cups herb-seasoned stuffing mix

3/4 cup shredded mozzarella or Monterey Jack cheese

1 Heat 2 inches water (salted, if desired) to boiling. Add zucchini. Heat to boiling; reduce heat. Cover and simmer 8 to 10 minutes or just until tender; drain. Cool slightly. Cut each zucchini lengthwise in half.

2 Spoon out pulp. Chop coarsely. Place zucchini, cut sides up, in ungreased baking dish, 13 × 9 inches.

3 Heat oven to 350°F.

4 Cook onion in margarine in 10-inch skillet, stirring frequently, until onion is tender. Stir in chopped pulp, chiles, pimientos and stuffing mix.

5 Divide stuffing mixture among zucchini halves. Sprinkle each with about 1 tablespoon cheese. Bake uncovered 30 to 35 minutes or until hot.

1 Serving: Calories 145 (Calories from Fat 70); Fat 8g (Saturated 2g); Cholesterol 5mg; Sodium 330mg; Carbohydrate 14g (Dietary Fiber 2g); Protein 6g

Pacific Green Beans

Photo on page 179

5 servings | Prep Time: 25 minutes | Start to Finish: 25 minutes

Herbs grow in abundance in the mild climate of the Pacific Northwest. Summer savory, with its peppery flavor, is often served there with mild green beans.

1 lb fresh green beans

1 small onion, finely chopped (1/4 cup)

1 tablespoon margarine, butter or bacon fat

1/4 cup water

1/4 teaspoon salt

2 teaspoons chopped fresh or 1/2 teaspoon dried summer savory leaves

1 tablespoon chopped fresh parsley

1 Cut beans into 1 1/2-inch pieces or leave whole.

2 Cook onion in margarine in 3-quart saucepan over medium heat, stirring frequently, until onion is tender.

3 Stir in beans, water and salt. Heat to boiling; reduce heat. Cover and simmer, stirring occasionally, until beans are crisp-tender, 10 to 13 minutes for pieces or 13 to 16 minutes for whole beans.

4 Stir in summer savory and parsley.

1 Serving: Calories 40 (Calories from Fat 21); Fat 2g (Saturated 1g); Cholesterol 0mg; Sodium 140mg; Carbohydrate 7g (Dietary Fiber 4g); Protein 1g

Skillet Acorn Squash

4 servings | Prep Time: 20 minutes | Start to Finish: 40 minutes

Tender, colorful acorn squash is coated in a heavenly mixture of orange juice, brown sugar and cinnamon.

1 large acorn squash (2 lb)

$1/4$ cup pecan pieces

$1/2$ cup orange juice

2 tablespoons packed brown sugar

1 tablespoon margarine or butter

$1/4$ teaspoon ground cinnamon

1 Cut squash lengthwise in half. Remove seeds and fibers. Cut each half crosswise into $1/2$-inch slices.

2 Heat pecans in 12-inch skillet over medium heat, stirring constantly, until lightly browned; remove from skillet.

3 Mix orange juice, brown sugar, margarine and cinnamon in skillet. Stir in squash. Heat to boiling; reduce heat. Cover and simmer 10 minutes; turn squash. Cover and simmer 5 to 8 minutes longer or until squash is tender. Sprinkle with pecans.

1 Serving: Calories 180 (Calories from Fat 71); Fat 8g (Saturated 1g); Cholesterol 0mg; Sodium 41mg; Carbohydrate 29g (Dietary Fiber 3g); Protein 2g

COUNTRY COOKING WISDOM

Super Squash

Acorn Squash and all winter squashes—butternut, buttercup, and spaghetti—have hard, thick skins and seeds. The hard skin protects the flesh and allows it to be stored longer than summer squash. The deep yellow to orange flesh is firmer than that of summer squash and therefore requires longer cooking. Select squash that are heavy in relation to size, with good yellow-orange color and hard, tough rinds with no soft spots.

Country Fried Cabbage

This flavorful dish is often served in late summer or fall when the large leafy heads of cabbage are harvested. It makes a great side dish for ham, pork or poultry.

2 tablespoons bacon fat or vegetable oil

1 medium head green or red cabbage, shredded (1½ lb)

2 tablespoons whipping cream

1½ teaspoons lemon juice or vinegar

Salt and pepper

1 Heat bacon fat in 10-inch skillet. Add cabbage. Cook over low heat, stirring frequently, until light brown. Cover and cook about 5 minutes longer, stirring occasionally, until crisp-tender.

2 Stir in whipping cream and lemon juice. Heat until whipping cream is hot. Sprinkle with salt and pepper.

1 Serving: Calories 135 (Calories from Fat 83); Fat 9g (Saturated 4g); Cholesterol 15mg; Sodium 198mg; Carbohydrate 11g (Dietary Fiber 4g); Protein 2g

Corn Pudding

Corn on the cob is a time-honored American favorite. But corn *off* the cob can be just as wonderful! In the summer, use just-picked corn to make this simple, creamy pudding. Be sure to scrape all the pulp and milk from the cob.

4 medium ears corn*

2 tablespoons sugar

2 tablespoons all-purpose flour

½ teaspoon salt

Dash of pepper

2 eggs

1¼ cups milk

2 tablespoons margarine or butter, melted

½ teaspoon ground nutmeg

1 Heat oven to 350°F. Grease 1-quart casserole or soufflé dish.

2 Cut enough kernels from corn to measure 2 cups. (Scrape ears with knife to extract all pulp and milk.)

3 Mix the corn, sugar, flour, salt and pepper in 2-quart bowl. Stir in eggs. Stir in milk and margarine. Pour into casserole. Sprinkle with nutmeg.

4 Set casserole in baking pan on middle oven rack. Pour hot water into pan until about 1½ inches deep. Bake 50 to 55 minutes or until knife inserted halfway between center and edge comes out clean.

2 cups frozen whole kernel corn, thawed, or 1 can (16 oz) whole kernel corn, drained, can be substituted for the fresh corn.

1 Serving: Calories 125 (Calories from Fat 53); Fat 5g (Saturated 2g); Cholesterol 55mg; Sodium 220mg; Carbohydrate 14g (Dietary Fiber 1g); Protein 4g

Cheesy Grits

8 servings | Prep Time: 15 minutes | Start to Finish: 1 hour 10 minutes

Hominy is corn that has its hulls removed, so it cooks up soft with a little texture. You will find it in the hot cereal aisle, near the oatmeal. For a cheesier flavor, select a sharp Cheddar instead of mild.

2 cups milk

2 cups water

1 teaspoon salt

$1/4$ teaspoon pepper

1 cup uncooked hominy quick grits

$1^1/2$ cups shredded Cheddar cheese (6 oz)

3 green onions, sliced ($1/4$ cup)

2 eggs, slightly beaten

1 tablespoon margarine or butter

$1/4$ teaspoon paprika

1 Heat oven to 350°F. Grease $1^1/2$-quart casserole.

2 Heat milk, water, salt and pepper to boiling in 2-quart saucepan. Gradually add grits, stirring constantly; reduce heat. Simmer uncovered about 5 minutes, stirring frequently, until thick. Stir in cheese and onions. Stir 1 cup of the hot mixture into eggs, then stir egg mixture into remaining hot mixture in saucepan.

3 Pour hot mixture into casserole. Dot with margarine and sprinkle with paprika. Bake uncovered 35 to 40 minutes or until set. Let stand 10 minutes.

1 Serving: Calories 220 (Calories from Fat 100); Fat 11g (Saturated 6g); Cholesterol 80mg; Sodium 490mg; Carbohydrate 19g (Dietary Fiber 0g); Protein 11g

Hush Puppies

About 4 dozen hush puppies | Prep Time: 20 minutes | Start to Finish: 20 minutes

Southern Fried Catfish (page 128) and these hush puppies are a great combination. Use a frying thermometer to make sure the oil is the right temperature so your pups are golden and light.

Vegetable oil

$1^1/2$ cups cornmeal

$1/2$ cup all-purpose flour

$1/4$ cup shortening

1 cup milk

2 tablespoons finely chopped onion

2 teaspoons baking powder

1 teaspoon sugar

1 teaspoon salt

$1/2$ teaspoon baking soda

$1/4$ to $1/2$ teaspoon ground red pepper (cayenne)

1 egg

1 Heat oil (1 inch) in Dutch oven to 375°F.

2 Mix remaining ingredients. Drop by teaspoonfuls into hot oil. Fry about 1 minute, turning once, until golden brown; drain.

1 Hush Puppy: Calories 50 (Calories from Fat 25); Fat 3g (Saturated 1g); Cholesterol 5mg; Sodium 85mg; Carbohydrate 5g (Dietary Fiber 0g); Protein 1g

Corn and Pepper Cakes

6 servings   Prep Time: 25 minutes   Start to Finish: 25 minutes

If you don't have fresh corn on hand, one 10-oz package of frozen whole-kernel corn, cooked, can be substituted. That makes it easy to enjoy these yummy cakes all year long.

4 medium ears corn

1/2 cup all-purpose flour

1/4 cup milk

1 tablespoon sugar

1/2 teaspoon salt

1/8 teaspoon pepper

2 eggs, separated

1 small bell pepper, finely chopped (about 1/2 cup)

1/2 cup vegetable oil

Sour cream, if desired

1 Cut enough kernels from corn to measure 2 cups (scrape ears with knife to extract all pulp and milk).

2 Beat flour, milk, sugar, salt, pepper and egg yolks in medium bowl. Stir in corn and bell pepper.

3 Beat egg whites until stiff and glossy. Fold corn mixture into egg whites.

4 Heat oil in 10-inch skillet. Drop corn mixture by tablespoonfuls into hot oil. Fry about 30 seconds on each side or until golden brown. Serve with sour cream.

1 Serving: Calories 220 (Calories from Fat 100); Fat 11g (Saturated 2g); Cholesterol 70mg; Sodium 230mg; Carbohydrate 22g (Dietary Fiber 2g); Protein 5g

Crispy Potato Pancakes

12 pancakes | Prep Time: 15 minutes | Start to Finish: 15 minutes

A dollop of sour cream or applesauce is all you need to top these tasty pancakes. Grilled kielbasa or Polish sausage makes this meal just perfect.

1 lb peeled large baking potatoes, shredded

1/2 cup beer or milk

1/4 cup all-purpose flour

1 small onion, finely chopped (1/4 cup)

2 tablespoons finely chopped parsley

1/2 teaspoon salt

1/4 teaspoon pepper

1 egg

2 to 3 tablespoons vegetable oil

Applesauce, if desired

1 Mix all ingredients except oil until well blended.

2 Heat oil on griddle or in large skillet until hot. Spread about 1/4 cup batter on griddle for each pancake. Cook on medium-high heat 2 minutes on each side or until crispy; keep warm. Add more oil to griddle, if necessary. Serve with applesauce.

1 Pancake: Calories 90 (Calories from Fat 25); Fat 3g (Saturated 1g); Cholesterol 15mg; Sodium 105mg; Carbohydrate 15g (Dietary Fiber 1g); Protein 2g

Bountiful Twice-Baked Potatoes

Photo on page 162

8 servings | Prep Time: 25 minutes | Start to Finish: 1 hour 55 minutes

These potatoes can be ready when you are! Once made, you can refrigerate them for up to 24 hours. Just increase the final baking time to 30 minutes. You can freeze them, too, then pop them in the oven, uncovered, for about 40 minutes.

2 lb unpeeled large baking potatoes

1/4 to 1/2 cup milk

1/4 cup margarine or butter, softened

1/4 teaspoon salt

Dash of pepper

1 cup shredded Cheddar cheese (4 oz)

1 tablespoon chopped fresh chives

1 Heat oven to 375°F. Gently scrub potatoes, but do not peel. Pierce potatoes several times with fork to allow steam to escape. Bake 1 hour to 1 hour 15 minutes or until potatoes feel tender when pierced with fork; removed. Increase oven temperature to 400°F.

2 Cut potatoes lengthwise in half. Scoop out inside, leaving a thin shell. Mash pulp in medium bowl until no lumps remain. Add milk in small amounts, beating after each addition (amount of milk needed to make potatoes smooth and fluffy depends on kind of potatoes used).

3 Add margarine, salt and pepper. Beat vigorously until potatoes are light and fluffy. Stir in cheese and chives. Fill potato shells with mashed potatoes. Place on ungreased cookie sheet.

4 Bake about 20 minutes or until hot.

1 Serving: Calories 180 (Calories from Fat 100); Fat 11g (Saturated 4g); Cholesterol 15mg; Sodium 280mg; Carbohydrate 16g (Dietary Fiber 1g); Protein 5g

Basil-Baked New Potatoes

6 servings   Prep Time: 5 minutes   Start to Finish: 1 hour 20 minutes

Keep the skin on—the potato peel has lots of flavor and nutrients, so don't remove it if you don't have to.

2½ lb new potatoes (14 to 18)

3 medium green onion, finely chopped (¼ cup)

2 tablespoons chopped fresh or 2 teaspoons dried basil leaves

2 tablespoons olive or vegetable oil

1 Heat oven to 350°F. Spray rectangular pan, 13 × 9 inches, with cooking spray.

2 Place potatoes in pan. Sprinkle with onions and basil. Drizzle with oil and stir to coat.

3 Bake uncovered about 1 hour 15 minutes, stirring occasionally, until potato skins are crispy and potatoes are tender.

1 Serving: Calories 185 (Calories from Fat 45); Fat 5g (Saturated 1g); Cholesterol 0mg; Sodium 10mg; Carbohydrate 35g (Dietary Fiber 3g); Protein 3g

COUNTRY COOKING WISDOM
Nice New Potatoes

New potatoes appear in trendy restaurants and gourmet recipes—so what are they? They're simply young potatoes that haven't had time to convert their sugar fully into starch, so they have a crisp, waxy texture and an extra-thin skin. Choose nicely shaped, smooth and firm potatoes with unblemished skins (some are very delicate). Also, choose potatoes of similar size, about 1½ inches in diameter, for even cooking success.

Garlic Smashed Potatoes

Photo on page 102

6 servings | **Prep Time: 20 minutes** | **Start to Finish: 1 hour 20 minutes**

Looking for a scrumptious twist on mashed potatoes? The Yukon Gold potatoes have a beautiful golden color, and the roasted garlic adds a subtle sweet flavor to the potatoes. We're sure you'll find them delicious.

2 lb unpeeled Yukon Gold or russet potatoes (6 medium)

1 bulb garlic

2 tablespoons olive or vegetable oil

1 teaspoon chopped fresh or ¼ teaspoon dried oregano leaves

½ teaspoon salt

⅓ to ½ cup milk

¼ cup chopped fresh chives

1 Heat oven to 375°F.

2 Pierce potatoes with fork to allow steam to escape. Cut ¼-inch slice from top of garlic bulb to expose cloves. Carefully remove most of the paperlike skin, leaving the bulb intact and the cloves unpeeled. Wrap garlic in foil. Bake potatoes and garlic about 1 hour or until potatoes are tender.

3 Heat oil and oregano over medium heat 2 to 3 minutes or until oregano is fragrant.

4 Open garlic pack to cool. Cut potatoes in half. Carefully spoon potatoes in large bowl. Save skins for another use or discard. Separate garlic cloves and press the cloves slightly to squeeze the garlic out; discard skin. Place garlic in bowl and add oil mixture and salt.

5 Mash potatoes until no lumps remain. Beat in milk in small amounts (amount of milk needed to make potatoes smooth and fluffy depends on kind of potatoes used). Beat vigorously until potatoes are light and fluffy. Stir in chives.

1 Serving: Calories 155 (Calories from Fat 45); Fat 5g (Saturated 1g); Cholesterol 2mg; Sodium 190mg; Carbohydrate 26g (Dietary Fiber 2g); Protein 3g

Roasted Rosemary-Onion Potatoes

4 servings | Prep Time: 10 minutes | Start to Finish: 35 minutes

Instead of French fries, try this as a side. Roasted potatoes, redolent with rosemary and sweet onion, are a great partner for any sandwich, burger or even breakfast eggs!

1⅓ lb potatoes (4 medium)

1 small onion, finely chopped (¼ cup)

2 tablespoons olive or vegetable oil

2 tablespoons chopped fresh or 2 teaspoons dried rosemary leaves

1 teaspoon chopped fresh or ¼ teaspoon dried thyme leaves

¼ teaspoon salt

⅛ teaspoon pepper

1 Heat oven to 450°F. Grease jelly roll pan, 15 × 10 inches.

2 Cut potatoes into 1-inch chunks.

3 Mix onion, oil, rosemary, thyme, salt and pepper in large bowl. Add potatoes and toss to coat. Spread potatoes in single layer in pan.

4 Bake uncovered 20 to 25 minutes, turning occasionally, until potatoes are light brown and tender when pierced with fork.

1 Serving: Calories 150 (Calories from Fat 65); Fat 7g (Saturated 1g); Cholesterol 0mg; Sodium 140mg; Carbohydrate 22g (Dietary Fiber 2g); Protein 2g

Duchess Potatoes

12 servings | Prep Time: 15 minutes | Start to Finish: 1 hour 5 minutes

These potatoes are as elegant as they are delicious—delicate pillows of baked, golden mashed potatoes. Think of this side dish the next time you are having a roast. And if company is coming, these beauties can be made ahead of time. Just pop them in the oven before serving.

4 lb peeled potatoes
   (12 medium)

$2/3$ to 1 cup milk

$1/2$ cup margarine, butter or
   spread, softened

$1/2$ teaspoon salt

Dash of pepper

4 eggs, beaten

Margarine, butter or spread,
   melted

1 Cut potatoes into large pieces or leave whole. Heat 1 inch water (salted if desired) to boiling in Dutch oven. Add potatoes. Cover and heat to boiling; reduce heat. Cook whole potatoes 30 to 35 minutes, pieces 20 to 25 minutes, or until tender; drain. Shake Dutch oven gently over low heat to dry potatoes.

2 Heat oven to 425°F. Grease cookie sheet.

3 Mash potatoes until no lumps remain. Beat in milk in small amounts (amount of milk needed to make potatoes smooth and fluffy depends on kind of potatoes used). Add $1/2$ cup margarine, the salt and pepper. Beat vigorously until potatoes are light and fluffy. Add eggs and beat until blended.

4 Drop potato mixture by spoonfuls into 12 mounds on cookie sheet. Or place in decorating bag with star tip and form rosettes or pipe a border around meat or fish. Brush with melted margarine. Bake about 15 minutes or until light brown.

1 Serving: Calories 240 (Calories from Fat 115); Fat 13g (Saturated 3g); Cholesterol 70mg; Sodium 260mg; Carbohydrate 28g (Dietary Fiber 2g); Protein 5g

Creamy Scalloped Potatoes

6 servings | Prep Time: 15 minutes | Start to Finish: 2 hours 25 minutes

Make it your way with either peeled or unpeeled potatoes. This creamy side is the perfect partner for pork chops.

2 lb boiling or baking potatoes (6 medium)

4 tablespoons margarine or butter

1 small onion, finely chopped ($\frac{1}{4}$ cup)

3 tablespoons all-purpose flour

1 teaspoon salt

$\frac{1}{4}$ teaspoon pepper

2$\frac{1}{2}$ cups milk

1 Heat oven to 350°F. Grease bottom and sides of 2-quart casserole with shortening.

2 Scrub potatoes; peel, if desired. Cut into enough thin slices to measure 4 cups.

3 Melt 3 tablespoons of the margarine in 2-quart saucepan over medium heat. Cook onion in margarine about 2 minutes, stirring occasionally, until tender. Stir in flour, salt and pepper. Cook, stirring constantly, until smooth and bubbly; remove from heat.

4 Stir in milk. Heat to boiling, stirring constantly. Boil and stir 1 minute.

5 Spread potatoes in casserole. Pour sauce over potatoes. Dot with remaining 1 tablespoon margarine.

6 Cover and bake 50 minutes. Uncover and bake 1 hour to 1 hour 10 minutes longer or until potatoes are tender. Let stand 5 to 10 minutes before serving.

1 Serving: Calories 190 (Calories from Fat 98); Fat 11g (Saturated 3g); Cholesterol 10mg; Sodium 528mg; Carbohydrate 16g (Dietary Fiber 4g); Protein 7g

Marbled Potatoes and Carrots

4 to 5 servings   Prep Time: 15 minutes   Start to Finish: 40 minutes

Comfort food at its tastiest—homemade mashed potatoes swirled with sweet cooked carrots flavored with dill weed.

2 medium peeled potatoes ($^2/_3$ lb), cut into pieces

4 medium carrots, sliced (2 cups)

4 to 6 tablespoons milk

3 teaspoons margarine, butter or spread

$^1/_4$ teaspoon salt

$^1/_4$ teaspoon dried dill weed

1 Heat 1 inch water (salted, if desired) to boiling in 1-quart saucepan. Add potatoes. Cover and heat to boiling; reduce heat. Cook 20 to 25 minutes or until tender; drain. Shake pan gently over low heat to dry potatoes.

2 While potatoes are cooking, heat 1 inch water (salted, if desired) to boiling in 1-quart saucepan. Add carrots. Cover and heat to boiling; reduce heat. Cook about 15 minutes or until very tender; drain.

3 Mash potatoes until no lumps remain. Beat in 2 to 3 tablespoons of the milk (amount of milk needed to make potatoes smooth and fluffy depends on kind of potatoes used) in small amounts. Add 2 tablespoons margarine and $^1/_4$ teaspoon salt. Beat vigorously until potatoes are light and fluffy. Cover to keep warm.

4 Mash carrots until no lumps remain. Beat in remaining 2 to 3 tablespoons milk. Beat in 1 teaspoon margarine and the dill weed.

5 Spoon potato mixture into half of small serving bowl. Spoon carrot mixture into other half. Pull a small rubber spatula through mixtures to create a marbled design.

1 Serving: Calories 105 (Calories from Fat 25); Fat 3g (Saturated 1g); Cholesterol 2mg; Sodium 200mg; Carbohydrate 20g (Dietary Fiber 3g); Protein 2g

Candied Sweet Potatoes

Photo on page 186

4 servings | Prep Time: 10 minutes | Start to Finish: 45 minutes

While often present on a Thanksgiving table, these tender sweet bites shouldn't be just for the holidays. They are as delicious alongside salty ham as they are with a roast turkey.

2 lb unpeeled sweet potatoes or yams (6 medium)*

1/2 cup packed brown sugar

3 tablespoons margarine or butter

3 tablespoons water

1/2 teaspoon salt

1 Heat enough water (salted if desired) to cover potatoes to boiling. Add potatoes. Cover and heat to boiling; reduce heat. Boil 30 to 35 minutes or until tender. Drain and cool slightly. Slip off skins. Cut potatoes into 1/2-inch slices.

2 Heat remaining ingredients in 8-inch skillet over medium heat, stirring constantly, until smooth and bubbly. Add potato slices; stir gently until glazed and hot.

*1 can (23 oz) sweet potatoes or yams, drained and cut into 1/2-inch slices, can be substituted for the sweet potatoes.

1 Serving: Calories 330 (Calories from Fat 78); Fat 9g (Saturated 2g); Cholesterol 0mg; Sodium 463mg; Carbohydrate 62g (Dietary Fiber 6g); Protein 4g

Brandy Sweet Potatoes: Substitute brandy for the water.

Orange Sweet Potatoes: Substitute orange juice for the water and add 1 tablespoon grated orange peel.

Pineapple Sweet Potatoes: Omit water, add 1 can (8.25 oz) crushed pineapple in syrup, undrained.

Spicy Sweet Potatoes: Stir 1/2 teaspoon ground cinnamon or 1/4 teaspoon ground allspice, cloves, mace or nutmeg into brown sugar mixture in skillet.

COUNTRY COOKING WISDOM

You Say Potato

Sweet potatoes and yams are similar in many ways, but they are actually from different plant species. Sweet potatoes are often called yams. True yams, which are not widely marketed and are seldom grown in the United States, are similar in size and shape. Yams contain more natural sugar and have a higher moisture content. Sweet potatoes are richer in vitamins A and C.

Hoppin' John

6 servings | Prep Time: 5 minutes | Start to Finish: 3 hours

In South Carolina and neighboring states, it just wouldn't be a proper New Year's Day without Hoppin' John. This southern favorite is said to bring good luck for the coming year. Some believe Hoppin' John got its name because hungry children used to hop impatiently around the table as they waited for supper. Others contend that it was named after the custom of inviting a guest to eat by saying, "Hop in, John."

1 cup dried black-eyed peas (½ lb)

3½ cups water

¼ lb slab bacon, lean salt pork or smoked pork

1 onion, sliced

¼ to ½ teaspoon very finely chopped fresh hot chile or ⅛ to ¼ teaspoon crushed red pepper

½ cup uncooked regular long grain rice

1 teaspoon salt

Pepper

1 Heat peas and water to boiling in 2-quart saucepan; boil 2 minutes. Remove from heat. Cover and let stand 1 hour.

2 Cut bacon into 8 pieces. Stir bacon, onion and hot chile pepper into peas. Heat to boiling; reduce heat. Cover and simmer until peas are tender, 1 hour to 1 hour 30 minutes.

3 Stir in rice, salt and pepper. Cover and simmer, stirring occasionally, until rice is tender, about 25 minutes. Stir in additional water, if necessary, to cook rice.

1 Serving: Calories 130 (Calories from Fat 25); Fat 3g (Saturated 1g); Cholesterol 5mg; Sodium 480mg; Carbohydrate 23g (Dietary Fiber 3g); Protein 6g

Penne with Roasted Tomatoes and Garlic

4 servings | Prep Time: 10 minutes | Start to Finish: 1 hour 10 minutes

Garlic has long been associated with health and vitality. With that in mind, this recipe provides a wealth of health! A bulb of garlic may seem like a lot, but when roasted, garlic becomes mellow and sweet, with a butter-soft texture.

¼ cup olive or vegetable oil

8 to 10 roma (plum) tomatoes, cut in half

1 teaspoon sugar

¼ teaspoon salt

Freshly ground pepper

1 bulb garlic, unpeeled

2 cups uncooked penne pasta (8 oz)

¼ cup chopped fresh or 1 tablespoon dried basil leaves

4 oz feta cheese, crumbled

1 Heat oven to 300°F. Cover cookie sheet with foil; generously brush with 1 tablespoon of the oil.

2 Arrange tomato halves, cut sides up, in single layer on cookie sheet. Brush with 4 teaspoons of the oil. Sprinkle with sugar, salt and pepper.

3 Cut ½ inch off top of garlic bulb; drizzle 2 teaspoons of the oil over garlic bulb. Wrap in foil; place on cookie sheet with tomatoes.

4 Bake 55 to 60 minutes or until garlic is soft when pierced with a knife and tomatoes have begun to shrivel; cool slightly.

5 Cook and drain pasta as directed on package.

6 Squeeze garlic into remaining 1 tablespoon oil and mash until smooth. Toss with pasta. Add tomato halves and basil; toss. Top with cheese. Serve immediately.

1 Serving: Calories 450 (Calories from Fat 190); Fat 21g (Saturated 6g); Cholesterol 25mg; Sodium 470mg; Carbohydrate 55g (Dietary Fiber 3g); Protein 13g

COUNTRY COOKING WISDOM

Penne Pasta

Penne is a short-cut pasta, about 1¼ inches long. Tubular in shape with slanted cuts at both ends, penne can have a smooth or grooved finish. It is narrower than mostaccioli. The word *penne* means "feather," indicating either the lightness of the noodle or the transversally cut shape that resembles the wing of a bird. It is excellent with tomato and vegetable sauces.

Creamy Fettuccine Alfredo

6 servings | Prep Time: 15 minutes | Start to Finish: 15 minutes

For a creative touch, top with toasted walnuts, roasted red bell pepper strips, or chopped Kalamata olives instead of the parsley.

8 oz uncooked fettuccine

1/2 cup margarine or butter

1/2 cup whipping cream

3/4 cup grated Parmesan cheese

1/2 teaspoon salt

Dash of pepper

Chopped fresh parsley

1 Cook and drain fettuccine as directed on package.

2 While fettuccine is cooking, heat margarine and whipping cream in 2-quart saucepan over low heat, stirring constantly, until margarine is melted. Stir in cheese, salt and pepper.

3 Pour sauce over fettuccine and stir until fettuccine is well coated. Sprinkle with parsley.

I Serving: Calories 380 (Calories from Fat 235); Fat 26g (Saturated 9g); Cholesterol 65mg; Sodium 600mg; Carbohydrate 26g (Dietary Fiber 1g); Protein 9g

Macaroni and Cheese

6 servings | Prep Time: 25 minutes | Start to Finish: 50 minutes

Add extra pep to this favorite recipe by using pizza-flavored or jalapeño pepper cheese.

1 package (7 oz) elbow macaroni (2 cups)

1/4 cup margarine or butter

1/4 cup all-purpose flour

1/2 teaspoon salt

1/4 teaspoon pepper

1/4 teaspoon ground mustard

1/4 teaspoon Worcestershire sauce

2 cups milk

2 cups shredded or cubed sharp Cheddar cheese (8 oz)

1 Heat oven to 350°F.

2 Cook macaroni as directed on package.

3 While macaroni is cooking, melt margarine in 3-quart saucepan over low heat. Stir in flour, salt, pepper, mustard and Worcestershire sauce. Cook over low heat, stirring constantly, until mixture is smooth and bubbly; remove from heat.

4 Stir in milk. Heat to boiling, stirring constantly. Boil and stir 1 minute. Stir in cheese. Cook, stirring occasionally, until cheese is melted.

5 Drain macaroni. Gently stir macaroni into cheese sauce. Pour into ungreased 2-quart casserole. Bake uncovered 20 to 25 minutes or until bubbly.

I Serving: Calories 445 (Calories from Fat 205); Fat 23g (Saturated 11g); Cholesterol 45mg; Sodium 540mg; Carbohydrate 42g (Dietary Fiber 1g); Protein 18g

Spanish Rice

Photo on page 111

| 6 servings | Prep Time: 10 minutes | Start to Finish: 40 minutes |

Looking for a flavor fiesta? Instead of regular tomato sauce, use an herbed or other specially flavored tomato sauce to add even more excitement to the rice.

2 tablespoons vegetable oil

I cup uncooked regular long-grain rice

I medium onion, chopped (1/2 cup)

2 1/2 cups water

1 1/2 teaspoons salt

3/4 teaspoon chili powder

1/8 teaspoon garlic powder

I small green bell pepper, chopped (1/2 cup)

I can (8 oz) tomato sauce

1 Heat oil in 10-inch skillet over medium heat. Cook rice and onion in oil about 5 minutes, stirring frequently, until rice is golden brown and onion is tender.

2 Stir in remaining ingredients. Heat to boiling; reduce heat to low. Cover and simmer about 30 minutes, stirring occasionally, until rice is tender.

I Serving: Calories 180 (Calories from Fat 45); Fat 5g (Saturated Ig); Cholesterol 0mg; Sodium 770mg; Carbohydrate 32g (Dietary Fiber Ig); Protein 3g

Cranberry–Wild Rice Bake

| 8 servings | Prep Time: 15 minutes | Start to Finish: 2 hours 50 minutes |

Ruby red dried cranberries enhance this robust rice dish that complements pork, turkey or game. It's also a nice change from, or addition to, Thanksgiving stuffing.

I cup uncooked wild rice

2 1/2 cups water

I tablespoon margarine or butter

I medium onion, chopped (1/2 cup)

I cup sliced mushrooms (3 oz)

2 1/2 cups chicken broth, heated

1/4 teaspoon salt

2 cloves garlic, finely chopped

I cup dried cranberries

1 Heat oven to 350°F. Grease square baking dish, 8 × 8 inches, with shortening.

2 Place wild rice in wire strainer. Run cold water through rice, lifting rice with fingers to clean thoroughly. Heat rice and water to boiling in 2-quart saucepan, stirring occasionally; reduce heat to low. Cover and simmer 30 minutes; drain.

3 Melt margarine in 10-inch skillet over medium heat. Cook onion and mushrooms in margarine, stirring occasionally, until onion is tender.

4 Combine rice and onion mixture in baking dish. Mix broth, salt and garlic and pour over rice mixture.

5 Cover and bake 1 hour 15 minutes. Stir in cranberries. Cover and bake 15 to 20 minutes longer or until liquid is absorbed.

I Serving: Calories 120 (Calories from Fat 20); Fat 2g (Saturated 0g); Cholesterol 0mg; Sodium 85mg; Carbohydrate 24g (Dietary Fiber 2g); Protein 4g

Spring Rice Medley

This rice dish is packed with healthful vegetables—asparagus, zucchini, broccoli, bell pepper, tomato, beans and peas—and flavored with saffron.

1 lb asparagus, cut into 2-inch pieces	4 cups cooked rice
3 cups broccoli flowerets (8 oz)	2 large tomatoes, coarsely chopped and seeded (2 cups)
2 teaspoons olive or vegetable oil	3/4 teaspoon salt
1 medium red bell pepper cut into 1/4-inch strips	1/2 teaspoon saffron threads or 1/4 teaspoon ground turmeric
1 medium zucchini, sliced (2 cups)	2 cans (15 to 16 oz each) garbanzo beans, rinsed and drained
1 medium onion, chopped (1/2 cup)	1 package (10 oz) frozen green peas, thawed

1 Cook asparagus and broccoli in enough boiling water to cover in 2-quart saucepan about 4 minutes or until crisp-tender; drain.

2 Heat oil in Dutch oven over medium-high heat. Cook asparagus, broccoli, bell pepper, zucchini and onion in oil about 5 minutes, stirring occasionally, until onion is crisp-tender.

3 Stir in remaining ingredients. Cook about 5 minutes, stirring frequently, until hot.

1 Serving: Calories 400 (Calories from Fat 45); Fat 5g (Saturated 1g); Cholesterol 0mg; Sodium 599mg; Carbohydrate 74g (Dietary Fiber 14g); Protein 18g

Cranberry-Raspberry Salad

12 servings | Prep Time: 10 minutes | Start to Finish: 12 hours 10 minutes

The tang of cranberry and the fruity coolness of the lemon gelatin make this salad a hit at any meal. It will become a favorite of yours on the Thanksgiving table.

2 packages (12 oz each) cranberry-orange sauce

1 package (12 oz) cranberry-raspberry sauce

1 package (6 oz) lemon-flavored gelatin

2 cups boiling water

Watercress, if desired

Cranberries, if desired

1 Lightly oil 6$\frac{1}{2}$-cup ring mold.

2 Mix cranberry sauces together in large bowl. Dissolve gelatin in boiling water and stir into cranberry sauces. Pour into mold. Cover and refrigerate overnight.

3 Unmold salad on serving plate. Garnish with watercress and cranberries.

1 Serving: Calories 190 (Calories from Fat 0); Fat 0g (Saturated 0g); Cholesterol 0mg; Sodium 60mg; Carbohydrate 49g (Dietary Fiber 2g); Protein 1g

Rice Stuffing

8 servings | Prep Time: 10 minutes | Start to Finish: 55 minutes

Bacon and paprika flavor this medley of rice, vegetables, nuts and raisins. Not just for turkeys, this stuffing can also be served with a crown roast of pork, pork chops or chicken.

1 medium stalk celery (with leaves), chopped ($\frac{1}{2}$ cup)

1 small onion, chopped ($\frac{1}{4}$ cup)

2 tablespoons margarine or butter

$\frac{1}{2}$ teaspoon salt

$\frac{1}{8}$ teaspoon pepper

2 cups cooked rice

$\frac{1}{2}$ cup chopped walnuts

$\frac{1}{3}$ cup raisins

$\frac{1}{4}$ teaspoon paprika

4 slices bacon, crisply cooked and crumbled

1 Cook celery, onion, margarine, salt and pepper in 10-inch skillet, stirring frequently, until celery is tender; remove from heat. Stir in remaining ingredients.

2 Use to stuff one 10- to 12-lb turkey. Or to bake stuffing separately, grease 3-quart baking dish. Place stuffing in dish. Cover with lid or foil and bake at 325°F for 30 minutes, uncover and bake 15 minutes longer.

1 Serving: Calories 164 (Calories from Fat 83); Fat 9g (Saturated 2g); Cholesterol 3mg; Sodium 260mg; Carbohydrate 18g (Dietary Fiber 1g); Protein 4g

Chestnut Stuffing

10 servings | Prep Time: 10 minutes | Start to Finish: 1 hour 15 minutes

A traditional Victorian-era chestnut stuffing is most commonly associated with Thanksgiving turkey. Look for fresh chestnuts around Thanksgiving, when they usually become available. When preparing this dish at other times of the year, opt for frozen, canned or jarred chestnuts. Their distinctive flavor makes this recipe absolutely delicious.

1 lb chestnuts

3 medium stalks celery (with leaves), chopped (1½ cups)

1 large onion, finely chopped (1 cup)

1 cup margarine or butter

7 cups soft bread cubes (about 10 slices bread)

1½ teaspoons salt

2 tablespoons chopped fresh or 1½ teaspoons dried sage leaves

1 tablespoon chopped fresh or 1 teaspoon dried thyme leaves

½ teaspoon pepper

1 Cut X shape on rounded side of each chestnut. In 6-quart Dutch oven, heat chestnuts and enough water to cover to boiling. Boil uncovered 10 minutes; drain. Remove shells and skins. Return chestnuts to Dutch oven, cover with water and heat to boiling. Boil uncovered 10 minutes; drain and chop.

2 Cook celery, onion and margarine in 10-inch skillet, stirring frequently, until celery and onion is tender. Stir in about ⅓ of the bread cubes. Turn mixture into deep bowl. Add remaining bread cubes, the salt, sage, thyme, pepper and chestnuts; toss.

3 Use to stuff one 10- to 12-lb turkey. Or to bake stuffing separately, grease 3-quart baking dish. Place stuffing in dish. Cover with lid or foil and bake at 325°F for 30 minutes, then uncover and bake 15 minutes longer.

1 Serving: Calories 308 (Calories from Fat 174); Fat 19g (Saturated 4g); Cholesterol 0mg; Sodium 740mg; Carbohydrate 31g (Dietary Fiber 1g); Protein 3g

COUNTRY COOKING WISDOM

Sensational Stuffings

Stuffing—or dressing, as it is sometimes called—has been a common sight on American tables since colonial times. Usually well seasoned, and based on a mixture of bread crumbs or cubes, it is used to stuff poultry, fish, meat and vegetables. While stuffing may offer the advantage of "stretching" a particular dish, we usually make it because it tastes so good!

Corn Bread Stuffing

16 servings | Prep Time: 15 minutes | Start to Finish: 1 hour

Corn bread stuffing was one of the favorite stuffings in earlier times because its ingredients were plentiful. This recipe is based on one that African Americans in the South used, but it also shows the influences of Native Americans and white sharecroppers. Simple and basic, it reflects the limited resources available to the cook

2 medium stalks celery (with leaves), chopped (1 cup)

1 large onion, chopped (1 cup)

1/2 cup margarine or butter

5 cups crumbled corn bread

3 cups soft bread cubes (about 4 slices bread)

1/2 cup chicken broth

2 teaspoons poultry seasoning

1/2 teaspoon salt

1/2 teaspoon ground sage

1/2 teaspoon ground thyme

1/4 teaspoon pepper

1 Cook celery, onion and margarine in Dutch oven over medium-high heat about 3 minutes, stirring frequently, until celery is tender. Stir in corn bread and bread cubes. Cook, about 10 minutes, stirring occasionally, until bread is golden brown; remove from heat. Add remaining ingredients; toss.

2 Use to stuff one 10- to 12-lb turkey. Or to bake stuffing separately, grease 3-quart baking dish. Place stuffing in dish. Cover with lid or foil and bake at 325°F for 30 minutes, then uncover and bake 15 minutes longer.

1 Serving: Calories 163 (Calories from Fat 79); Fat 9g (Saturated 2g); Cholesterol 17mg; Sodium 421mg; Carbohydrate 18g (Dietary Fiber 1g); Protein 3g

Marinated Tomato Slices

4 servings | Prep Time: 5 minutes | Start to Finish: 35 minutes

Tomatoes go with just about everything! For a richer flavor, cover the tomatoes and marinate them in the refrigerator overnight.

1/4 cup chopped fresh or 2 tablespoons dried basil leaves

6 tablespoons olive oil

2 tablespoons red wine vinegar

2 large tomatoes, sliced

1 Mix all ingredients except tomatoes.

2 Pour mixture over tomatoes in glass bowl. Chill for at least 30 minutes.

1 Serving: Calories 60 (Calories from Fat 45); Fat 5g (Saturated 1g); Cholesterol 0mg; Sodium 10mg; Carbohydrate 4g (Dietary Fiber 1g); Protein 1g

Country Potato Salad

Photo on page 165

10 servings | Prep Time: 10 minutes | Start to Finish: 4 hours 45 minutes

Marinating the potatoes in the dressing beforehand makes this a flavorful potato salad and one of the most requested favorites. Instead of the Cooked Salad Dressing, 1 cup of mayonnaise or salad dressing can be mixed in.

2 lb peeled potatoes (6 medium)

1/4 cup Italian dressing

Cooked Salad Dressing (right) or 1 cup mayonnaise

2 medium stalks celery, sliced (1 cup)

1 medium cucumber, chopped (1 cup)

1 large onion, chopped (1 cup)

6 radishes, thinly sliced (1/2 cup)

4 hard-cooked eggs, chopped

1 Heat 1 inch water (salted, if desired) to boiling. Add potatoes. Cover and heat to boiling; reduce heat. Cook 30 to 35 minutes or until tender. Drain and cool slightly.

2 Cut potatoes into cubes (about 6 cups). Toss warm potatoes with Italian dressing in 4-quart glass or plastic bowl. Cover and refrigerate at least 4 hours. Make Cooked Salad Dressing.

3 Add celery, cucumber, onion, radishes and eggs to potatoes. Pour Cooked Salad Dressing over top and toss. Refrigerate until chilled. Immediately refrigerate any remaining salad.

Cooked Salad Dressing

2 tablespoons all-purpose flour
1 tablespoon sugar
1 teaspoon ground mustard
3/4 teaspoon salt
1/4 teaspoon pepper
1 egg yolk, slightly beaten
3/4 cup milk
2 tablespoons vinegar
1 tablespoon margarine or butter

1 Mix flour, sugar, mustard, salt and pepper in 1-quart saucepan. Mix egg yolk and milk and slowly stir into flour mixture. Cook over medium heat, stirring constantly, until mixture thickens and boils. Boil and stir 1 minute; remove from heat.

2 Stir in vinegar and margarine. Place plastic wrap directly on surface. Refrigerate until cool, at least 1 hour.

1 Serving: Calories 290 (Calories from Fat 200); Fat 22g (Saturated 4g); Cholesterol 100mg; Sodium 210mg; Carbohydrate 20g (Dietary Fiber 2g); Protein 5g

COUNTRY COOKING WISDOM

Simple Seeding

The easiest way to seed a cucumber is to use a small melon baller. Cut the cucumber in half lengthwise and, starting at one end, scoop it into the seeds and slide down the length of the cucumber.

Hot German Potato Salad

5 servings | Prep Time: 30 minutes | Start to Finish: 1 hour 5 minutes

Salty bacon melds with sweetened vinegar to create a flavorful dressing for potatoes.

1½ lb potatoes (4 medium)

3 slices bacon

1 medium onion, chopped (½ cup)

1 tablespoon all-purpose flour

1 tablespoon sugar

1 teaspoon salt

¼ teaspoon celery seed

Dash of pepper

½ cup water

¼ cup vinegar

1 Heat 1 inch water (salted if desired) to boiling. Add potatoes. Cover and heat to boiling; reduce heat. Cook 30 to 35 minutes or until tender; drain. Cut into thin slices and keep warm.

2 Cook bacon in 8-inch skillet until crisp; remove bacon and drain.

3 Cook and stir onion in bacon fat until tender. Stir in flour, sugar, salt, celery seed and pepper. Cook over low heat, stirring constantly, until bubbly; remove from heat. Stir in water and vinegar. Heat to boiling, stirring constantly. Boil and stir 1 minute; remove from heat.

4 Crumble bacon into hot mixture, then add warm potatoes. Cook, stirring gently to coat potato slices, until hot and bubbly.

1 Serving: Calories 199 (Calories from Fat 57); Fat 2g (Saturated 2g); Cholesterol 9mg; Sodium 587mg; Carbohydrate 31g (Dietary Fiber 2g); Protein 5g

Classic Creamy Potato Salad

10 servings | Prep Time: 10 minutes | Start to Finish: 4 hours 45 minutes

Create a picnic anywhere, anytime, with this creamy potato salad. For a summery flavor and a cool crunch, we stir in ½ cup each thinly sliced radishes, chopped cucumber and chopped bell pepper.

2 lb boiling potatoes (6 medium)

1½ cups mayonnaise or salad dressing

1 tablespoon vinegar

1 tablespoon yellow mustard

1 teaspoon salt

¼ teaspoon pepper

2 medium stalks celery, chopped (1 cup)

1 medium onion, chopped (½ cup)

4 hard-cooked eggs, chopped

1 Heat 1 inch water (salted, if desired) to boiling. Add potatoes. Cover and heat to boiling; reduce heat to low. Boil gently 30 to 35 minutes or until potatoes are tender; cool slightly. Cut into cubes (about 6 cups).

2 Mix mayonnaise, vinegar, mustard, salt and pepper in large glass or plastic bowl. Add potatoes, celery and onion; toss. Stir in eggs. Cover and refrigerate at least 4 hours. Cover and refrigerate any remaining salad.

1 Serving: Calories 350 (Calories from Fat 250); Fat 28g (Saturated 5g); Cholesterol 105mg; Sodium 480mg; Carbohydrate 21g (Dietary Fiber 2g); Protein 5g

Cold Cucumber Salad

12 servings | Prep Time: 15 minutes | Start to Finish: 15 minutes

When the temperature is too hot to handle, try whipping up this cool salad. Even better, you can make it a day ahead of time. This is the perfect side for deli subs or anything hot off the grill.

1/2 cup sugar

1/3 cup water

1 teaspoon white pepper

1/2 teaspoon salt

1 1/2 cups cider vinegar

4 large cucumbers, peeled and thinly sliced

1/4 cup chopped fresh parsley

1 Mix sugar, water, white pepper and salt in medium saucepan. Heat mixture over medium-high heat to boiling and boil until sugar is dissolved. Remove from heat and cool. Stir in vinegar.

2 Pour mixture over cucumber slices. Sprinkle with parsley. Cover and refrigerate until ready to serve.

1 Serving: Calories 50 (Calories from Fat 0); Fat 0g (Saturated 0g); Cholesterol 0mg; Sodium 100mg; Carbohydrate 13g (Dietary Fiber 1g); Protein 1g

Seven-Layer Salad

6 servings | Prep Time: 20 minutes | Start to Finish: 2 hours 20 minutes

This salad is a little mix of everything: crunchy, sweet, smoky and tangy. For less fat and fewer calories, but still great flavor, use turkey bacon and low-fat or fat-free salad dressing.

6 cups bite-size pieces mixed salad greens

2 medium stalks celery, thinly sliced (1 cup)

12 radishes, thinly sliced (1 cup)

5 medium green onions, sliced

12 slices bacon, crisply cooked and crumbled

1 package (10 oz) frozen green peas, thawed

1 1/2 cups mayonnaise or salad dressing

1/2 cup grated Parmesan cheese or shredded Cheddar cheese (2 oz)

1 Place salad greens in large glass bowl. Layer celery, radishes, onions, bacon and peas on salad greens.

2 Spread mayonnaise over peas, covering top completely and sealing to edge of bowl. Sprinkle with cheese.

3 Cover and refrigerate at least 2 hours to blend flavors but no longer than 12 hours. Toss before serving, if desired. Cover and refrigerate any remaining salad.

1 Serving: Calories 550 (Calories from Fat 480); Fat 53g (Saturated 10g); Cholesterol 50mg; Sodium 720mg; Carbohydrate 11g (Dietary Fiber 3g); Protein 10g

Antipasto Salad

6 servings | Prep Time: 15 minutes | Start to Finish: 15 minutes

Have fun choosing the different ingredients for this salad. Consider shopping at an Italian market, specialty store or deli.

¼ cup Italian olives

8 oz fresh mozzarella cheese, drained and cubed

4 oz sliced Italian salami

4 oz sliced Italian capicolla, prosciutto or fully cooked smoked Virginia ham

4 oz marinated Italian peppers

1 jar (8 oz) marinated mushrooms, drained

¼ cup chopped fresh basil leaves

Vinaigrette (right)

1 Arrange all ingredients except basil and Vinaigrette on 6 salad plates. Sprinkle with fresh basil.

2 Prepare Vinaigrette; drizzle over salad.

Vinaigrette

⅓ cup olive oil

3 tablespoons red wine vinegar

1 clove garlic, crushed

Mix all ingredients in small bowl.

1 Serving: Calories 345 (Calories from Fat 245); Fat 27g (Saturated 9g); Cholesterol 45mg; Sodium 1,080mg; Carbohydrate 6g (Dietary Fiber 1g); Protein 20g

Heartland Three-Bean Salad

12 servings | Prep Time: 15 minutes | Start to Finish: 3 hours 15 minutes

Three-bean salads are picnic favorites. If desired, add lima beans to this recipe and enjoy a four-bean salad!

1 can (16 oz) cut green beans, drained

1 can (16 oz) cut wax beans, drained

1 can (15 oz) kidney beans, drained

1 cup thinly sliced onion, cut in half

1 small bell pepper, finely chopped (½ cup)

2 tablespoons chopped fresh parsley

⅔ cup vinegar

½ cup sugar

⅓ cup vegetable oil

½ teaspoon pepper

½ teaspoon salt

2 slices bacon, crisply cooked and crumbled

1 Mix beans, onion, bell pepper and parsley in 3-quart bowl.

2 Mix remaining ingredients except bacon in 1½-quart saucepan. Heat to boiling, stirring occasionally. Pour over beans; stir.

3 Cover and refrigerate, stirring occasionally, at least 3 hours or until chilled. Just before serving, sprinkle with bacon.

1 Serving: Calories 160 (Calories from Fat 65); Fat 7g (Saturated 1g); Cholesterol 0mg; Sodium 400mg; Carbohydrate 23g (Dietary Fiber 4g); Protein 5g

Old-Fashioned Coleslaw

Photo on page 75

8 servings | Prep Time: 25 minutes | Start to Finish: 3 hours 25 minutes

Coleslaw is not an American invention. It is thought to have been brought to this country by either German or Dutch immigrants. The Dutch called their salad *koolsla* (cabbage salad). This recipe blends sweet-and-tangy flavor with the richness of sour cream. If you prefer, you can leave out the carrot and bell pepper and toss in a chopped tart apple and ¼ cup crumbled blue cheese for an apple-cheese slaw.

- 3 tablespoons sugar
- 2 tablespoons all-purpose flour
- 1 teaspoon ground mustard
- ½ teaspoon salt
- ⅛ teaspoon ground red pepper (cayenne)
- 1 egg
- ¾ cup water
- ¼ cup lemon juice
- 1 tablespoon margarine or butter
- ¼ cup sour cream
- 1 lb green cabbage, shredded or finely chopped (6 cups)
- 1 medium carrot, shredded (1 cup)
- 1 small bell pepper, finely chopped (½ cup)

1 Mix sugar, flour, mustard, salt and red pepper in heavy 1-quart saucepan. Beat in egg. Stir in water and lemon juice gradually until well blended. Cook over low heat 13 to 15 minutes, stirring constantly, until thick and smooth; remove from heat.

2 Stir in margarine until melted. Place plastic wrap directly on surface of dressing and refrigerate about 2 hours or until cool. Stir in sour cream.

3 Mix dressing, cabbage, carrot and bell pepper; toss well. Refrigerate at least 1 hour but no longer than 24 hours.

1 Serving: Calories 85 (Calories from Fat 35); Fat 4g (Saturated 1g); Cholesterol 30mg; Sodium 190mg; Carbohydrate 12g (Dietary Fiber 2g); Protein 2g

COUNTRY COOKING WISDOM

Sour Cream Savvy

Sour cream is cream that's commercially cultured with lactic acid to give a tangy flavor. Regular sour cream is 18 to 20 percent butterfat. Reduced-fat sour cream is made from half-and-half and can be substituted for regular sour cream in most recipes. Fat-free sour cream has all the fat removed and may not be successful in all recipes that call for regular sour cream.

Sweet-Sour Coleslaw

Photo on page 174

6 servings | **Prep Time: 20 minutes** | **Start to Finish: 20 minutes**

The Pennsylvania Dutch, originally from southern Germany, use a boiled sweet-sour dressing on both coleslaw and potato salad to give them a nice, tangy flavor that goes with the crunch of the cabbage. The secret to their classic boiled dressing is to cook it quickly and not let the eggs clump. For the best flavor, this coleslaw should be covered and refrigerated for 2 to 4 hours before serving.

1 egg

1/4 cup sugar

1/4 cup vinegar

2 tablespoons water

2 tablespoons margarine or butter

1 teaspoon salt

1/2 teaspoon ground mustard

1 lb green cabbage, finely shredded or chopped (4 cups)

1 small bell pepper, chopped (1/2 cup)

1 Beat egg until thick and lemon-colored.

2 Heat sugar, vinegar, water, margarine, salt and mustard to boiling, stirring constantly. Gradually stir at least half of the hot mixture into egg, then stir into hot mixture in saucepan.

3 Cook over low heat about 5 minutes, stirring constantly, until thickened. Pour over cabbage and bell pepper; toss.

1 Serving: Calories 80 (Calories from Fat 35); Fat 4g (Saturated 1g); Cholesterol 2mg; Sodium 350mg; Carbohydrate 10g (Dietary Fiber 1g); Protein 2g

Classic Crunchy Coleslaw

8 servings | **Prep Time: 15 minutes** | **Start to Finish: 15 minutes**

This mayonnaise- and sour cream–based recipe for coleslaw is creamy, crunchy and not too sweet. The coleslaw keeps well for several days in the refrigerator. Just keep it tightly covered.

1/2 cup sour cream or plain yogurt

1/4 cup mayonnaise or salad dressing

1 teaspoon sugar

1/2 teaspoon dry mustard

1/2 teaspoon seasoned salt

1/8 teaspoon pepper

1 lb green cabbage, finely shredded or chopped (4 cups)

1 small onion, chopped (1/4 cup)

Paprika, if desired

Dill weed, if desired

1 Mix sour cream, mayonnaise, sugar, mustard, seasoned salt and pepper. Toss with cabbage and onion.

2 Sprinkle with paprika or dried dill weed.

1 Serving: Calories 125 (Calories from Fat 100); Fat 11g (Saturated 3g); Cholesterol 20mg; Sodium 180mg; Carbohydrate 6g (Dietary Fiber 2g); Protein 2g

Peas and Cheese Salad

6 servings | Prep Time: 10 minutes | Start to Finish: 1 hour 10 minutes

Here's an exciting twist on vegetable salads. You'll delight in fresh peas tossed with Cheddar cheese, celery, sweet pickles and hard-cooked eggs in a creamy sweet mayonnaise dressing.

1/3 to 1/2 cup mayonnaise or salad dressing

1/2 teaspoon salt

1/2 teaspoon yellow mustard

1/4 teaspoon sugar

1/8 teaspoon pepper

2 cups cooked shelled fresh green peas*

1 cup diced mild Cheddar or Colby cheese

1 medium stalk celery, thinly sliced (1/2 cup)

3 sweet pickles, chopped (1/4 cup)

2 tablespoons finely chopped onion

2 hard-cooked eggs, chopped

Lettuce leaves, if desired

1 Mix mayonnaise, salt, mustard, sugar and pepper in 2 1/2-quart bowl.

2 Add peas, cheese, celery, pickles and onion; toss. Stir in eggs. Cover and refrigerate at least 1 hour or until chilled. Serve on lettuce leaves. Immediately refrigerate any remaining salad.

*1 package (10 oz) frozen green peas, thawed and drained, can be substituted for the fresh green peas.

1 Serving: Calories 240 (Calories from Fat 160); Fat 18g (Saturated 6g); Cholesterol 100mg; Sodium 500mg; Carbohydrate 10g (Dietary Fiber 3g); Protein 9g

Kidney Bean and Cheese Salad: Substitute 1 can (15 oz) kidney beans, rinsed and drained, for the fresh green peas.

Cranberry Salad Mold

8 servings | Prep Time: 15 minutes | Start to Finish: 3 hours 15 minutes

This salad nicely rounds out a meal of pork or poultry.

3/4 cup boiling water

1 package (4-serving size) raspberry-flavored gelatin

1/2 cup coarsely chopped nuts

1/3 cup chopped celery

1 can (16 oz) whole berry cranberry sauce

1 can (8.25 oz) crushed pineapple in syrup, undrained

Salad greens, if desired

1 Pour boiling water on gelatin in 2-quart bowl; stir until gelatin is dissolved.

2 Stir in remaining ingredients. Pour mixture into 5-cup mold.

3 Refrigerate until firm; unmold. Garnish with salad greens.

1 Serving: Calories 187 (Calories from Fat 49); Fat 5g (Saturated 1g); Cholesterol 0mg; Sodium 55mg; Carbohydrate 35g (Dietary Fiber 2g); Protein 2g

Avocado-Citrus Salad

4 servings | Prep Time: 10 minutes | Start to Finish: 10 minutes

You'll love the fresh, delicious combination of rich, creamy avocado, tart grapefruit, and tangy orange in the spectacular salad.

2 tablespoons lime juice

2 tablespoons olive oil

1 tablespoon chopped fresh mint leaves

Lettuce leaves

2 small avocados, sliced

1 grapefruit, peeled and sliced

1 large orange, peeled and sliced

1 small red onion, chopped (¼ cup)

1 Mix lime juice, olive oil and mint; reserve.

2 Line 4 salad plates with lettuce. Arrange avocado, grapefruit and orange slices on lettuce. Sprinkle with red onion. Drizzle with reserved lime juice mixture.

1 Serving: Calories 270 (Calories from Fat 184); Fat 20g (Saturated 3g); Cholesterol 0mg; Sodium 9mg; Carbohydrate 23g (Dietary Fiber 10g); Protein 3g

COUNTRY COOKING WISDOM

Amazing Avocados

With their creamy, buttery flavor and healthy, monosaturated fats, avocados fit well into any wholesome meal plan. They were first named alligator pears due to the shape and skin of the Haas avocado. Today, many varieties are available—from the pear-shaped and rough, black-skinned to the rounder, green, smooth-skinned Fuerte or Florida avocado. Be sure avocados are fully ripe, easily yielding to pressure, before cutting.

The easiest way to remove the pit is to cut the avocado lengthwise in half around the pit. Carefully and firmly strike the exposed pit with the sharp edge of a knife. While grasping the avocado, twist the knife to loosen and remove the pit.

Mandarin Salad

6 servings | Prep Time: 20 minutes | Start to Finish: 20 minutes

The nutty almonds and sweet mandarin slices blend perfectly together in this most requested salad. Add flavor and texture with some grilled chicken pieces or cooked shrimp.

¼ cup sliced almonds

1 tablespoon plus 1 teaspoon sugar

Sweet-Sour Dressing (right)

½ small head lettuce, torn into bite-size pieces (3 cups)

½ bunch romaine, torn into bite-size pieces (3 cups)

2 medium stalks celery, chopped (1 cup)

2 medium green onions, thinly sliced (2 tablespoons)

1 can (11 oz) mandarin orange segments, drained

1 Cook almonds and sugar in 1-quart saucepan over low heat, stirring constantly, until sugar is melted and almonds are coated. Cool and break apart.

2 Make Sweet-Sour Dressing.

3 Toss almonds, dressing and remaining ingredients.

Sweet-Sour Dressing

¼ cup vegetable oil

2 tablespoons sugar

2 tablespoons white vinegar

1 tablespoon chopped fresh parsley

½ teaspoon salt

Dash of pepper

Dash of red pepper sauce

Shake all ingredients in tightly covered container. Refrigerate until serving.

1 Serving: Calories 165 (Calories from Fat 100); Fat 11g (Saturated 2g); Cholesterol 0mg; Sodium 200mg; Carbohydrate 16g (Dietary Fiber 1g); Protein 1g

COUNTRY COOKING WISDOM

Thickening Agents

Gelatin is an odorless and colorless powder whose thickening agents are released when it is mixed with hot liquid. Gelatin is pure protein, processed from beef and veal bones and cartilage or pig skin. Agar-agar, made from seaweed, is a vegetarian alternative.

Wilted Spinach Salad

Photo on page 102

6 servings | **Prep Time: 10 minutes** | **Start to Finish: 10 minutes**

This warm spinach salad boasts bacon and onions tossed in a lemon dressing with a hint of nutmeg—simply delicious.

1 medium onion, chopped (½ cup)

1 slice bacon, cut up

1 clove garlic, finely chopped

2 tablespoons margarine or butter

2 tablespoons olive or vegetable oil

½ teaspoon salt

¼ teaspoon pepper

¼ teaspoon ground nutmeg

1 lb spinach

Juice of 1 medium lemon (2 tablespoons)

1 Cook onion, bacon and garlic in margarine and oil in Dutch oven over medium heat until bacon is crisp; reduce heat. Stir in salt, pepper and nutmeg.

2 Add spinach and toss just until spinach is wilted. Drizzle with lemon juice.

1 Serving: Calories 121 (Calories from Fat 92); Fat 10g (Saturated 2g); Cholesterol 3mg; Sodium 330mg; Carbohydrate 6g (Dietary Fiber 2g); Protein 3g

Perfection Salad

6 servings | **Prep Time: 15 minutes** | **Start to Finish: 3 hours 15 minutes**

Popular at family gatherings, this delicious recipe is easy to make ahead and adds a pretty color and a cool, refreshing flavor to a robust country meal.

1 cup boiling water

1 package (4-serving size) lemon-flavored gelatin

1 cup cold water

2 tablespoons lemon juice or vinegar

1 teaspoon salt

1 cup finely diced celery

1 cup finely shredded green cabbage

⅓ cup chopped sweet pickles

2 tablespoons finely chopped pimientos

1 Pour boiling water on gelatin in 2-quart bowl; stir until gelatin is dissolved. Stir in cold water, lemon juice and salt. Refrigerate until slightly thickened but not set.

2 Stir in remaining ingredients. Pour into 4-cup mold or 6 individual molds. Refrigerate until firm; unmold.

1 Serving: Calories 30 (Calories from Fat 0); Fat 0g (Saturated 0g); Cholesterol 0mg; Sodium 516mg; Carbohydrate 7g (Dietary Fiber 7g); Protein 1g

CHAPTER SIX

Warm Up the Oven

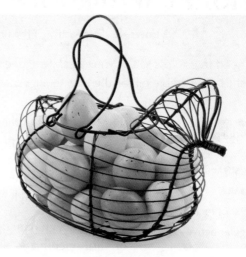

BAKED GOODS ARE A CHERISHED PART OF ANY MEAL, WHETHER BREAKFAST, LUNCH OR DINNER. THEY'RE GREATLY APPRECIATED BETWEEN MEALS TOO!

After all, who can resist a fresh baked cookie and tall glass of milk? We have classic cookies as well as some new offerings. And how about the smell of freshly baked bread? Mmmm, the aroma fills the house with memories as family members clamor to get the first slice. Here you'll find plenty of breads, whether you like to make them the old-fashioned way or opt for the bread machine to do the work. The quick breads and muffins offer a speedier but just as delicious alternative.

Traditional White Bread

2 loaves, 16 slices each | Prep time: 35 minutes | Start to Finish: 2 hours 55 minutes

Do you have a need to use less salt in your diet? If so, decrease sugar to 2 tablespoons and salt to 4 teaspoons. Substitute vegetable oil for the shortening. Each rising time will be 10 to 15 minutes shorter.

6 to 7 cups all-purpose or bread flour

3 tablespoons sugar

1 tablespoon salt

2 tablespoons shortening

2 packages regular active dry yeast

2¼ cups very warm water (120°F to 130°F)

Margarine or butter, melted

1 Mix 3½ cups of the flour, the sugar, salt, shortening and yeast in large bowl. Add warm water. Beat with electric mixer on low speed 1 minute, scraping bowl frequently. Beat on medium speed 1 minute, scraping bowl frequently. Stir in enough remaining flour, 1 cup at a time, to make dough easy to handle.

2 Turn dough onto lightly floured surface. Knead about 10 minutes or until smooth and elastic. Place in greased bowl and turn greased side up. Cover and let rise in warm place 40 to 60 minutes or until double. (Dough is ready if indentation remains when touched.)

3 Grease bottoms and sides of 2 loaf pans, 8 × 4 or 9 × 5 inches, with shortening.

4 Punch down dough and divide in half. Flatten each half with hands or rolling pin into rectangle, 18 × 9 inches, on lightly floured surface. Roll dough up tightly, beginning at 9-inch side, to form a loaf. Press with thumbs to seal after each turn. Pinch edge of dough into roll to seal. Press each end with side of hand to seal. Fold ends under loaf. Place seam side down in pan. Brush loaves lightly with margarine. Cover and let rise in warm place 25 to 50 minutes or until double.

5 Move oven rack to low position so that tops of pans will be in center of oven. Heat oven to 425°F.

6 Bake 25 to 30 minutes or until loaves are deep golden brown and sound hollow when tapped. Remove from pans to cooling rack. Brush loaves with margarine; cool.

1 **Slice**: Calories 90 (Calories from Fat 10); Fat 1g (Saturated 0g); Cholesterol 0mg; Sodium 200mg; Carbohydrate 19g (Dietary Fiber 1g); Protein 2g

Honey–Whole Wheat Bread

2 loaves, 16 slices each | Prep time: 35 minutes | Start to Finish: 3 hours 10 minutes

Who can resist freshly baked bread, with the goodness of whole wheat kissed with honey? Since this recipe makes two loaves, there is one to eat and one to freeze or give away!

3 cups stone-ground whole wheat or graham flour

1/3 cup honey

1/4 cup shortening

1 tablespoon salt

2 packages regular active dry yeast

2 1/4 cups very warm water (120°F to 130°F)

3 to 4 cups all-purpose or bread flour

Margarine or butter, melted, if desired

1 Mix whole wheat flour, honey, shortening, salt and yeast in large bowl. Add warm water. Beat with electric mixer on low speed 1 minute, scraping bowl frequently. Beat on medium speed 1 minute, scraping bowl frequently. Stir in enough all-purpose flour, 1 cup at a time, to make dough easy to handle.

2 Turn dough onto lightly floured surface. Knead about 10 minutes or until smooth and elastic. Place in greased bowl and turn greased side up. Cover and let rise in warm place 40 to 60 minutes or until double. (Dough is ready if indentation remains when touched.)

3 Grease bottoms and sides of 2 loaf pans, 8 × 4 or 9 × 5 inches, with shortening.

4 Punch down dough and divide in half. Flatten each half with hands or rolling pin into rectangle, 18 × 9 inches, on lightly floured surface. Roll dough up tightly, beginning at 9-inch side, to form a loaf. Press with thumbs to seal after each turn. Pinch edge of dough into roll to seal. Press each end with side of hand to seal. Fold ends under loaf. Place seam side down in pan. Brush loaves lightly with margarine. Cover and let rise in warm place 35 to 50 minutes or until double.

5 Move oven rack to low position so that tops of pans will be in center of oven. Heat oven to 375°F.

6 Bake 40 to 45 minutes or until loaves are deep golden brown and sound hollow when tapped. Remove from pans to cooling rack. Brush loaves with margarine, cool.

1 Slice: Calories 105 (Calories from Fat 20); Fat 2g (Saturated 1g); Cholesterol 0mg; Sodium 210mg; Carbohydrate 21g (Dietary Fiber 2g); Protein 3g

Garden Wheat Batter Bread

I loaf, 16 slices | Prep time: 20 minutes | Start to Finish: 1 hour 30 minutes

Studded with carrots and parsley, this hearty bread is the perfect accompaniment to a piping hot bowl of soup or stew.

2 cups whole wheat flour

1 package quick active dry yeast

1 teaspoon salt

1¼ cups water

2 tablespoons honey

2 tablespoons margarine or butter

1 cup all-purpose or unbleached flour

1 small carrot, finely shredded (¼ cup)

1 tablespoon chopped fresh parsley

Margarine or butter, melted, if desired

1 Mix whole wheat flour, yeast and salt in 3-quart bowl.

2 Heat water, honey and margarine in 1-quart saucepan over medium-low heat until very warm (120°F to 130°F). Add to wheat flour mixture. Beat with electric mixer on low speed until moistened, scraping bowl occasionally. Beat 3 minutes on medium speed. (By hand, beat 300 vigorous strokes.)

3 Stir in all-purpose flour, carrot and parsley. Scrape batter from side of bowl. Cover and let rise in warm place about 20 minutes or until double.

4 Generously grease loaf pan, 8 × 4 or 9 × 5 inches. Stir down batter by beating about 25 strokes. Smooth and pat batter in loaf pan with floured hands. Cover and let rise in warm place about 15 minutes or until double.

5 Heat oven to 375°F. Bake 30 to 35 minutes or until loaf sounds hollow when tapped. Immediately remove from pan to cooling rack. Brush top with melted margarine; cool on wire rack.

1 Serving: Calories 105 (Calories from Fat 16); Fat 2g (Saturated 1g); Cholesterol 0mg; Sodium 165mg; Carbohydrate 19g (Dietary Fiber 2g); Protein 3g

Brown Bread

1 loaf, 24 slices   Prep time: 20 minutes   Start to Finish: 2 hours 50 minutes

Rye flour, which can be found in smaller bags where other flours are found, adds a hearty denseness to the bread. This is a great bread to serve with any soup or stew that has lots of broth to sop up.

½ cup all-purpose or rye flour

½ cup cornmeal

½ cup whole wheat flour

½ cup currants or chopped raisins

1 cup buttermilk

⅓ cup molasses

1 teaspoon baking soda

1 teaspoon grated orange peel

½ teaspoon salt

1 Grease loaf pan, 8 × 4 inches.

2 Beat all ingredients in 3-quart bowl with electric mixer on low speed 30 seconds, scraping bowl constantly. Beat on medium speed 30 seconds longer, scraping bowl constantly. Pour into pan. Cover tightly with foil.

2 Place pan on rack in Dutch oven or steamer; pour boiling water into Dutch oven to level of rack. Cover Dutch oven and heat over low heat. Keep water boiling about 2 hours 30 minutes or until toothpick inserted in center of bread comes out clean. (Add boiling water during steaming, if necessary.)

4 Remove pan from Dutch oven. Immediately remove bread from pan. Serve warm.

1 Slice: Calories 50 (Calories from Fat 0); Fat 0g (Saturated 0g); Cholesterol 0mg; Sodium 115mg; Carbohydrate 12g (Dietary Fiber 1g); Protein 1g

Herb Foccacia

6 foccacia   Prep time: 30 minutes   Start to Finish: 2 hours 15 minutes

The fresh herbs used in the glaze for this bread enliven its wonderful, homey flavor. Make this traditional Italian bread the day before you plan on using it, and warm before serving.

2 packages regular active dry yeast

¼ teaspoon sugar

1 cup warm water (105°F to 115°F)

3 cups all-purpose flour

1 small onion, finely chopped (¼ cup)

3 tablespoons vegetable oil

1 teaspoon salt

Herb Glaze (below right)

1 Mix yeast, sugar and water in small bowl. Let stand 5 minutes.

2 Blend remaining ingredients except Herb Glaze in large bowl. Stir in yeast mixture to form a soft dough. Turn dough out onto floured surface. Knead dough 5 minutes until smooth and elastic. Place dough in greased bowl. Cover and let rise in warm place 1 hour.

3 Grease baking sheet. Punch dough down and divide evenly into 6 pieces. Shape each piece into 5-inch circle. Place on baking sheet. Cover and let rise 20 minutes.

4 Heat oven to 400°F. Prepare Herb Glaze. Brush top of each bread with Herb Glaze. Bake 15 to 18 minutes or until light golden brown.

Herb Glaze

1 tablespoon chopped fresh or ½ teaspoon dried thyme leaves
1 tablespoon chopped fresh or ½ teaspoon dried basil leaves
1 egg, beaten

Mix all ingredients.

1 Foccacia: Calories 300 (Calories from Fat 70); Fat 8g (Saturated 1g); Cholesterol 35mg; Sodium 410mg; Carbohydrate 50g (Dietary Fiber 2g); Protein 9g

COUNTRY COOKING WISDOM

Kneading Know-How

Kneading develops the gluten in flour and makes breads, biscuits and other baked goods have an even texture and a smooth, rounded top. One way to knead is by hand—the traditional way. To knead by hand, press the dough with the heels of your hands, pushing the dough away from your body. Move the dough a quarter turn and repeat. Or use a standard countertop electric mixer with a dough-hook attachment. Bread loaves may have slightly less volume than those kneaded by hand.

A heavy-duty electric mixer produces loaves with higher volumes. Just follow the manufacturer's instructions for the size of the recipe that the mixer can handle—usually given in cups of flour—as well as mixing times.

WARM UP THE OVEN   **237**

Raisin-Oatmeal Bread

| 1 loaf, 16 slices | Prep time: 30 minutes | Start to Finish: 3 hours 45 minutes |

Use this bread to make unforgettable slices of warm, golden French toast, kissed with brown sugar and sweet, plump raisins.

1½ cups water

1½ teaspoons salt

1½ cups quick-cooking oats

⅓ cup packed brown sugar

1 tablespoon shortening

1 package regular active dry yeast

¼ cup warm water (105°F to 115°F)

½ cup raisins

3 to 3¼ cups all-purpose flour

1 egg white, slightly beaten

2 tablespoons quick-cooking oats

1 Heat 1½ cups water and salt to boiling in 3-quart saucepan. Stir in 1½ cups oats, the brown sugar and shortening. Remove from heat and cool to lukewarm. Dissolve yeast in ¼ cup warm water. Stir into oat mixture. Stir in raisins. Mix in flour with spoon (dough will be sticky).

2 Turn dough onto lightly floured surface. Knead about 10 minutes or until smooth and elastic. Place in greased bowl and turn greased side up. Cover and let rise in warm place (85°F) until double, about 1 hour 30 minutes. (If kitchen is cool, place dough on a rack over a bowl of hot water and cover completely with a towel.)

3 Grease loaf pan, 9 × 5 inches. Punch down dough and shape into rounded loaf. Place in pan. Brush top with egg white; sprinkle with 2 tablespoons oats. Cover and let rise in warm place about 1 hour or until double.

4 Heat oven to 375°F. Bake 40 to 45 minutes or until dark brown. Remove from pan; cool on cooling rack.

1 Slice: Calories 155 (Calories from Fat 20); Fat 2g (Saturated 0g); Cholesterol 0mg; Sodium 230mg; Carbohydrate 32g (Dietary Fiber 2g); Protein 4g

COUNTRY COOKING WISDOM

Crust Choices

Use these simple steps before baking to create the crust of your choice:

- For a shiny crust, brush the top of the bread with an egg or egg white beaten with a little water. If desired, sprinkle with poppy, caraway or sesame seed or rolled oats.

- For a softer, deep golden brown crust, brush with softened butter or margarine.

- For a crisp crust, brush or spray lightly with water.

- For a soft, tender crust, brush with milk.

Almond Honey–Whole Wheat Bread

1-lb Recipe, 8 slices | Prep time: 10 minutes | Start to Finish: 3 hours 40 minutes

Bread machines make it possible to have homemade bread with the press of a button! Savory almonds and honey combine to make this bread remarkable.

1-lb Recipe (8 slices)

$2/3$ cup water

2 tablespoons honey

1 tablespoon margarine or butter, softened

1 cup bread flour

1 cup whole wheat flour

2 tablespoons toasted slivered almonds

$3/4$ teaspoon salt

1 teaspoon bread machine yeast

1½-lb Recipe (12 slices)

1 cup plus 2 tablespoons water

3 tablespoons honey

2 tablespoons margarine or butter, softened

1½ cups bread flour

1½ cups whole wheat flour

¼ cup toasted slivered almonds

1 teaspoon salt

1½ teaspoons bread machine yeast

1 Make 1-lb Recipe with bread machines that use 2 cups flour, or make 1½-lb Recipe with bread machines that use 3 cups flour.

2 Measure carefully, placing all ingredients in bread machine pan in the order recommended by the manufacturer.

3 Select Whole Wheat or Basic/White cycle. Use Medium or Light crust color. Remove baked bread from pan and cool on cooling rack.

1 Slice (1-lb Recipe): Calories 160 (Calories from Fat 35); Fat 4g (Saturated 1g); Cholesterol 0mg; Sodium 200mg; Carbohydrate 29g (Dietary Fiber 2g); Protein 4g

Sunflower Seven-Grain Bread

1 loaf, 16 slices | Prep time: 30 minutes | Start to Finish: 3 hours

Using ready-to-eat seven-grain cereal eliminates the need to buy seven different grains to make this wholesome bread.

1½ cups all-purpose* or bread flour

3 tablespoons packed brown sugar

2 tablespoons vegetable oil

1½ teaspoons salt

1 package regular or quick active dry yeast

1 cup very warm water (120°F to 130°F)

1½ cups 7-grain ready-to-eat cereal

½ cup raw sunflower nuts

1 to 1½ cups whole wheat flour

Vegetable oil

1 Mix all-purpose flour, brown sugar, 2 tablespoons oil, the salt and yeast in large bowl. Add warm water. Beat with electric mixer on low speed 1 minute, scraping bowl frequently. Beat on medium speed 1 minute, scraping bowl frequently.

2 Stir in cereal and nuts. Stir in enough whole wheat flour, ½ cup at a time, to make dough easy to handle.

3 Turn dough onto lightly floured surface. Knead about 10 minutes or until smooth and elastic. Place in greased bowl and turn greased side up. Cover and let rise in warm place about 1 hour or until double. Dough is ready if indentation remains when touched.

4 Grease bottom and sides of loaf pan, 8 × 4 or 9 × 5 inches, with shortening.

5 Punch down dough. Flatten with hands or rolling pin into rectangle, 18 × 9 inches, on lightly floured surface. Roll dough up tightly, beginning at 9-inch side, to form a loaf. Press with thumbs to seal after each turn. Pinch edge of dough into roll to seal. Press each end with side of hand to seal. Fold ends under loaf. Place seam side down in pan. Brush loaves lightly with oil. Cover and let rise in warm place 45 to 60 minutes or until double.

6 Move oven rack to low position so that tops of pans will be in center of oven. Heat oven to 400°F.

7 Bake 25 to 30 minutes or until loaf is deep golden brown and sounds hollow when tapped. Remove from pans to cooling rack; cool.

*If using self-rising flour, omit salt.

1 Slice: Calories 140 (Calories from Fat 35); Fat 4g (Saturated 1g); Cholesterol 0mg; Sodium 200mg; Carbohydrate 25g (Dietary Fiber 3g); Protein 4g

Pull-Apart Bread

The delightful pull-apart loaf is also known as monkey bread or bubble loaf. For fun variations, after rolling the balls in butter, roll them in a cinnamon and sugar mixture or in a savory blend of fragrant herbs.

3½ to 3¾ cups all-purpose flour

2 tablespoons sugar

½ teaspoon salt

1 package regular active dry yeast

1 cup milk

¼ cup margarine or butter

1 egg

¼ cup margarine or butter, melted

1 Grease 12-cup fluted tube or angel food (tube) cake pan, 10 × 4 inches.

2 Mix 1½ cups of the flour, the sugar, salt and yeast in 3-quart bowl. Heat milk and ¼ cup margarine in 1-quart saucepan over medium-low heat, stirring frequently, until very warm (120°F to 130°F). Add milk mixture and egg to flour mixture. Beat with electric mixer on low speed until moistened, then beat 3 minutes on medium speed. Stir in enough remaining flour to make dough easy to handle.

3 Turn dough onto lightly floured surface. Knead about 5 minutes or until smooth and elastic. Shape dough into 24 balls. Dip each ball of dough into the melted margarine. Layer evenly in pan. Cover and let rise in warm place 20 to 30 minutes or until double.

4 Heat oven to 350°F. Bake 25 to 30 minutes or until golden brown. Cool 2 minutes; invert onto heatproof serving plate. Serve warm.

1 Serving: Calories 220 (Calories from Fat 80); Fat 9g (Saturated 2g); Cholesterol 20mg; Sodium 220mg; Carbohydrate 31g (Dietary Fiber 1g); Protein 5g

COUNTRY COOKING WISDOM

Rise to the Occasion

For perfectly risen bread each time, grease a large bowl—bread dough will double in size—with shortening or cooking spray. Add the dough, turning it so all sides are greased. Cover the bowl with plastic wrap and do one of the following:

- Set the bowl in a warm, draft-free place.
- Place the covered bowl on a wire rack over a bowl of hot water.
- Fill a microwavable measuring cup with water, and microwave until the water boils. Set the covered bowl of dough in the microwave with the steaming water. It's a nice toasty-warm, humid place, especially if you keep your home cool.

Praline Bread

I loaf, 24 slices | Prep time: 25 minutes | Start to Finish: I hour 30 minutes

Pralines—pecans suspended in a rich golden brown sugar mixture—are a southern specialty. Here they add a sweet crunch to this tender bread.

2 cups all-purpose or unbleached flour

I teaspoon baking powder

¹/₂ teaspoon salt

¹/₂ cup (1 stick) margarine or butter, softened

¹/₂ cup granulated sugar

¹/₂ cup packed brown sugar

I teaspoon vanilla

¹/₂ teaspoon maple extract

2 eggs

³/₄ cup milk

I cup chopped pecans, toasted

1 Heat oven to 350°F. Grease bottom only of loaf pan, 8 × 4 or 9 × 5 inches.

2 Mix flour, baking powder and salt; reserve.

3 Beat margarine and the sugars in 3-quart bowl with electric mixer on medium speed until light and fluffy. Beat in vanilla, maple extract and 1 egg. Beat in remaining egg. Beat in reserved flour mixture alternately with milk on low speed, beating well after each addition.

4 Reserve 2 tablespoons pecans. Mix remaining pecans into batter; pour into pan. Finely chop reserved pecans; sprinkle over batter.

5 Bake 55 to 65 minutes or until toothpick inserted in center comes out clean. Cool 10 minutes; remove from pan. Cool completely before slicing.

I Slice: Calories 150 (Calories from Fat 73); Fat 8g (Saturated 2g); Cholesterol 20mg; Sodium 115mg; Carbohydrate 18g (Dietary Fiber 1g); Protein 2g

Traditional Corn Bread

12 servings | Prep time: 15 minutes | Start to Finish: 45 minutes

Corn bread is one of America's favorite quick breads. Easy and quick to make, it's a hearty way to satisfy a longing for warm-from-the-oven homemade bread. Delicious when hot, corn bread is also wonderful when cooled, sliced and thickly spread with butter or jam, or when toasted the next day.

1½ cups yellow cornmeal
½ cup all-purpose flour
¼ cup shortening
1½ cups buttermilk
2 teaspoons baking powder
1 teaspoon sugar
1 teaspoon salt
½ teaspoon baking soda
2 eggs

1 Heat oven to 450°F. Grease round pan, 9 inches, or square pan, 8 × 8 inches. Mix all ingredients; beat vigorously 30 seconds.

2 Pour batter into pan. Bake 25 to 30 minutes or until golden brown. Serve warm.

1 Serving: Calories 140 (Calories from Fat 55); Fat 6g (Saturated 2g); Cholesterol 38mg; Sodium 370mg; Carbohydrate 19g (Dietary Fiber 1g); Protein 4g

Chile-Cheese Corn Bread

9 servings | Prep time: 15 minutes | Start to Finish: 40 minutes

This zesty corn bread is full of delicious Tex-Mex flavor. Serve it with all of your Southwestern favorites—it's especially good with a big bowl of hot chili!

1 cup all-purpose flour
1 cup yellow cornmeal
1 cup shredded Cheddar cheese (4 oz)
1 cup cooked fresh whole kernel corn*
¼ cup shortening
1 cup milk
2 tablespoons sugar
4 teaspoons baking powder
½ teaspoon salt
1 can (4 oz) chopped green chiles, drained
1 egg

1 Heat oven to 425°F. Grease square pan, 9 × 9 inches.

2 Mix all ingredients until moistened. Beat vigorously 30 seconds. Pour into pan.

3 Bake until golden brown, 20 to 25 minutes.

*1 can (7 oz) whole kernel corn, drained, or 1 cup frozen whole kernel corn, thawed and drained, can be substituted for fresh corn.

1 Serving: Calories 240 (Calories from Fat 96); Fat 11g (Saturated 5g); Cholesterol 37mg; Sodium 648mg; Carbohydrate 30g (Dietary Fiber 2g); Protein 7g

Blueberry Streusel Muffins

12 muffins | Prep time: 20 minutes | Start to Finish: 45 minutes

No streusel for you? That's fine. You can make these muffins without the streusel topping if you like—the baking time will be the same.

Streusel Topping (right)

1 cup milk

¼ cup vegetable oil

½ teaspoon vanilla

1 egg

2 cups all-purpose or whole wheat flour

⅓ cup sugar

3 teaspoons baking powder

½ teaspoon salt

1 cup fresh or canned (drained) blueberries*

1 Heat oven to 400°F. Grease bottoms only of 12 regular-size muffin cups or line with paper baking cups.

2 Make Streusel Topping; set aside.

3 Beat milk, oil, vanilla and egg in large bowl. Stir in flour, sugar, baking powder and salt all at once just until flour is moistened (batter will be lumpy). Fold in blueberries. Divide batter evenly among muffin cups. Sprinkle each with about 2 teaspoons Streusel Topping.

4 Bake 20 to 25 minutes or until golden brown. Immediately remove from pan to cooling rack. Serve warm if desired.

Streusel Topping

2 tablespoons firm stick margarine or butter

¼ cup all-purpose flour

2 tablespoons packed brown sugar

¼ teaspoon ground cinnamon

Cut margarine into flour, brown sugar and cinnamon in medium bowl, using pastry blender or crisscrossing 2 knives, until crumbly.

¾ cup frozen (thawed and well drained) blueberries can be substituted for the fresh or canned blueberries.

1 Muffin: Calories 195 (Calories from Fat 70); Fat 8g (Saturated 1g); Cholesterol 20mg; Sodium 250mg; Carbohydrate 29g (Dietary Fiber 1g); Protein 3g

Brown Sugar Muffins

12 muffins | Prep time: 20 minutes | Start to Finish: 40 minutes

Make these easy and delicious muffins on a morning when you want to wake up the family with enticing smells wafting from the kitchen.

1 cup quick-cooking oats

1/2 cup milk

3/4 cup packed brown sugar

1/4 cup margarine or butter, melted

1 egg

1 cup all-purpose flour

1/2 cup chopped walnuts

2 teaspoons baking powder

1 Heat oven to 400°F. Grease 12 regular-size muffin cups or line with paper baking cups.

2 Mix oats, milk and brown sugar in large bowl; let stand 5 minutes. Add margarine and egg; blend well. Stir in remaining ingredients just until moistened.

3 Divide butter evenly among muffin cups filling two-thirds full. Bake 15 to 20 minutes or until toothpick inserted in center comes out clean.

1 Muffin: Calories 195 (Calories from Fat 70); Fat 8g (Saturated 1g); Cholesterol 20mg; Sodium 150mg; Carbohydrate 28g (Dietary Fiber 1g); Protein 4g

Apple-Buckwheat Muffins

18 muffins | Prep time: 15 minutes | Start to Finish: 45 minutes

Not only are these robust muffins—with bits of juicy apples and crunchy nuts—great for breakfast, you can also serve them piping hot for lunch, with a bowl of hearty soup.

1 1/2 cups all-purpose flour

1/2 cup buckwheat or whole wheat flour

1/2 cup sugar

1 tablespoon baking powder

1/4 teaspoon salt

3/4 cup apple juice

1/4 cup margarine or butter, melted

1 egg

1 cup chopped walnuts

1 large tart apple, peeled, cored and chopped

1 Heat oven to 400°F. Grease bottoms only of 18 regular-size muffin cups or line with paper baking cups.

2 Mix all-purpose flour, buckwheat flour, sugar, baking powder and salt in large bowl. Stir in apple juice, margarine and egg just until blended (batter will be lumpy). Stir in walnuts and chopped apple.

3 Divide batter evenly among muffin cups, filling two-thirds full. Bake 20 to 25 minutes or until toothpick inserted in center comes out clean. Cool 5 minutes; remove from pan.

1 Muffin: Calories 145 (Calories from Fat 65); Fat 7g (Saturated 1g); Cholesterol 10mg; Sodium 150mg; Carbohydrate 19g (Dietary Fiber 1g); Protein 3g

Praline-Peach Muffins

12 muffins | Prep time: 20 minutes | Start to Finish: 40 minutes

When the sweet aroma of fresh, ripe peaches welcomes you at the supermarket, you'll be glad you have this recipe. If you are planning on using fresh peaches, be sure to choose freestone peaches instead of clingstone. Freestone peaches will release the pit without much effort.

Topping (right)
$\frac{1}{2}$ cup packed brown sugar
$\frac{1}{2}$ cup milk
$\frac{1}{3}$ cup vegetable oil
1 teaspoon vanilla
1 egg
$1\frac{2}{3}$ cups all-purpose flour
2 teaspoons baking powder
$\frac{1}{4}$ teaspoon salt
1 cup chopped fresh or frozen (thawed and drained) or canned (well drained) peaches
$\frac{1}{2}$ cup coarsely chopped pecans

1 Heat oven to 400°F. Grease bottoms only of 12 regular-size muffin cups or line with paper baking cups.

2 Make Topping; set aside. Beat brown sugar, milk, oil, vanilla and egg in large bowl. Stir in flour, baking powder and salt just until flour is moistened. Fold in peaches and pecans.

3 Divide batter evenly among muffin cups (cups will be almost full). Sprinkle with topping.

4 Bake 18 to 20 minutes or until golden brown. Immediately remove from pan to cooling rack. Serve warm if desired.

Topping

1 tablespoon firm margarine or butter
$\frac{1}{4}$ cup packed brown sugar
$\frac{1}{4}$ cup chopped pecans

Cut margarine into remaining ingredients, using pastry blender or crisscrossing 2 knives, until crumbly.

1 Muffin: Calories 245 (Calories from Fat 115); Fat 13g (Saturated 2g); Cholesterol 20mg; Sodium 160mg; Carbohydrate 30g (Dietary Fiber 1g); Protein 3g

Mountain Bran Muffins

12 muffins | Prep time: 15 minutes | Start to Finish: 35 minutes

Freshly baked muffins from a homemade mix can be a real boon to busy families. This handy mix—based on a cherished bran bread recipe from the Colorado mountains—can be stored in a cool, dry place. The next time you're longing for a rich, moist bran muffin packed with walnuts and raisins, you'll be all ready to go! The Mountain Bran Mix makes about 7½ cups of the mix—which is enough for 3 dozen muffins!

1 cup buttermilk

1 egg

2½ cups Mountain Bran Mix (below right)

½ cup chopped walnuts

½ cup raisins

1 Heat oven to 400°F. Grease bottoms only of 12 regular-size muffin cups or line with paper baking cups.

2 Beat buttermilk and egg in large bowl. Stir in Mountain Bran Mix just until moistened. Fold in walnuts and raisins.

3 Divide batter evenly among muffin cups (about seven-eighths full). Bake 18 to 20 minutes or until golden brown or toothpick inserted in center comes out clean. Let stand 3 minutes; remove muffins from pan.

Mountain Bran Mix

3 cups all-purpose flour
3 cups bran cereal shreds, finely crushed
2 cups packed brown sugar
1½ teaspoons baking soda
1½ teaspoons baking powder
1½ teaspoons salt
½ cup shortening

Mix flour, cereal, brown sugar, baking soda, baking powder and salt in 4-quart bowl. Cut shortening into mixture, using pastry blender or crisscrossing 2 knives, until mixture resembles coarse crumbs. Cover and store in cool, dry place no longer than 1 month.

1 Muffin: Calories 190 (Calories from Fat 65); Fat 7g (Saturated 1g); Cholesterol 20mg; Sodium 220mg; Carbohydrate 31g (Dietary Fiber 3g); Protein 4g

Strawberry Muffins

Stir a little honey into some softened butter and serve it with these muffins, fresh from the oven. It's delicious!

3/4 cup milk

1/2 cup vegetable oil

1 tablespoon grated orange peel

1 egg

2 cups all-purpose flour

1 cup chopped strawberries

1/3 cup sugar

1 tablespoon baking powder

1/4 teaspoon salt

Pecan Streusel Topping (right)

1 Heat oven to 400°F. Grease 12 regular-size muffin cups or line with paper baking cups.

2 Mix milk, oil, orange peel and egg in large bowl until well blended. Stir in remaining ingredients except Pecan Streusel Topping, just until moistened.

3 Make Pecan Streusel Topping. Divide batter evenly among muffin cups, filling two-thirds full. Sprinkle batter with Pecan Streusel Topping. Bake 15 to 20 minutes or until toothpick inserted in center comes out clean.

Pecan Streusel Topping

1/2 cup chopped pecans
1/2 cup packed brown sugar
1/4 cup all-purpose flour
2 tablespoons melted margarine or butter

Mix all ingredients in large bowl until well blended.

1 Muffin: Calories 285 (Calories from Fat 135); Fat 15g (Saturated 2g); Cholesterol 20mg; Sodium 210mg; Carbohydrate 35g (Dietary Fiber 1g); Protein 4g

Sweet Corn Bread Muffins

12 muffins   Prep time: 15 minutes   Start to Finish: 40 minutes

Cornmeal is available in textures ranging from fine to coarse. You'll find grocery stores commonly carry a finely ground cornmeal, which will make a light, soft bread. The coarser cornmeals, often called stone-ground, give breads a stronger flavor and coarser texture. Stone-ground cornmeal is delicious in this recipe.

1 cup milk

¼ cup margarine or butter, melted

1 egg

1¼ cups cornmeal

1 cup all-purpose flour

½ cup sugar

1 tablespoon baking powder

½ teaspoon salt

1 Heat oven to 400°F. Grease bottoms only of 12 regular-size muffin cups or line with paper baking cups.

2 Beat milk, margarine and egg in 3-quart bowl. Stir in remaining ingredients all at once just until flour is moistened (batter will be lumpy).

3 Divide batter evenly among muffin cups, filling about three-fourths full. Bake 20 to 25 minutes or until golden brown and toothpick inserted in center comes out clean.

1 Muffin: Calories 175 (Calories from Fat 45); Fat 5g (Saturated 1g); Cholesterol 20mg; Sodium 290mg; Carbohydrate 29g (Dietary Fiber 1g); Protein 4g

Easy Garlic-Cheese Biscuits

10 to 12 biscuits   Prep time: 5 minutes   Start to Finish: 15 minutes

These melt-in-your-mouth biscuits are good with any meal. The next time you make them, experiment with a different cheese, such as smoky Cheddar or pizza mozzarella.

2 cups Original Bisquick

⅔ cup milk

½ cup shredded Cheddar cheese (2 oz)

¼ cup margarine or butter, melted

¼ teaspoon garlic powder

1 Heat oven to 450°F.

2 Mix Bisquick, milk and cheese to make a soft dough. Beat vigorously 30 seconds. Drop 10 to 12 spoonfuls dough onto ungreased cookie sheet.

3 Bake 8 to 10 minutes or until golden brown. Mix margarine and garlic powder. Brush on warm biscuits before removing from cookie sheet. Serve warm.

1 Biscuit: Calories 160 (Calories from Fat 90); Fat 10g (Saturated 3g); Cholesterol 10mg; Sodium 440mg; Carbohydrate 15g (Dietary Fiber 0g); Protein 3g

Easy Garlic-Cheese Biscuits *(top)* and
Sweet Corn Bread Muffins *(bottom)*

Buttermilk Biscuits

About 10 biscuits   Prep time: 15 minutes   Start to Finish: 30 minutes

Buttermilk makes these biscuits tender and flavorful. The secret to fluffy biscuits is not overworking the dough. Once the shortening is cut into the flour, just a few quick stirs should make the dough form into a ball.

- 1/2 cup shortening
- 2 cups all-purpose flour
- 1 tablespoon sugar
- 2 teaspoons baking powder
- 1 teaspoon salt
- 1/4 teaspoon baking soda
- About 3/4 cup buttermilk

1 Heat oven to 450°F.

2 Cut shortening into remaining ingredients except buttermilk in large bowl, using pastry blender or crisscrossing 2 knives, until mixture resembles fine crumbs. Stir in just enough buttermilk so dough leaves side of bowl and forms a ball.

3 Turn dough onto lightly floured surface. Knead lightly 10 times. Roll or pat 1/2 inch thick. Cut with floured 2 1/2-inch biscuit cutter. Place about 1 inch apart on ungreased cookie sheet.

4 Bake 10 to 12 minutes or until golden brown. Immediately remove from cookie sheet. Serve hot.

1 Biscuit: Calories 200 (Calories from Fat 100); Fat 11g (Saturated 3g); Cholesterol 2mg; Sodium 390mg; Carbohydrate 22g (Dietary Fiber 0g); Protein 3g

Baking Powder Biscuits

12 biscuits   Prep time: 15 minutes   Start to Finish: 30 minutes

Add a bit of extra flavor to your biscuits by stirring in 2 teaspoons chopped fresh or 3/4 teaspoon dried dill weed or basil with the flour.

- 1/2 cup shortening
- 2 cups all-purpose flour
- 1 tablespoon sugar
- 3 teaspoons baking powder
- 1 teaspoon salt
- 3/4 cup milk

1 Heat oven to 450°F.

2 Cut shortening into flour, sugar, baking powder and salt in medium bowl, using pastry blender or crisscrossing 2 knives, until mixture resembles fine crumbs. Stir in milk until dough leaves side of bowl (dough will be soft and sticky).

3 Turn dough onto lightly floured surface. Knead lightly 10 times. Roll or pat 1/2 inch thick. Cut with floured 2 1/2-inch biscuit cutter. Place on ungreased cookie sheet about 1 inch apart for crusty sides, touching for soft sides.

4 Bake 10 to 12 minutes or until golden brown. Immediately remove from cookie sheet. Serve warm.

1 Biscuit: Calories 160 (Calories from Fat 80); Fat 9g (Saturated 2g); Cholesterol 5mg; Sodium 310mg; Carbohydrate 18g (Dietary Fiber 0g); Protein 2g

Beaten Biscuits

24 biscuits | Prep time: 15 minutes | Start to Finish: 35 minutes

The beaten biscuit is a tradition down South that dates all the way back to the 1800s. Most biscuits are flaky and tender, but the beaten biscuit is hard and crisp. This texture is made when the dough is beaten until it is smooth and elastic. Our suggestion of a wooden spoon or mallet also works well for the beatings. If you put baked ham in a biscuit, you'll be recreating the ham-and-biscuit combination first found in the southern colonies.

¼ cup shortening
2 cups all-purpose flour
2 teaspoons sugar
½ teaspoon salt
¼ teaspoon baking powder
¾ to 1 cup cold water

1 Heat oven to 400°F.

2 Cut shortening into flour, sugar, salt and baking powder in a large bowl, using pastry blender or crisscrossing 2 knives, until mixture resembles coarse crumbs. Stir in ¾ cup water, then stir in additional water to make a stiff dough.

3 Turn dough onto lightly floured board. Beat dough with wooden spoon or mallet 5 minutes, turning and folding dough constantly. Roll or pat dough to ¼-inch thickness. Cut with 2-inch biscuit cutter.

4 Place biscuits on ungreased cookie sheet; prick tops with fork. Bake 18 to 20 minutes or until golden brown.

1 Biscuit: Calories 55 (Calories from Fat 20); Fat 2g (Saturated 1g); Cholesterol 0mg; Sodium 55mg; Carbohydrate 8g (Dietary Fiber 0g); Protein 1g

Popovers

Crusty on the outside and soft and moist on the inside, popovers are the perfect mate with roasts, beef stew or any meal where there's a little juice to sop.

1 cup all-purpose flour
1 cup milk
¼ teaspoon salt
2 eggs

1 Heat oven to 450°F. Generously grease six 6-oz custard cups.

2 Mix all ingredients with hand beater just until smooth (do not overbeat). Fill cups about half full. Bake 20 minutes.

3 Reduce oven temperature to 350°F. Bake 20 minutes longer. Immediately remove from cups. Serve hot.

1 Popover: Calories 120 (Calories from Fat 25); Fat 3g (Saturated 1g); Cholesterol 75mg; Sodium 140mg; Carbohydrate 18g (Dietary Fiber 0g); Protein 5g

COUNTRY COOKING WISDOM

What's the Pop in Popovers?

Who can resist these puffy muffin-shaped breads served piping-hot from the oven? Do you know how they got their name? The batter, usually baked in muffin tins or special popover pans, rises and seems to pop over the sides of the pan during the baking process.

These crusty breads have been around a long time. The first occurrence of the word in print was back in 1876. Early American bakers liked them because they were much quicker to make than yeast breads, which required long rising times. Popovers are very similar to the English Yorkshire pudding and a close relative of the cream puff.

Chocolate Brownies

16 brownies   Prep time: 10 minutes   Start to Finish: 1 hour 55 minutes

You can make colorful Thanksgiving turkeys, festive holiday wreaths or delicate Valentine hearts, but any day you bake up these brownies becomes a holiday.

2/3 cup margarine or butter

5 oz unsweetened baking chocolate, cut into pieces

1³/4 cups sugar

2 teaspoons vanilla

3 eggs

1 cup all-purpose flour

1 cup chopped walnuts

Fudge Frosting (page 274), if desired

1 Heat oven to 350°F. Grease bottom and sides of square pan, 9 × 9 inches, with shortening.

2 Melt margarine and chocolate in 1-quart saucepan over low heat, stirring constantly. Cool slightly.

3 Beat sugar, vanilla and eggs in medium bowl with electric mixer on high speed 5 minutes. Beat in chocolate mixture on low speed. Beat in flour just until blended. Stir in walnuts. Spread in pan.

4 Bake 40 to 45 minutes or just until brownies begin to pull away from sides of pan. Cool completely in pan on cooling rack. Spread with Fudge Frosting. Cut into about 2-inch squares.

1 Brownie: Calories 300 (Calories from Fat 160); Fat 18g (Saturated 5g); Cholesterol 40mg; Sodium 100mg; Carbohydrate 32g (Dietary Fiber 2g); Protein 4g

Cashew Brownie Bars

36 bars   Prep time: 15 minutes   Start to Finish: 1 hour 50 minutes

Using a brownie mix to start with makes it a snap to cook up these rich, nutty bars at a moment's notice.

1 package (15.5 oz) Betty Crocker fudge brownie mix

Brown Butter Frosting (below)

1 oz unsweetened chocolate

1 tablespoon butter

1/2 cup chopped cashews

1 Bake Fudgy or Cake-like Brownies as directed on package. Cool.

2 Prepare Brown Butter Frosting; spread over bars. Melt chocolate and butter over low heat. When cool, spread over frosting; sprinkle with nuts. When topping is set, cut into bars, 2¼ × 1 inch.

Brown Butter Frosting

1/4 cup butter

2 cups confectioners' sugar

2 tablespoons half-and-half

1 teaspoon vanilla

In 1-quart saucepan, heat butter over medium heat until delicate brown. Blend in sugar. Beat in half-and-half and vanilla until smooth and of spreading consistency.

1 Bar: Calories 120 (Calories from Fat 45); Fat 5g (Saturated 2g); Cholesterol 5mg; Sodium 65mg; Carbohydrate 17g (Dietary Fiber 0g); Protein 2g

Pepper-Cheese Twists

18 twists   Prep time: 15 minutes   Start to Finish: 30 minutes

Freshly ground black pepper adds a nice spice kick to the twists. These are easy to make ahead. Just cover them tightly with plastic wrap and refrigerate until ready to bake. They go great with clam chowder or tomato soup.

½ package (17.25 oz) frozen puff pastry dough, thawed

1 egg, beaten

1 cup shredded Cheddar cheese

2 teaspoons black pepper

1 Heat oven to 425°F.

2 Roll sheet of dough into 18 × 12-inch rectangle. Brush with beaten egg. Sprinkle cheese over half of rectangle. Fold remaining half over cheese and press edges to seal.

3 Brush dough with egg and sprinkle with pepper. Cut pastry lengthwise into ½-inch strips. Twist strips and place on cookie sheet. Bake 10 to 12 minutes or until light golden brown.

1 Twist: Calories 110 (Calories from Fat 70); Fat 8g (Saturated 2g); Cholesterol 18mg; Sodium 75mg; Carbohydrate 6g (Dietary Fiber 0g); Protein 3g

Lemon Squares

25 squares | Prep time: 15 minutes | Start to Finish: 1 hour 45 minutes

You'll love these tart, creamy lemon bars. Be sure to grate the lemon peel first. Then firmly roll the lemon on your countertop before squeezing, to get the most juice from it.

1 cup all-purpose flour

½ cup margarine or butter, softened

¼ cup powdered sugar

1 cup granulated sugar

2 teaspoons grated lemon peel, if desired

2 tablespoons lemon juice

½ teaspoon baking powder

¼ teaspoon salt

2 eggs

1 Heat oven to 350°F.

2 Mix flour, margarine and powdered sugar. Press in ungreased square pan, 8 × 8 or 9 × 9 inches, building up ½-inch edges.

3 Bake crust 20 minutes.

4 Beat remaining ingredients with electric mixer on high speed about 3 minutes or until light and fluffy. Pour over hot crust.

5 Bake 25 to 30 minutes or until no indentation remains when touched lightly in center. Cool in pan on cooling rack. Cut into about 1½-inch squares.

1 Square: Calories 90 (Calories from Fat 35); Fat 4g (Saturated 1g); Cholesterol 15mg; Sodium 80mg; Carbohydrate 13g (Dietary Fiber 0g); Protein 1g

Russian Tea Cakes

About 4 dozen cookies | Prep time: 20 minutes | Start to Finish: 32 minutes

The powdered sugar gives these cookies a wonderful melt-in-your-mouth texture. Walnuts or almonds are often used when making these cookies, which are also known as Mexican Wedding Cakes. Try toasting the nuts very lightly for a more pronounced flavor.

1 cup margarine or butter, softened

½ cup powdered sugar

1 teaspoon vanilla

2¼ cups all-purpose flour

¾ cup finely chopped nuts

¼ teaspoon salt

Powdered sugar

1 Heat oven to 400°F.

2 Mix margarine, ½ cup powdered sugar and the vanilla in large bowl. Stir in flour, nuts and salt.

3 Shape dough into 1-inch balls. Place about 1 inch apart on ungreased cookie sheet.

4 Bake 10 to 12 minutes or until set but not brown. Remove from cookie sheet. Cool slightly on cooling rack.

5 Roll warm cookies in powdered sugar; cool on cooling rack. Roll in powdered sugar again.

1 Cookie: Calories 75 (Calories from Fat 45); Fat 5g (Saturated 1g); Cholesterol 0mg; Sodium 55mg; Carbohydrate 7g (Dietary Fiber 0g); Protein 1g

Raisin Crisscross Cookies *(left, page 263)*;
Snickerdoodles *(bottom middle, page 262)*;
Joe Froggers *(top middle, page 263)* and
Chocolate Chip Cookies *(right)*

Chocolate Chip Cookies

About 3½ dozen cookies | Prep time: 20 minutes | Start to Finish: 35 minutes

Make someone's day a little bit brighter by sharing these all-American cookies with them. Don't forget it's best to wash them down with a nice glass of cold milk!

1½ cups margarine or butter, softened

1¼ cups granulated sugar

1¼ cups packed brown sugar

1 tablespoon vanilla

2 eggs

4 cups all-purpose flour

2 teaspoons baking soda

½ teaspoon salt

2 cups coarsely chopped nuts, if desired

1 bag (24 oz) semisweet chocolate chips (4 cups)

1 Heat oven to 375°F.

2 Beat margarine, sugars, vanilla and eggs in large bowl with electric mixer on medium speed, or mix with spoon. Stir in flour, baking soda and salt (dough will be stiff). Stir in nuts and chocolate chips.

3 Drop dough by level ¼ cupfuls or #16 cookie/ice-cream scoop about 2 inches apart onto ungreased cookie sheet. Flatten slightly with fork.

4 Bake 13 to 15 minutes or until light brown (centers will be soft). Cool 1 to 2 minutes on cookie sheet; remove from cookie sheet to cooling rack.

1 Cookie: Calories 240 (Calories from Fat 110); Fat 12g (Saturated 4g); Cholesterol 15mg; Sodium 170mg; Carbohydrate 32g (Dietary Fiber 1g); Protein 2g

Farm-Style Oatmeal Cookies

About 7 dozen cookies | Prep time: 20 minutes | Start to Finish: 40 minutes

Buttermilk is the secret ingredient to these delicious cookies. Warm from the oven with a glass of milk, they make the perfect after-school snack.

2 cups packed brown sugar

1 cup lard or shortening

½ cup buttermilk

1 teaspoon vanilla

4 cups quick-cooking oats

1¾ cups all-purpose or whole wheat flour

1 teaspoon baking soda

¾ teaspoon salt

1 Heat oven to 375°F.

2 Mix brown sugar, lard, buttermilk and vanilla in 3-quart bowl. Stir in remaining ingredients.

3 Shape dough into 1-inch balls. Place about 3 inches apart on ungreased cookie sheet. Flatten cookies with bottom of glass dipped in water.

4 Bake until golden brown, 8 to 10 minutes. Immediately remove from cookie sheet.

1 Cookie: Calories 70 (Calories from Fat 3); Fat 3g (Saturated 1g); Cholesterol 2mg; Sodium 40mg; Carbohydrate 10g (Dietary Fiber 1g); Protein 1g

Oatmeal-Raisin Cookies

About 3 dozen cookies | Prep time: 20 minutes | Start to Finish: 30 minutes

Looking for something to replace the raisins? Try dried cherries or dried cranberries for a refreshing change of pace.

²/₃ cup granulated sugar

²/₃ cup packed brown sugar

¹/₂ cup margarine or butter, softened

¹/₂ cup shortening

1 teaspoon baking soda

1 teaspoon ground cinnamon

1 teaspoon vanilla

¹/₂ teaspoon baking powder

¹/₂ teaspoon salt

2 eggs

3 cups quick-cooking or old-fashioned oats

1 cup all-purpose flour

1 cup raisins, chopped nuts or semisweet chocolate chips, if desired

1 Heat oven to 375°F.

2 Mix all ingredients except oats, flour and raisins in large bowl. Stir in oats, flour and raisins.

3 Drop dough by rounded tablespoonfuls about 2 inches apart onto ungreased cookie sheet.

4 Bake 9 to 11 minutes or until light brown. Immediately remove from cookie sheet. Cool on cooling rack.

1 Cookie: Calories 120 (Calories from Fat 55); Fat 6g (Saturated 1g); Cholesterol 10mg; Sodium 110mg; Carbohydrate 15g (Dietary Fiber 1g); Protein 2g

Snickerdoodles

Photo on page 260

About 6 dozen cookies | Prep time: 10 minutes | Start to Finish: 20 minutes

Get the kids involved with these fun cookies by having them help roll the dough in the cinnamon-sugar mixture.

1¹/₂ cups sugar

¹/₂ cup margarine or butter, softened

¹/₂ cup shortening

2 eggs

2³/₄ cups all-purpose flour

2 teaspoons cream of tartar

1 teaspoon baking soda

¹/₄ teaspoon salt

2 tablespoons sugar

2 teaspoons ground cinnamon

1 Heat oven to 400°F.

2 Mix 1¹/₂ cups sugar, the margarine, shortening and eggs thoroughly in 3-quart bowl. Stir in flour, cream of tartar, baking soda and salt until blended. Shape dough by rounded teaspoonfuls into balls.

3 Mix 2 tablespoons sugar and the cinnamon. Roll balls in sugar mixture. Place about 2 inches apart on ungreased cookie sheet. Bake 8 to 10 minutes or until set. Immediately remove from cookie sheet.

1 Cookie: Calories 65 (Calories from Fat 25); Fat 3g (Saturated 1g); Cholesterol 5mg; Sodium 45mg; Carbohydrate 8g (Dietary Fiber 0g); Protein 1g

Raisin Crisscross Cookies

Photo on page 260

About 3 dozen cookies **Prep time: 20 minutes** **Start to Finish: 30 minutes**

A potato masher dipped into flour is also a quick way to flatten these cookies.

$3/4$ cup sugar

$1/4$ cup shortening

$1/4$ cup margarine or butter, softened

1 egg

$1/2$ teaspoon lemon extract or vanilla

$13/4$ cups all-purpose flour

$3/4$ teaspoon cream of tartar

$3/4$ teaspoon baking soda

$1/4$ teaspoon salt

1 cup raisins

1 Heat oven to 400°F.

2 Mix sugar, shortening, margarine, egg and lemon extract in large bowl. Stir in remaining ingredients.

3 Shape dough by rounded teaspoonfuls into balls. Place 3 inches apart on ungreased cookie sheet. Flatten in crisscross pattern with fork dipped in flour.

4 Bake 8 to 10 minutes or until light brown. Remove from cookie sheet. Cool on cooling rack.

1 Cookie: Calories 75 (Calories from Fat 25); Fat 3g (Saturated 1g); Cholesterol 10mg; Sodium 55mg; Carbohydrate 12g (Dietary Fiber 0g); Protein 0g

Joe Froggers

Photo on page 260

About 3 dozen cookies **Prep time: 20 minutes** **Start to Finish: 40 minutes**

Be careful not to overwork the dough while rolling out these tasty treats.

1 cup sugar

$1/2$ cup shortening

1 cup dark molasses

$1/2$ cup water

4 cups all-purpose flour

$11/2$ teaspoons salt

$11/2$ teaspoons ground ginger

1 teaspoon baking soda

$1/2$ teaspoon ground cloves

$1/2$ teaspoon ground nutmeg

$1/4$ teaspoon ground allspice

Sugar

1 Mix 1 cup sugar, the shortening, molasses and water in 3-quart bowl. Stir in remaining ingredients except sugar. Cover and refrigerate at least 2 hours.

2 Heat oven to 375°F.

3 Roll dough $1/4$ inch thick on well-floured cloth-covered board. Cut into 3-inch circles; sprinkle with sugar. Place about $1/2$ inches apart on ungreased cookie sheet.

4 Bake 10 to 12 minutes or until almost no indentation remains when touched. Cool 2 minutes; remove from cookie sheet. Cool completely.

1 Cookie: Calories 123 (Calories from Fat 25); Fat 3g (Saturated 1g); Cholesterol 0mg; Sodium 137mg; Carbohydrate 23g (Dietary Fiber 0g); Protein 1g

CHAPTER SEVEN

Homespun Desserts

PERFECT ENDINGS TO PERFECT MEALS OR AN ELEGANT FINISH TO A LOVELY EVENING INVITES THESE MEMORABLE DESSERTS TO YOUR TABLE.

You'll find a winning array of scrumptious treats for any grand finale. Moist cakes thick with creamy frosting, fruit studded cobblers and crisps ready for a scoop of vanilla ice cream, fruit pies and desserts oozing with summer sweetness—they're all here, waiting to be served.

Applesauce Cake

16 servings   Prep time: 15 minutes   Start to Finish: 2 hours 15 minutes

The applesauce in this recipe makes this one-bowl cake moist and delicious. Want a really yummy idea? Serve with warmed caramel topping drizzled over each slice. Pure heaven!

2 1/2 cups all-purpose flour

1 1/2 cups unsweetened applesauce

1 1/4 cups sugar

1/2 cup margarine or butter, softened

1/2 cup water

1 1/2 teaspoons baking soda

1 1/2 teaspoons pumpkin pie spice

1 teaspoon salt

3/4 teaspoon baking powder

2 eggs

1 cup raisins

2/3 cup chopped nuts

Maple-Nut Buttercream Frosting or Cream Cheese Frosting (right), if desired

1 Heat oven to 350°F. Grease bottom and sides of rectangular pan, 13 × 9 inches, or 2 round pans, 8 or 9 inches, with shortening; lightly flour.

2 Beat all ingredients except raisins, nuts and frosting in large bowl with electric mixer on low speed 30 seconds, scraping bowl constantly. Beat on high speed 3 minutes, scraping bowl occasionally. Stir in raisins and nuts. Pour into pan(s).

3 Bake rectangular pan 45 to 50 minutes, round pans 40 to 45 minutes, or until toothpick inserted in center comes out clean. Cool rectangular pan on wire rack. Cool round pans 10 minutes; remove to cooling rack. Cool completely.

4 Make Maple-Nut Buttercream Frosting or Cream Cheese Frosting. Frost rectangle or fill and frost layers.

Maple-Nut Buttercream Frosting

3 cups powdered sugar

1/3 cup margarine or butter, softened

1/2 cup maple-flavored syrup

1 to 2 tablespoons milk

1/4 cup finely chopped nuts

Mix powdered sugar and margarine in medium bowl. Stir in syrup and milk. Beat until smooth and spreadable. Stir in nuts.

Cream Cheese Frosting

1 package (8 oz) cream cheese, softened

1/4 cup margarine or butter, softened

2 teaspoons milk

1 teaspoon vanilla

4 cups powdered sugar

Beat cream cheese, margarine, milk and vanilla in medium bowl with electric mixer on low speed until smooth. Gradually beat in powdered sugar on low speed, 1 cup at a time, until smooth and spreadable.

1 Serving: Calories 265 (Calories from Fat 90); Fat 10g (Saturated 2g); Cholesterol 25mg; Sodium 350mg; Carbohydrate 42g (Dietary Fiber 1g); Protein 3g

Williamsburg Orange Cake

12 servings | Prep time: 10 minutes | Start to Finish: 2 hours 10 minutes

Studded with nuts and raisins, these rich vanilla layers are delicious topped with orange-scented buttercream.

2½ cups all-purpose flour or 2¾ cups cake flour

1½ cups sugar

1½ teaspoons baking soda

¾ teaspoon salt

1½ cups buttermilk

½ cup margarine or butter, softened

¼ cup shortening

3 eggs

1½ teaspoons vanilla

1 cup golden raisins, cut up

½ cup finely chopped nuts

1 tablespoon grated orange peel

Williamsburg Butter Frosting (right)

1 Heat oven to 350°F. Grease and flour rectangular pan, 13 × 9 inches.

2 Beat all ingredients except frosting in large bowl on low speed 30 seconds, scraping bowl constantly. Beat on high speed 3 minutes, scraping bowl occasionally. Pour into pan.

3 Bake rectangular pan 45 to 50 minutes, layers 30 to 35 minutes, or until toothpick inserted in center comes out clean; cool. Prepare Williamsburg Butter Frosting and frost cake.

Williamsburg Butter Frosting

½ cup margarine or butter, softened

4½ cups powdered sugar

4 to 5 tablespoons orange-flavored liqueur or orange juice

1 tablespoon grated orange peel

Mix margarine and powdered sugar. Beat in liqueur and orange peel.

1 Serving: Calories 500 (Calories from Fat 170); Fat 19g (Saturated 4g); Cholesterol 40mg; Sodium 420mg; Carbohydrate 78g (Dietary Fiber 1g); Protein 5g

COUNTRY COOKING WISDOM

Got Buttermilk?

Buttermilk adds a creamy, slightly tangy flavor to cakes, but it's not something you typically have on hand. As a substitute for buttermilk, add 1 tablespoon lemon juice or white vinegar to each cup of milk called for in the recipe. Let stand for 5 minutes to thicken.

Burnt-Sugar Chiffon Cake

16 servings | Prep time: 20 minutes | Start to Finish: 90 minutes

Chiffon cake is very close to our hearts. Harry Baker, a California insurance salesman, developed this wonderfully light and rich cake in 1927 but would not part with his secret ingredient for more than twenty years. He decided to share the identity of his secret ingredient—vegetable oil—with Betty Crocker after listening to "Betty Crocker's Cooking School of the Air." The year 1948 saw the chiffon cake trumpeted as "the cake discovery of the century!"

3 cups sugar

¾ cup boiling water

2 cups all-purpose flour

1 tablespoon baking powder

¾ teaspoon salt

½ cup vegetable oil

7 egg yolks

¼ cup cold water

1 teaspoon vanilla

7 or 8 egg whites (1 cup)

½ teaspoon cream of tartar

Burnt Sugar Frosting (below right)

1 Heat 1½ cups of the sugar in 10-inch heavy skillet over medium-low heat until sugar begins to melt. Continue cooking, stirring occasionally, until completely melted and medium brown; remove from heat. Slowly stir in boiling water until smooth. (If any lumps remain, return to heat and melt.) Cool; reserve for cake and frosting.

2 Move oven rack to lowest position. Heat oven to 325°F. Mix flour, remaining 1½ cups sugar, the baking powder and salt in medium bowl.

3 Beat in oil, egg yolks, ½ cup of the burnt sugar mixture, the cold water and vanilla until smooth. Beat egg whites and cream of tartar in large bowl until stiff peaks form. Gradually pour egg yolk mixture over beaten whites, gently folding just until blended. Pour into ungreased angel food cake (tube) pan, 10 × 4 inches.

4 Bake 60 to 65 minutes or until top springs back when touched lightly. Immediately invert pan onto heatproof funnel; let hang until cake is completely cool. Remove from pan.

5 Prepare Burnt Sugar Frosting and frost cake.

Burnt Sugar Frosting

4 cups powdered sugar

½ cup margarine or butter

Reserved burnt sugar mixture

2 teaspoons vanilla

4 tablespoons whipping cream

Mix powdered sugar and margarine. Stir in reserved burnt sugar mixture (from step 1 above) and the vanilla. Stir in whipping cream, 1 tablespoon at a time, until of spreading consistency.

1 Serving: Calories 475 (Calories from Fat 142); Fat 16g (Saturated 4g); Cholesterol 95mg; Sodium 298mg; Carbohydrate 80g (Dietary Fiber 0g); Protein 5g

Lemon-Filled Coconut Cake

16 servings | Prep time: 30 minutes | Start to Finish: 2 hours 15 minutes

Decadent! That's the only word to describe this scrumptious cake. Vanilla-and-coconut-flavored cake layers are coated with a rich lemon filling, then surrounded by sweet whipped cream. Don't expect to have leftovers!

Lemon Filling (below right)

2¼ cups all-purpose flour

1⅔ cups granulated sugar

⅔ cup shortening

1¼ cups milk

3½ teaspoons baking powder

1 teaspoon salt

1 teaspoon vanilla

5 egg whites

1 cup flaked or shredded coconut

1 cup whipping cream

¼ cup powdered sugar

1 Make Lemon Filling. Press plastic wrap onto hot filling. Refrigerate about 1 hour, or until set.

2 Heat oven to 350°F. Grease and flour 2 round pans, 8 or 9 inches.

3 Beat flour, granulated sugar, shortening, milk, baking powder, salt and vanilla in 3-quart bowl with electric mixer on low speed 30 seconds, scraping bowl constantly. Beat on high speed 2 minutes, scraping bowl occasionally. Beat in egg whites on high speed 2 minutes, scraping bowl occasionally. Stir in coconut. Pour into pans.

4 Bake 30 to 35 minutes or until toothpick inserted in center comes out clean or top springs back when touched lightly. Cool 10 minutes; remove from pans. Cool completely on cooling rack.

5 Beat whipping cream and powdered sugar in chilled 1½-quart bowl until stiff. Fill layers with Lemon Filling and frost with whipped cream; refrigerate. Immediately refrigerate any remaining cake.

Lemon Filling

¾ cup sugar

3 tablespoons cornstarch

¼ teaspoon salt

¾ cup water

1 tablespoon margarine or butter

1 teaspoon finely grated lemon peel

⅓ cup lemon juice

2 to 4 drops yellow food color, if desired

1 Mix sugar, cornstarch and salt in 1½-quart saucepan. Gradually stir in water. Cook over medium heat, stirring constantly, until mixture thickens and boils. Boil 5 minutes, stirring frequently; remove from heat.

2 Stir in margarine and lemon peel until margarine is melted. Gradually stir in lemon juice and food color.

1 Serving: Calories 360 (Calories from Fat 150); Fat 17g (Saturated 2g); Cholesterol 20mg; Sodium 340mg; Carbohydrate 51g (Dietary Fiber 2g); Protein 4g

Raspberry Jam Cake

16 servings | Prep time: 30 minutes | Start to Finish: 2 hours 30 minutes

This spice-laden jam cake hails from the South. You'll find that blackberry is the jam of choice in Texas and the western states, but in the Appalachian Mountain region, raspberry is favorite. One thing every one agrees on is that the buttery caramel frosting is just perfect!

1 cup margarine or butter, softened

1/2 cup granulated sugar

1/2 cup packed brown sugar

4 eggs

1 jar (10 oz) red raspberry preserves

3 1/4 cups all-purpose flour

1 teaspoon baking powder

1 teaspoon baking soda

1 teaspoon ground nutmeg

1 teaspoon ground cinnamon

1/2 teaspoon salt

1/4 teaspoon ground cloves

1 cup buttermilk

1 cup chopped pecans

Caramel Frosting (right)

1 Heat oven to 350°F. Grease and flour angel food cake tube pan, 10 × 4 inches.

2 Beat margarine and sugars in 3-quart bowl with electric mixer on medium speed, scraping bowl constantly, until blended. Beat on high speed 1 minute. Beat in eggs and preserves until well blended. (Mixture will appear curdled.)

3 Mix in flour, baking powder, baking soda, nutmeg, cinnamon, salt, and cloves alternately with buttermilk, beginning and ending with flour mixture, until well blended. Stir in pecans. Pour into pan.

4 Bake 70 to 75 minutes or until toothpick inserted in center comes out clean and top springs back when touched lightly. Cool 10 minutes; remove from pan. Cool completely on cooling rack.

5 Make Caramel Frosting and frost cake.

Caramel Frosting

1/2 stick margarine or butter
1 cup packed brown sugar
1/4 cup milk
2 cups powdered sugar

1 Heat margarine in 2-quart saucepan until melted.

2 Stir in brown sugar. Heat to boiling, stirring constantly. Boil and stir over low heat 2 minutes; stir in milk. Heat to boiling; remove from heat. Cool to lukewarm.

3 Gradually stir in powdered sugar. Beat until smooth and of spreading consistency. If frosting becomes too stiff, stir in additional milk, 1 teaspoon at a time.

1 Serving: Calories 529 (Calories from Fat 217); Fat 24g (Saturated 5g); Cholesterol 55mg; Sodium 422mg; Carbohydrate 75g (Dietary Fiber 2g); Protein 6g

Red Devil's Food Cake

16 servings | Prep time: 20 minutes | Start to Finish: 2 hours 10 minutes

This rich, dense chocolate cake gets its name from the color of the cake. Often, cooks would add red food color to the cake, similar to red velvet cake. We've eliminated this step as the chocolate gives the cake a red hue. Frost to your family's liking with either of the creamy, traditional frostings below.

1²/₃ cup all-purpose flour or 2 cups cake flour

1 cup granulated sugar

¹/₂ cup packed brown sugar

¹/₂ cup shortening

1¹/₂ cups buttermilk

1¹/₂ teaspoons baking soda

1 teaspoon salt

1 teaspoon vanilla

2 eggs

2 oz unsweetened chocolate, melted and cooled

Creamy Vanilla Frosting or Chocolate Frosting (right), if desired

1 Heat oven to 350°F. Grease and flour 2 round pans, 8 or 9 inches, or rectangular pan, 13 × 9 inches.

2 Beat all ingredients except frosting with electric mixer on low speed 30 seconds, scraping bowl constantly. Beat on high speed 3 minutes, scraping bowl occasionally. Pour into pan(s).

3 Bake round pans 30 to 35 minutes, rectangular pan 35 to 40 minutes, or until toothpick inserted in center comes out clean. Cool layers 10 minutes; remove from pans. Cool completely on cooling rack.

4 Make Creamy Vanilla Frosting or Chocolate Frosting. Fill and frost layers or frost top of rectangular pan.

Creamy Vanilla Frosting

3 cups powdered sugar

¹/₃ cup margarine or butter, softened

1¹/₂ teaspoons vanilla

About 2 tablespoons milk

Mix powdered sugar and margarine. Stir in vanilla and milk. Beat until smooth and of spreading consistency.

Chocolate Frosting

¹/₃ cup margarine or butter, softened

2 oz unsweetened chocolate, melted and cooled

2 cups powdered sugar

1¹/₂ teaspoons vanilla

About 2 tablespoons milk

Mix margarine and chocolate. Stir in powdered sugar. Beat in vanilla and milk until smooth and of spreading consistency.

1 serving (with Vanilla Frosting): Calories 350 (Calories from Fat 114); Fat 13g (Saturated 5g); Cholesterol 30mg; Sodium 345mg; Carbohydrate 54g (Dietary Fiber 2g); Protein 3g

Best Chocolate Cake with Fudge Frosting

12 to 16 servings | Prep time: 20 minutes | Start to Finish: 2 hours 15 minutes

Looking for a great cake to make for someone's birthday? Here it is! For a special color and flavor treat, serve a few raspberries with each slice!

2 cups all-purpose flour

2 cups sugar

$^1/_2$ cup shortening

$^3/_4$ cup water

$^3/_4$ cup buttermilk

1 teaspoon baking soda

1 teaspoon salt

1 teaspoon vanilla

$^1/_2$ teaspoon baking powder

2 eggs

4 oz unsweetened chocolate, melted and cooled

Fudge Frosting (right)

1 Heat oven to 350°F. Grease and flour rectangular pan, 13 × 9 inches, 3 round pans, 8 inches, or 2 round pans, 9 inches.

2 Beat all ingredients except Fudge Frosting in large bowl with electric mixer on low speed 30 seconds, scraping bowl constantly. Beat on high speed 3 minutes, scraping bowl occasionally. Pour into pan(s).

3 Bake rectangular pan 40 to 45 minutes, round pans 30 to 35 minutes, or until toothpick inserted in center comes out clean. Cool round pans 10 minutes; remove from pans. Cool completely.

4 Make Fudge Frosting; frost cake. Fill layers with $^1/_3$ cup frosting; frost side and top with remaining frosting.

Fudge Frosting

2 cups sugar

$^1/_2$ cup shortening

3 oz unsweetened chocolate

$^2/_3$ cup milk

$^1/_2$ teaspoon salt

2 teaspoons vanilla

Mix all ingredients except vanilla in 2½-quart saucepan. Heat to rapid boil, stirring occasionally. Boil 1 minute without stirring. Place saucepan in bowl of ice and water. Beat until frosting is smooth and of spreading consistency. Stir in vanilla.

1 Serving: Calories 620 (Calories from Fat 250); Fat 28g (Saturated 10g); Cholesterol 40mg; Sodium 450mg; Carbohydrate 89g (Dietary Fiber 3g); Protein 6g

COUNTRY COOKING WISDOM

Frosting Footnote

A good frosting is smooth and lustrous and can hold a swirl. It's soft enough to spread on a cake without running down the sides. If a creamy frosting is too thick, it can pull and tear the cake surface as you frost, leaving you with crumbs in your frosting. To make thick frosting thinner, add a few drops of water or milk.

Angel Food Cake with Chocolate Glaze

16 servings | Prep time: 20 minutes | Start to Finish: 3 hours

If you're looking for a delicious dessert that's the skinny on fat and cholesterol, look no further. Angel food cake boasts zero to both! Serve it with cut-up fresh fruit or berries and a dollop of fluffy whipped topping, and it will be a favorite with both young and old.

1½ cups powdered sugar
1 cup cake flour
1½ cups egg whites (about 12)
1½ teaspoons cream of tartar
1 cup granulated sugar
1½ teaspoons vanilla
½ teaspoon almond extract
¼ teaspoon salt
Chocolate Glaze (below right)

1 Move oven rack to lowest position. Heat oven to 375°F.

2 Mix powdered sugar and flour; set aside.

3 Beat egg whites and cream of tartar in large bowl with electric mixer on medium speed until foamy. Beat in granulated sugar, 2 tablespoons at a time, on high speed, adding vanilla, almond extract and salt with the last addition of sugar. Continue beating until stiff and glossy meringue forms. Do not underbeat.

4 Sprinkle sugar-flour mixture, ¼ cup at a time, over meringue, folding in just until sugar-flour mixture disappears. Push batter into ungreased angel food cake (tube) pan, 10 × 4 inches. Cut gently through batter with metal spatula.

5 Bake 30 to 35 minutes or until cracks feel dry and top springs back when touched lightly. Immediately turn pan upside down onto heatproof funnel or bottle. Let stand about 2 hours or until cake is completely cool. Loosen side of cake with knife or long, metal spatula; remove from pan.

6 Prepare Chocolate Glaze; spread or drizzle top of cake.

Chocolate Glaze

½ cup semisweet chocolate chips
2 tablespoons margarine or butter
2 tablespoons corn syrup
1 to 2 teaspoons hot water

Heat chocolate chips, margarine and corn syrup in 1-quart saucepan over low heat, stirring constantly, until chocolate chips are melted; cool slightly. Stir in hot water, 1 teaspoon at a time, until consistency of thick syrup.

1 Serving: Calories 180 (Calories from Fat 25); Fat 3g (Saturated 1g); Cholesterol 0mg; Sodium 95mg; Carbohydrate 35g (Dietary Fiber 0g); Protein 3g

Velvet Crumb Cake

8 servings   Prep time: 20 minutes   Start to Finish: 1 hour

Enjoy the moment while it lasts! Nothing tastes better than the velvety sensation of this longtime favorite recipe melting on your tastebuds. Even better, you can make this cake in one pan. The broiled topping makes it a little crunchy, adding a pleasant texture to this tender cake.

1½ cups Original Bisquick

½ cup sugar

½ cup milk or water

2 tablespoons shortening

1 teaspoon vanilla

1 egg

Broiled Topping (below right)

1 Heat oven to 350°F. Grease and flour square pan, 8 × 8 or 9 × 9 inches, or round pan, 9 inches.

2 Beat all ingredients except Broiled Topping in large bowl with electric mixer on low speed 30 seconds, scraping bowl constantly. Beat on medium speed 4 minutes, scraping bowl occasionally. Pour into pan.

3 Bake 9-inch square pan 25 to 30 minutes, 8-inch square or 9-inch round pan 30 to 35 minutes, or until toothpick inserted in center comes out clean; cool slightly.

4 Make Broiled Topping; spread over cake. Set oven control to broil. Broil cake about 3 inches from heat 3 minutes or until topping is golden brown.

Broiled Topping

½ cup flaked coconut

⅓ cup packed brown sugar

¼ cup chopped nuts

3 tablespoons margarine or butter, softened

2 tablespoons milk

Mix all ingredients in a medium bowl.

1 Serving: Calories 310 (Calories from Fat 145); Fat 16g (Saturated 5g); Cholesterol 30mg; Sodium 400mg; Carbohydrate 39g (Dietary Fiber 1g); Protein 3g

COUNTRY COOKING WISDOM

Coffee Klatch

This cake is perfect paired with hot, steaming mugs of café au lait. To prepare, make 1 strong cup of coffee. In a small saucepan, heat 1 cup milk. Cook just until a thin film forms on the surface, stirring constantly to prevent sticking. Fill large mugs halfway full with coffee. Top off with the hot milk.

Bonnie Butter Cake

| 16 servings | Prep time: 20 minutes | Start to Finish: 2 hours 10 minutes |

Bonnie Butter Cake has been around for many years, a testament to the delicious flavor and delicate texture of this cake. Treat yourself and use real butter for a rich, old-fashioned taste!

1³/₄ cups sugar

²/₃ cup margarine or butter, softened

1¹/₂ teaspoons vanilla

2 eggs

3 cups cake flour or 1²/₃ cups all-purpose flour

2¹/₂ teaspoons baking powder

1 teaspoon salt

1¹/₄ cups milk

Fudge Frosting (page 274)

1 Heat oven to 350°F. Grease bottom and sides of rectangular pan, 13 × 9 inches, or 2 round pans, 9 inches; lightly flour.

2 Beat sugar, margarine, vanilla and eggs in large bowl with electric mixer on low speed 30 seconds, scraping bowl constantly. Beat on high speed 5 minutes, scraping bowl occasionally. Beat in flour, baking powder and salt alternately with milk on low speed. Pour into pan(s).

3 Bake rectangular pan 45 to 50 minutes, round pans 30 to 35 minutes, or until toothpick inserted in center comes out clean. Cool rectangular pan on wire rack. Cool round pans 10 minutes; remove to cooling rack. Cool completely.

4 Make Fudge Frosting. Frost top of rectangular pan or fill and frost layers.

1 Serving: Calories 395 (Calories from Fat 135); Fat 15g (Saturated 8g); Cholesterol 50mg; Sodium 330mg; Carbohydrate 63g (Dietary Fiber 1g); Protein 4g

COUNTRY COOKING WISDOM

The Great Chocolate Meltdown

- Chocolate must be melted carefully because it can burn easily. Never heat dark chocolate above 120°F or white or milk chocolate above 110°F. Be sure to break up or chop chocolate bars or squares before melting.

- To melt, microwave uncovered in a microwavable dish or bowl on Medium (50%), stirring once every minute, just until melted. Some chocolate retains its shape when softened, so stir it frequently.

- Never get water in chocolate while it's melting. If this happens, the chocolate will get thick, lumpy and sometimes grainy—it's called "seizing." You'll think it's ruined.

- Seized chocolate can be "saved" by stirring in 1 teaspoon vegetable oil or shortening for every ounce of chocolate melted. (Don't use butter or margarine because they contain water.)

Oatmeal Spice Cake with Browned Butter Frosting

16 servings | Prep time: 15 minutes | Start to Finish: 2 hours 5 minutes

Sugar and spice and all things nice make this a cake to remember! Top with vanilla ice cream for a little à la mode. Keep an eye on the butter when you make the frosting. You'll have more control over the browning if you use a heavy skillet and just let the frosting get light golden brown to ensure it won't burn.

1½ cups all-purpose flour

1 cup quick-cooking oats

1 cup packed brown sugar

½ cup granulated sugar

1½ teaspoons baking soda

1 teaspoon ground cinnamon

½ teaspoon salt

½ teaspoon ground nutmeg, if desired

½ cup shortening

1 cup water

2 eggs

2 tablespoons molasses

Browned Butter Frosting (right)

1 Heat oven to 350°F.

2 Grease rectangular pan, 13 × 9 inches with shortening; lightly flour.

3 Beat all ingredients except Browned Butter Frosting in large bowl with electric mixer on low speed 30 seconds, scraping bowl constantly. Beat on high speed 3 minutes, scraping bowl occasionally. Pour into pan.

4 Bake 35 to 40 minutes or until toothpick inserted in center comes out clean. Cool in pan on cooling rack.

5 Make Browned Butter Frosting; spread on cake.

Browned Butter Frosting

⅓ cup butter

3 cups powdered sugar

1½ teaspoons vanilla

About 2 tablespoons milk

Heat butter over medium heat until delicate brown. Mix in powdered sugar. Beat in vanilla and enough milk until smooth and spreadable.

1 Serving: Calories 330 (Calories from Fat 100); Fat 11g (Saturated 4g); Cholesterol 35mg; Sodium 230mg; Carbohydrate 56g (Dietary Fiber 1g); Protein 3g

COUNTRY COOKING WISDOM

Frosting Finesse

Ever find your cakes always end up with crumbs in the frosting? Here's a simple way to prevent this. Apply a "crumb coat" of frosting to the cake. This is a very thin layer of frosting that seals the crumbs into the cake. First, using a pastry brush, sweep the crumbs from the surface. Then with a metal spatula, spread the thin layer (about ½ cup for entire cake) over cake surface. If time permits, chill the cake for 30 minutes. Then with a clean spatula, spread the remaining frosting over the crumb coat.

Silver White Cake

16 servings | Prep time: 15 minutes | Start to Finish: 2 hours 10 minutes

The silver white cake topped with a rich, chocolate frosting makes this a first-class cake. Why not polish up that silver platter that you've stored away and put it to good use?

2¼ cups all-purpose or 2½ cups cake flour

1⅔ cups sugar

⅔ cup shortening

1¼ cups milk

3½ teaspoons baking powder

1 teaspoon salt

1 teaspoon vanilla or almond extract

5 egg whites

Mocha Frosting (below right)

1 Heat oven to 350°F. Grease bottom and sides of rectangular pan, 13 × 9 inches, 2 round pans, 9 inches, or 3 round pans, 8 inches, with shortening; lightly flour.

2 Beat all ingredients except egg whites and Mocha Frosting in large bowl with electric mixer on low speed 30 seconds, scraping bowl constantly. Beat on high speed 2 minutes, scraping bowl occasionally.

3 Beat in egg whites on high speed 2 minutes, scraping bowl occasionally. Pour into pan(s).

4 Bake rectangular pan 40 to 45 minutes, 9-inch round pans 30 to 35 minutes, 8-inch round pans 23 to 28 minutes, or until toothpick inserted in center comes out clean or until cake springs back when touched lightly in center. Cool rectangular pan on wire rack. Cool round pans 10 minutes; remove to wire rack. Cool completely.

5 Make Mocha Frosting. Frost top of rectangular pan or fill and frost layers.

Mocha Frosting

3 cups powdered sugar

2½ teaspoons powdered instant coffee

⅓ cup stick margarine or butter, softened

2 teaspoons vanilla

3 oz unsweetened baking chocolate, melted and cooled

2 to 3 tablespoons milk

Mix all ingredients except milk in medium bowl. Stir in milk until smooth and spreadable.

1 Serving: Calories 235 (Calories from Fat 80); Fat 9g (Saturated 3g); Cholesterol 2mg; Sodium 270mg; Carbohydrate 36g (Dietary Fiber 0g); Protein 3g

Strawberry Shortcakes

6 shortcakes | Prep time: 30 minutes | Start to Finish: 1 hour 10 minutes

Who can resist tender shortcakes covered in sweet strawberries and topped off with a bit of whipped cream? It's what summer days are made for. Blueberries, raspberries, fresh peaches, kiwi and cherries also make wonderful fruits for these shortcakes.

1 quart strawberries, sliced
½ cup sugar
⅓ cup shortening
2 cups all-purpose flour
2 tablespoons sugar
3 teaspoons baking powder
1 teaspoon salt
¾ cup milk
Margarine or butter, softened
Sweetened whipped cream

1 Mix strawberries and ½ cup sugar. Let stand 1 hour.

2 Heat oven to 450°F.

3 Cut shortening into flour, 2 tablespoons of the sugar, the baking powder and salt in medium bowl, using pastry blender or crisscrossing 2 knives, until mixture looks like fine crumbs. Stir in milk just until blended.

4 Turn dough onto lightly floured surface. Gently smooth into a ball. Knead 20 to 25 times. Roll ½ inch thick. Cut into 3-inch squares or use floured 3-inch cutter. Place about 1 inch apart on ungreased cookie sheet.

5 Bake 10 to 12 minutes or until golden brown.

6 Split shortcakes horizontally in half while hot. Spread margarine on split sides. Fill with strawberries; replace tops. Top with strawberries and whipped cream.

1 Shortcake: Calories 400 (Calories from Fat 135); Fat 15g (Saturated 5g); Cholesterol 10mg; Sodium 630mg; Carbohydrate 63g (Dietary Fiber 8g); Protein 6g

Orchard Squares

Perfect for dessert or a midmorning coffee, these squares layer fresh fruits—peaches, pears, and apples—between tender toasted almond pastry. Yum!

Toasted Almond Pastry (below right)

$\frac{1}{3}$ to $\frac{2}{3}$ cup granulated sugar

$\frac{1}{3}$ cup all-purpose flour

$\frac{1}{2}$ teaspoon ground nutmeg

Dash of salt

3 cups sliced fresh peaches (3 medium)

3 cups sliced fresh pears (3 medium)

2 cups thinly sliced peeled tart apples (2 medium)

2 tablespoons lemon juice

2 tablespoons margarine or butter

$\frac{3}{4}$ cup powdered sugar

About 1 tablespoon milk or lemon juice

Ice cream, if desired

1 Make Toasted Almond Pastry. Gather into a ball; cut in half. Shape each half into flattened round on lightly floured cloth-covered surface. Roll 1 round into rectangle, 18 × 3 inches, with floured cloth-covered rolling pin. Fold pastry into quarters; unfold and ease into ungreased jelly roll pan, 15 × 10 inches.

2 Heat oven to 425°F.

3 Mix granulated sugar, flour, nutmeg and salt in large bowl. Stir in fruit. Turn into pastry-lined pan. Drizzle lemon juice over fruit. Dot with margarine.

4 Roll other round pastry into rectangle, 17 × 12 inches. Fold into quarters; cut slits so steam can escape. Place on fruit mixture and unfold; seal and flute.

5 Bake 35 to 40 minutes or until crust is brown and juice begins to bubble through slits in crust; cool slightly.

6 Mix powdered sugar and milk until smooth; drizzle over crust. Cut into about 3-inch squares. Serve warm with ice cream.

Toasted Almond Pastry

$1\frac{1}{4}$ cups shortening

$3\frac{1}{2}$ cups all-purpose flour

$\frac{1}{4}$ cup ground toasted almonds

1 teaspoon salt

8 to 9 tablespoons cold water

Cut shortening into flour, almonds and salt, using pastry blender or criss-crossing 2 knives, until particles are size of small peas. Sprinkle in water, 1 tablespoon at a time, tossing with fork until all flour is moistened and pastry almost cleans side of bowl (1 to 2 teaspoons water can be added, if necessary).

1 square: Calories 454 (Calories from Fat 156); Fat 17g (Saturated 6g); Cholesterol 0mg; Sodium 167mg; Carbohydrate 46g (Dietary Fiber 3g); Protein 4g

Citrus-Peach Shortcakes

6 shortcakes | Prep time: 20 minutes | Start to Finish: 1 hour

Shortcakes are an all-American dessert that showcases the fruits of the summer harvest. Each rich biscuit is layered with sweetened fresh fruit and topped with mounds of luscious whipped cream.

4 cups sliced peeled peaches (6 medium)

1 cup sugar

Citrus Glaze (below right)

2 cups all-purpose flour

2 tablespoons sugar

3 teaspoons baking powder

1/2 teaspoon salt

1 tablespoon grated orange peel

1/3 cup shortening

3/4 cup milk

1 1/2 teaspoons margarine or butter

Sweetened whipped cream, if desired

1 Mix peaches and 1 cup sugar; let stand 1 hour.

2 Make Citrus Glaze.

3 Heat oven to 450°F.

4 Mix flour, 2 tablespoons sugar, the baking powder and salt in 2-quart bowl. Mix in orange peel. Cut in shortening, using pastry blender or crisscrossing 2 knives, until mixture resembles fine crumbs. Stir in milk just until blended.

5 Gently smooth dough into ball on lightly floured cloth-covered surface; knead 20 to 25 times. Pat or roll about 1/4 inch thick. Cut into 12 circles with floured 3-inch cutter. Dot half of the circles with margarine; top with remaining circles. Place about 1 inch apart on ungreased cookie sheet.

6 Bake 12 to 15 minutes or until golden brown. Split shortcakes in half while hot. Fill and top with peaches; drizzle with Citrus Glaze. Top with whipped cream.

Citrus Glaze

1 cup sugar

1/3 cup orange juice

1 tablespoon grated orange peel

3 tablespoons lemon juice

1 teaspoon light corn syrup

Heat all ingredients to boiling in 1-quart saucepan. Reduce heat. Simmer about 15 minutes, or until mixture thickens slightly. Cool.

1 Shortcake: Calories 607 (Calories from Fat 120); Fat 13g (Saturated 5g); Cholesterol 3mg; Sodium 438mg; Carbohydrate 118g (Dietary Fiber 3g); Protein 6g

Pineapple Upside-Down Cake

9 servings | Prep time: 15 minutes | Start to Finish: 1 hour

This traditional cake is delicious served warm with a dollop of sweetened whipped cream. But don't limit this delectable dessert to pineapple. Try apricots, peaches or plums in its place.

1/4 cup margarine or butter

1 can (20 oz) sliced pineapple in syrup, drained (reserve 2 tablespoons syrup)

2/3 cup packed brown sugar

Maraschino cherries, if desired

1 1/2 cups cake flour or 1 1/4 cups all-purpose flour

1 cup granulated sugar

1/3 cup shortening

3/4 cup milk

1 1/2 teaspoons baking powder

1 teaspoon vanilla

1/2 teaspoon salt

1 egg

1 1/4 cups sweetened whipped cream

1 Heat oven to 350°F.

2 Heat margarine in 9-inch ovenproof skillet or square pan, 9 × 9 inches, in oven until melted. Stir reserved pineapple syrup into margarine. Sprinkle evenly with brown sugar. Arrange pineapple slices in margarine mixture. Place cherry in center of each pineapple slice.

3 Beat remaining ingredients except whipped cream in 3-quart bowl with electric mixer on low speed 30 seconds, scraping bowl constantly. Beat on high speed 3 minutes, scraping bowl occasionally. Pour evenly over pineapple slices.

4 Bake 40 to 45 minutes or until toothpick inserted in center comes out clean. Invert on heatproof platter. Leave skillet over cake a few minutes. Serve warm with whipped cream.

1 Serving: Calories 435 (Calories from Fat 172); Fat 19g (Saturated 8g); Cholesterol 45mg; Sodium 290mg; Carbohydrate 63g (Dietary Fiber 1g); Protein 4g

Apricot Upside-Down Cake: Substitute 1 can (17 oz) apricot halves for the pineapple slices.

Peach Upside-Down Cake: Substitute 1 can (16 oz) sliced peaches for the pineapple slices.

Plum Upside-Down Cake: Substitute 1 can (17 oz) plums, cut in half and pitted, for the pineapple slices.

Cranberry-Orange Pound Cake

16 servings | Prep time: 20 minutes | Start to Finish: 2 hours 35 minutes

Enjoy this moist, tender cake all year by purchasing bags of fresh cranberries in season and putting them in the freezer for later use. Quickly chop fresh or frozen cranberries, using a food processor with a metal blade.

1 package (18.25 oz) golden vanilla or yellow cake mix with pudding

1 package (4-serving size) vanilla instant pudding and pie filling mix

1 cup water

½ cup margarine or butter, melted

1 teaspoon grated orange peel

4 eggs

1½ cups fresh or frozen (do not thaw) cranberries, chopped

Orange Butter Sauce (right)

1 Heat oven to 350°F. Grease bottom and side of 12-cup bundt cake pan; lightly flour.

2 Beat cake mix (dry), pudding mix (dry), water, margarine, orange peel and eggs in large bowl with electric mixer on low speed 30 seconds, scraping bowl constantly. Beat on medium speed 2 minutes. Fold in cranberries. Spread in pan.

3 Bake 1 hour 5 minutes to 1 hour 10 minutes or until cake springs back when touched lightly in center. Cool 10 minutes; remove from pan. Cool completely.

4 Make Orange Butter Sauce. Serve warm with cake.

Orange Butter Sauce

1 cup sugar
1 tablespoon all-purpose flour
½ cup orange juice
½ cup butter (do not use margarine)

Mix sugar and flour in 1-quart saucepan. Stir in orange juice. Add butter. Cook over medium heat, stirring constantly, until thickened and bubbly.

1 Serving: Calories 340 (Calories from Fat 145); Fat 16g (Saturated 6g); Cholesterol 70mg; Sodium 400mg; Carbohydrate 47g (Dietary Fiber 0g); Protein 2g

Pumpkin Cheesecake

12 servings | Prep time: 20 minutes | Start to Finish: 4 hours 45 minutes

Try this tempting alternative to the traditional Thanksgiving pumpkin pie. The gingersnap crust adds a nice spice to the moist, rich cheesecake. Dot with whipped cream and garnish with pecan halves around the edges of the cake for a festive look.

1¼ cups gingersnap cookie crumbs (20 cookies)

¼ cup margarine or butter, melted

3 packages (8 oz each) cream cheese, softened

1 cup sugar

1 teaspoon ground cinnamon

1 teaspoon ground ginger

½ teaspoon ground cloves

1 can (16 oz) pumpkin

4 eggs

2 tablespoons sugar

12 walnut halves

¾ cup whipping cream

1   Heat oven to 350°F.

2   Mix cookie crumbs and margarine. Press evenly on bottom of springform pan, 9 × 3 inches. Bake 10 minutes; cool. Reduce oven temperature to 300°F.

3   Beat cream cheese, 1 cup sugar, the cinnamon, ginger and cloves in 4-quart bowl with electric mixer on medium speed until smooth and fluffy. Add pumpkin. Beat in eggs, one at a time, on low speed. Pour over crumb mixture.

4   Bake about 1 hour 15 minutes or until center is firm. Cool to room temperature. Cover and refrigerate at least 3 hours but no longer than 48 hours.

5   Cook 2 tablespoons sugar and the walnuts over medium heat until sugar is melted and nuts are coated. Immediately spread on a dinner plate or foil; cool. Carefully break nuts apart to separate, if necessary. Cover tightly and store at room temperature up to 3 days.

6   Loosen cheesecake from side of pan; remove side of pan. Beat whipping cream in chilled 1½-quart bowl until stiff. Pipe whipped cream around edge of cheesecake. Arrange walnuts on top. Refrigerate any remaining cheesecake immediately.

1 Serving: Calories 450 (Calories from Fat 290); Fat 32g (Saturated 17g); Cholesterol 150mg; Sodium 310mg; Carbohydrate 33g (Dietary Fiber 1g); Protein 8g

COUNTRY COOKING WISDOM

Toasting Tips

Toasting brings out the flavor and adds a wonderful dimension to any recipe that calls for nuts, coconut or sesame seed. A good doneness test, along with color, is when you can smell the toasted aroma. Use it as a signal to watch them carefully so they don't burn. Remove them immediately from the hot pan or skillet so they don't continue to toast and become too dark or scorch.

Cheesecake with Cherry Glaze

16 servings | Prep time: 35 minutes | Start to Finish: 5 hours

This "never fail" cheesecake is always a real crowd-pleaser. You might want to use a 15-oz can of cherry or blueberry pie filling instead of making the cherry glaze.

½ cup fine zwieback or graham cracker crumbs

1 tablespoon sugar

¼ teaspoon ground cinnamon

¼ teaspoon ground nutmeg

5 eggs, separated

1 cup sugar

2 packages (8 oz each) cream cheese, softened

1 cup sour cream

2 tablespoons all-purpose flour

1 teaspoon vanilla

Cherry Glaze (below right)

1 Heat oven to 275°F. Butter springform pan, 9 × 3 inches.

2 Mix crumbs, 1 tablespoon sugar, the cinnamon and nutmeg. Dust bottom and side of springform pan with crumb mixture.

3 Beat egg yolks in large bowl with electric mixer on high speed or until thick and lemon-colored. Gradually beat in 1 cup sugar. Beat in cream cheese until smooth. Beat in sour cream, flour and vanilla until smooth.

4 Beat egg whites in large bowl with electric mixer on high speed until stiff but not dry. Gently fold into cream cheese mixture. Pour into pan.

5 Bake 1 hour 10 minutes. Turn off oven and leave cheesecake in oven 1 hour. Cool in pan on wire rack 15 minutes. Refrigerate about 3 hours or until chilled.

6 Make Cherry Glaze. Spread over top of cheesecake. Refrigerate until glaze is set. Remove cheesecake from pan just before serving.

Cherry Glaze

1 can (16 oz) pitted red tart cherries, drained and liquid reserved

½ cup sugar

2 tablespoons cornstarch

Few drops red food color, if desired

Add enough water to reserved cherry liquid to measure 1 cup. Mix sugar and cornstarch in 1½-quart saucepan. Gradually stir in cherry liquid. Cook over medium heat, stirring constantly, until mixture thickens and boils. Boil and stir 1 minute; remove from heat. Stir in cherries and food color; cool.

1 Serving: Calories 275 (Calories from Fat 135); Fat 15g (Saturated 9g); Cholesterol 105mg; Sodium 115mg; Carbohydrate 30g (Dietary Fiber 0g); Protein 5g

Hot-Fudge Sundae Cake

Sound too good to be true? This moist, rich chocolate cake gets its name from the fact it makes its own sauce, which you can spoon over each warm, chocolatey piece. Wouldn't it be oh-so-good topped with fresh strawberries or sweetened whipped cream?

1 cup all-purpose flour
³/₄ cup granulated sugar
2 tablespoons baking cocoa
2 teaspoons baking powder
¹/₄ teaspoon salt
¹/₂ cup milk
2 tablespoons vegetable oil
1 teaspoon vanilla
1 cup chopped nuts, if desired
1 cup packed brown sugar
¹/₄ cup baking cocoa
1³/₄ cups very hot water
   Ice cream, if desired

1 Heat oven to 350°F.

2 Mix flour, granulated sugar, 2 tablespoons cocoa, the baking powder and salt in ungreased square pan, 9 × 9 inches. Mix in milk, oil and vanilla with fork until smooth. Stir in nuts. Spread in pan.

3 Sprinkle brown sugar and ¹/₄ cup cocoa over batter. Pour water over batter.

4 Bake 40 minutes or until top is dry.

5 Spoon warm cake into dessert dishes. Top with ice cream. Spoon sauce from pan onto each serving.

1 Serving: Calories 400 (Calories from Fat 100); Fat 11g (Saturated 5g); Cholesterol 30mg; Sodium 240mg; Carbohydrate 71g (Dietary Fiber 1g); Protein 5g

Peach-Custard Kuchen

9 servings   Prep time: 20 minutes   Start to Finish: 1 hour 5 minutes

This sweet peaches-and-cream dessert starts as an easy-to-whip-up base. Sprinkled with cinnamon-sugar, the peaches partially bake to release some of their juices before the creamy custard is poured over them to finish baking. Mmmmm.

1 cup all-purpose flour

2 tablespoons sugar

¼ teaspoon salt

⅛ teaspoon baking powder

¼ cup margarine or butter, softened

1½ cups sliced fresh peaches (3 medium)*

⅓ cup sugar

1 teaspoon ground cinnamon

2 egg yolks

1 cup whipping cream

1 Heat oven to 400°F.

2 Stir together flour, 2 tablespoons sugar, the salt and baking powder. Work in margarine until mixture is crumbly.

3 Pat mixture firmly and evenly in bottom and halfway up sides of ungreased square pan, 8 × 8 inches. Arrange peaches in pan. Mix ⅓ cup sugar and the cinnamon; sprinkle over peaches. Bake 15 minutes.

4 Blend egg yolks and whipping cream; pour over peaches. Bake 25 to 30 minutes or until custard is set and edges are light brown. Serve warm. Refrigerate any remaining dessert.

*1 package (8 oz) frozen sliced peaches, thawed and drained, or 1 can (16 oz) sliced peaches, drained, can be substituted for the fresh peaches.

1 Serving: Calories 245 (Calories from Fat 135); Fat 15g (Saturated 9g); Cholesterol 90mg; Sodium 115mg; Carbohydrate 25g (Dietary Fiber 1g); Protein 3g

Bread Pudding with Whiskey Sauce

8 servings   Prep time: 15 minutes   Start to Finish: 1 hour 10 minutes

Don't let day-old bread go to waste. In addition to white bread, try whole wheat, cinnamon-raisin, egg bread or other flavors of bread that appeal to you. For a family dessert, instead of the whiskey sauce, serve warm caramel sauce to drizzle over each warm, gooey serving.

2 cups milk

¼ cup margarine or butter

½ cup sugar

1 teaspoon ground cinnamon or nutmeg

¼ teaspoon salt

2 eggs, slightly beaten

6 cups dry bread cubes (about 8 slices bread)

½ cup raisins, if desired

Whiskey Sauce (below right)

1 Heat oven to 350°F.

2 Heat milk and margarine in 2-quart saucepan over medium heat until margarine is melted and milk is hot.

3 Mix sugar, cinnamon, salt and eggs in large bowl with wire whisk until well blended. Stir in bread cubes and raisins. Stir in milk mixture.

4 Pour into ungreased 1½-quart casserole or square baking dish, 8 × 8 inches. Place casserole in rectangular pan, 13 × 9 inches. Pour boiling water into rectangular pan until 1 inch deep.

5 Bake uncovered 40 to 45 minutes or until knife inserted 1 inch from edge of casserole comes out clean.

6 Make Whiskey Sauce. Serve sauce over warm bread pudding. Refrigerate any remaining dessert.

Whiskey Sauce

1 cup packed brown sugar

½ cup margarine or butter

3 to 4 tablespoons bourbon or 2 teaspoons brandy extract

Heat all ingredients to boiling in heavy 1-quart saucepan over medium heat, stirring constantly, until sugar is dissolved. Serve warm or cool.

1 Serving: Calories 665 (Calories from Fat 215); Fat 24g (Saturated 6g); Cholesterol 60mg; Sodium 1,020mg; Carbohydrate 101g (Dietary Fiber 3g); Protein 14g

Fresh Peach Cobbler

6 servings   Prep time: 20 minutes   Start to Finish: 50 minutes

Cobblers are a homey way to use fruit in season. Short on time? Try using blueberries instead—there's no peeling or pitting!

1/2 cup sugar

1 tablespoon cornstarch

1/4 teaspoon ground cinnamon

4 cups sliced peaches (6 medium)

1 teaspoon lemon juice

3 tablespoons shortening

1 cup all-purpose flour

1 tablespoon sugar

1 1/2 teaspoons baking powder

1/2 teaspoon salt

1/2 cup milk

Sweetened whipped cream, if desired

1   Heat oven to 400°F.

2   Mix 1/2 cup sugar, the cornstarch and cinnamon in 2-quart saucepan. Stir in peaches and lemon juice. Cook, stirring constantly, until mixture thickens and boils. Boil and stir 1 minute. Pour into ungreased 2-quart casserole. Keep peach mixture hot in oven.

3   Cut shortening into flour, 1 tablespoon sugar, the baking powder and salt in medium bowl, using pastry blender or crisscrossing 2 knives, until mixture looks like fine crumbs. Stir in milk. Drop dough by 6 spoonfuls onto hot peach mixture.

4   Bake 25 to 30 minutes or until topping is golden brown. Serve warm with sweetened whipped cream.

1 Serving: Calories 260 (Calories from Fat 65); Fat 7g (Saturated 2g); Cholesterol 5mg; Sodium 310mg; Carbohydrate 48g (Dietary Fiber 2g); Protein 3g

Blackberry Cobbler

8 servings | Prep time: 10 minutes | Start to Finish: 55 minutes

Cobblers are so named because they could be made quickly, or "cobbled together." Use whichever berry is abundant in your area; either blackberries or raspberries make this cobbler luscious.

4 cups fresh blackberries or raspberries

1 cup sugar

1 tablespoon cornstarch

1/2 teaspoon lemon juice

1 cup all-purpose flour

2 teaspoons baking powder

1/2 teaspoon salt

1/2 cup milk

1/4 cup (1/2 stick) margarine or butter, melted

1 egg

Sweetened whipped cream or whipping cream, if desired

1 Heat oven to 375°F.

2 Place blackberries in 2-quart ungreased casserole. Reserve 1 teaspoon of the sugar. Mix remaining sugar, the cornstarch and lemon juice and drizzle over blackberries; stir gently.

3 Mix flour, baking powder and salt in 2-quart bowl. Stir in milk, margarine and egg. Spread batter evenly over blackberries, sealing edge. Sprinkle with reserved sugar.

4 Bake uncovered 30 to 35 minutes or until topping is golden brown. Let stand 10 minutes before serving. Serve with sweetened whipped cream.

1 Serving: Calories 250 (Calories from Fat 61); Fat 7g (Saturated 2g); Cholesterol 26mg; Sodium 330mg; Carbohydrate 46g (Dietary Fiber 4g); Protein 3g

Blueberry Slump

The slump hails from New England and is a dish of fruit, usually berries, topped with biscuits. Cooked on the stove, the fruit stews while the biscuits cook to perfection.

1/2 cup sugar

2 tablespoons cornstarch

1/2 cup water

1 teaspoon lemon juice

4 cups blueberries

1 cup all-purpose flour

2 tablespoons sugar

1 1/2 teaspoons baking powder

1/4 teaspoon salt

1/4 teaspoon ground nutmeg

1/4 cup (1/2 stick) margarine or butter

1/3 cup milk

Cream, if desired

1 Mix 1/2 cup sugar and the cornstarch in 3-quart saucepan. Stir in water and lemon juice until well blended. Stir in blueberries. Cook over medium heat, stirring constantly, until mixture thickens and boils. Boil and stir 1 minute.

2 Mix flour, 2 tablespoons sugar, the baking powder, salt and nutmeg. Cut in margarine, using a pastry blender or crisscrossing 2 knives, until mixture resembles fine crumbs. Stir in milk. Drop dough by 6 spoonfuls onto hot blueberry mixture.

3 Cook uncovered over low heat 10 minutes; cover and cook 10 minutes longer. Serve with cream.

1 Serving (without cream): Calories 299 (Calories from Fat 77); Fat 9g (Saturated 2g); Cholesterol 1mg; Sodium 315mg; Carbohydrate 54g (Dietary Fiber 3g); Protein 3g

Rhubarb Crisp

Scented with orange, this tender rhubarb has a sweet topping that "crisps" during baking. Serve any leftovers for breakfast along with a dollop of vanilla yogurt.

1 1/3 cups granulated sugar

1/3 cup all-purpose flour

1/2 teaspoon grated orange peel

4 cups 1/2-inch pieces fresh rhubarb or 1 package (16 oz) frozen unsweetened rhubarb, thawed and well drained (2 cups)

1/2 cup all-purpose flour

1/4 cup packed brown sugar

1/4 cup margarine or butter, softened

1 Heat oven to 400°F.

2 Mix granulated sugar, 1/3 cup flour and the orange peel; toss with rhubarb until well coated. Arrange rhubarb mixture in greased square pan, 8 × 8 inches.

3 Mix 1/2 cup flour, the brown sugar and margarine with fork until crumbly. Sprinkle evenly over rhubarb mixture. Bake 35 to 40 minutes or until topping is golden brown and rhubarb is tender.

1 Serving: Calories 236 (Calories from Fat 47); Fat 5g (Saturated 1g); Cholesterol 0mg; Sodium 65mg; Carbohydrate 47g (Dietary Fiber 1g); Protein 2g

Standard Pastry

One-Crust Pie (9-inch)

1 cup all-purpose* or unbleached flour
$^1/_2$ teaspoon salt
$^1/_3$ cup plus 1 tablespoon shortening
2 to 3 tablespoons cold water

Two-Crust Pie (9-inch)

2 cups all-purpose* or unbleached flour
1 teaspoon salt
$^2/_3$ cup plus 2 tablespoons shortening
4 to 6 tablespoons cold water

1 In medium bowl, mix flour and salt. Cut in shortening, using pastry blender (or pulling 2 table knives through ingredients in opposite direction), until particles are size of small peas. Sprinkle with cold water, 1 tablespoon at a time, tossing with fork until all flour is moistened and pastry almost leaves side of bowl.

2 Gather pastry into a ball; shape into flattened round on lightly floured cloth-covered surface. (For Two-Crust Pie, divide pastry in half and shape into 2 rounds.) Wrap flattened round of pastry in plastic wrap and refrigerate about 45 minutes or until dough is firm and cold, yet pliable. If refrigerated longer, let pastry soften slightly before rolling.

3 Roll pastry on lightly floured surface, using floured rolling pin, into circle 2 inches larger than upside-down 9-inch glass pie plate or 3 inches larger than 10- or 11-inch tart pan. Fold pastry into fourths and place in plate; or roll pastry loosely around rolling pin and transfer to pie plate. Unfold or unroll pastry and ease into plate, pressing firmly against bottom and side and being careful not to stretch pastry. Continue with directions for One-Crust Pie or Two-Crust Pie.

If using self-rising flour, omit salt. Pie crusts made with self-rising flour differ in flavor and texture from those made with all-purpose flour.

1 Serving (using one crust): Calories 145 (Calories from Fat 90); Fat 10g (Saturated 3g); Cholesterol 0mg; Sodium 150mg; Carbohydrate 12g (Dietary Fiber 0g); Protein 2g

One-Crust Pie: Unbaked (for one-crust pies baked with a filling): *For pie,* trim overhanging edge of pastry 1 inch from rim of pie plate. Fold and roll pastry under,

even with plate; flute. *For tart,* trim overhanging edge of pastry even with top of tart pan. Fill and bake as directed in pie or tart recipe, or partially bake crust before adding filling as directed in next paragraph.

Partially Baked Partially bake pastry before adding filling: Heat oven to 425°F. Carefully line pastry with a double thickness of foil, gently pressing foil to bottom and side of pastry. Let foil extend over edge to prevent excessive browning. Bake 10 minutes; carefully remove foil and bake 2 to 4 minutes longer or until pastry *just begins* to brown and has become set. If crust bubbles, gently push bubbles down with back of spoon. Fill and bake as directed in recipe.

Baked (for one-crust pies baked completely before filling is added): Heat oven to 475°F. *For pie,* trim overhanging edge of pastry 1 inch from rim of pie plate. Fold and roll pastry under, even with plate; flute. *For tart,* trim overhanging edge of pastry even with top of tart pan. Prick bottom and side of pastry thoroughly with fork. Bake 8 to 10 minutes or until light brown; cool on wire rack.

Two-Crust Pie: Spoon desired filling into pastry-line 9-inch glass pie plate. Trim overhanging edge of bottom pastry $^1/_2$ inch from rim of plate. Roll other round of pastry. Fold top pastry into fourths and cut slits so steam can escape, or cut slits in pastry and roll pastry loosely around rolling pin.

Place pastry over filling and unfold or unroll. Trim overhanging edge of pastry 1 inch from rim of plate. Fold and roll top edge under lower edge, pressing on rim to seal; flute. Bake as directed in recipe.

Sour Cream–Raisin Pie

8 servings | Prep time: 30 minutes | Start to Finish: 3 hours 45 minutes

Using brown sugar instead of granulated sugar gives this meringue a light satiny beige color. Be decorative— use a spoon to spread and swoop the meringue up over the filling, forming soft points and swirls.

One-Crust 9-inch Baked Pie Shell (page 297)

1 cup plus 2 tablespoons sugar

1½ tablespoons cornstarch

¼ teaspoon salt

¾ teaspoon ground nutmeg

1½ cups sour cream

3 egg yolks

1½ cups raisins

1 tablespoon lemon juice

Brown Sugar Meringue (below right)

1 Prepare pastry and bake pie shell.

2 Heat oven to 400°F.

3 Mix sugar, cornstarch, salt and nutmeg in 2-quart saucepan. Stir in sour cream. Stir in egg yolks, raisins and lemon juice. Cook over medium heat, stirring constantly, until mixture thickens and boils. Boil and stir 1 minute. Pour into pie crust.

4 Make Brown Sugar Meringue. Spoon onto hot pie filling. Spread over filling, carefully sealing meringue to edge of crust to prevent shrinking or weeping.

5 Bake 8 to 10 minutes or until meringue is light brown. Cool away from draft for 2 hours. Cover and refrigerate or until serving time. Refrigerate any remaining pie after serving.

Brown Sugar Meringue

3 egg whites
¼ teaspoon cream of tartar
6 tablespoons packed brown sugar
½ teaspoon vanilla

Beat egg whites and cream of tartar in medium bowl with electric mixer on high speed until foamy. Beat in brown sugar, 1 tablespoon at a time, and continue beating until stiff and glossy. Do not underbeat. Beat in vanilla.

1 Serving: Calories 515 (Calories from Fat 190); Fat 21g (Saturated 10g); Cholesterol 115mg; Sodium 270mg; Carbohydrate 77g (Dietary Fiber 1g); Protein 6g

Classic Apple Pie

8 servings   Prep time: 25 minutes   Start to Finish: 1 hour 15 minutes

For a creamy Dutch Apple Pie, make extra-large slits in the top crust. Five minutes before the end of baking, pour ½ cup whipping cream through the slits in the crust.

Pastry for Two-Crust 9-inch Pie (page 297)

⅓ to ⅔ cup sugar

¼ cup all-purpose flour

½ teaspoon ground cinnamon

½ teaspoon ground nutmeg

Dash of salt

8 cups thinly sliced peeled tart apples (8 medium)

2 tablespoons margarine or butter

1 Heat oven to 425°F. Make pastry.

2 Mix sugar, flour, cinnamon, nutmeg and salt in large bowl. Stir in apples. Turn into pastry-lined pie plate. Dot with margarine.

3 Cover with top pastry that has slits cut in it; seal and flute. Cover edge with 3-inch strip of aluminum foil to prevent excessive browning.

4 Bake 40 to 50 minutes or until crust is brown and juice begins to bubble through slits in crust. Remove foil during last 15 minutes of baking. Cool in pie plate on wire rack. Serve warm if desired.

1 Serving: Calories 430 (Calories from Fat 215); Fat 24g (Saturated 6g); Cholesterol 0mg; Sodium 370mg; Carbohydrate 54g (Dietary Fiber 4g); Protein 4g

COUNTRY COOKING WISDOM

Frozen Favorites

When fruits are in their peak, consider making an extra pie or two and freezing them for later in the year. Follow these simple steps, and your pies will be perfect every time:

- For best results, the pie should be baked first. Then put it, uncovered, in the freezer. When it's completely frozen, wrap the pie tightly or put it in a resealable plastic freezer bag and pop it back in the freezer. Frozen baked fruit pies will keep up to 4 months.

- To serve a frozen two-crust pie, unwrap it and thaw at room temperature for 1 hour. Then heat the pie on the lowest rack in the oven at 375°F for 35 to 40 minutes or until warm.

- If you want to freeze pies unbaked, wrap and freeze the pie the same as a baked one. Don't cut slits in the top crust yet. Unbaked fruit pies will keep in the freezer up to 3 months. When you're ready to bake, unwrap and carefully cut slits in the still-frozen top crust. Do not thaw. Bake at 425°F for 15 minutes, then reduce the heat to 375°F and bake 30 to 45 minutes longer or until crust is golden brown and juice begins to bubble through the slits.

- Custard and cream pies don't freeze successfully.

Cranberry-Apple Pie

Apple-Praline Pie

8 servings   Prep time: 25 minutes   Start to Finish: 1 hour 25 minutes

This indulgent dessert combines apples and pecans between two pastry crusts covered with a luscious praline glaze.

Pastry for Two-Crust
10-inch Pie (page 297)
1 cup granulated sugar
1 cup chopped pecans
1/3 cup all-purpose flour
1 teaspoon ground cinnamon
1 teaspoon ground nutmeg
1/4 teaspoon salt
8 cups thinly sliced peeled tart apples (about 8 medium)
3 tablespoons margarine or butter
1/4 cup packed brown sugar
2 tablespoons half-and-half

1 Heat oven to 425°F. Make pastry.

2 Mix granulated sugar, 2/3 cup of the pecans, flour, cinnamon, nutmeg and salt in large bowl. Toss with apples. Turn into pastry-lined pie plate. Dot with margarine.

3 Cover with top crust that has slits cut in it; seal and flute. Cover edge with 2- to 3-inch strip of foil to prevent excessive browning. Bake 50 to 60 minutes or until crust is brown and juice begins to bubble through slits in crust. Remove foil during last 15 minutes of baking.

4 Mix brown sugar, remaining 1/3 cup pecans and the half-and-half in 1-quart saucepan. Cook over low heat, stirring constantly, until sugar is melted. Spread over hot pie.

1 Serving: Calories 712 (Calories from Fat 350); Fat 38g (Saturated 11g); Cholesterol 19mg; Sodium 419mg; Carbohydrate 86g (Dietary Fiber 5g); Protein 7g

Cranberry-Apple Pie

8 servings   Prep time: 25 minutes   Start to Finish: 1 hour 15 minutes

The beautiful color of cranberries pairs naturally with tart apples such as Granny Smith, Newtown Pippin, Crisps Pink or Jonagold.

Pastry for Two-Crust 9-inch
Pie (page 297)
1 3/4 cups sugar
1/4 cup all-purpose flour
3 cups sliced peeled tart apples (3 medium)
2 cups fresh or frozen (thawed) cranberries
2 tablespoons margarine or butter

1 Heat oven to 425°F. Make pastry.

2 Mix sugar and flour. In pastry-lined pie plate, alternate layers of apples, cranberries and sugar mixture, beginning and ending with apples. Dot with margarine.

3 Cover with top crust that has slits cut in it; seal and flute. Cover edge with 2- to 3-inch strip of aluminum foil to prevent excessive browning. Bake 40 to 50 minutes or until crust is brown. Remove foil during last 15 minutes of baking. Cool.

1 Serving: Calories 517 (Calories from Fat 185); Fat 21g (Saturated 7g); Cholesterol 13mg; Sodium 325mg; Carbohydrate 80g (Dietary Fiber 3g); Protein 4g

Green Tomato Pie

8 servings   Prep time: 25 minutes   Start to Finish: 1 hour 5 minutes

New Englanders, from colonial days up to the present, have made this pie when an early frost forced them to pick green tomatoes. If you find yourself with a large green tomato harvest, comfort yourself with a slice of this traditional pie.

Pastry for Two-Crust 9-inch Pie (page 297)

1¹/₃ cups sugar

¹/₄ cup plus 3 tablespoons all-purpose flour

1¹/₄ teaspoons ground nutmeg or ground cinnamon

1 teaspoon salt

4 cups green tomato slices

1¹/₄ teaspoons grated lemon peel

¹/₄ cup lemon juice

1 tablespoons butter or margarine

1 Heat oven to 425°F. Make pastry.

2 Mix sugar, flour, nutmeg and salt. Toss with tomatoes, lemon peel and lemon juice. Turn into pastry-lined pie plate. Dot with butter.

3 Cover with top crust; seal and flute. Cover edge with 2- to 3-inch strip of aluminum foil to prevent excessive browning.

4 Bake 35 to 40 minutes or until crust is brown and juice begins to bubble through slits in crust. Remove foil during last 15 minutes of baking. Serve warm.

1 Serving: Calories 464 (Calories from Fat 175); Fat 19g (Saturated 8g); Cholesterol 17mg; Sodium 604mg; Carbohydrate 68g (Dietary Fiber 2g); Protein 5g

Key Lime Pie

8 servings   Prep time: 25 minutes   Start to Finish: 2 hours 25 minutes

Key Lime Pie hails from the Florida Keys, which is the only place where the special yellow Key limes will grow. But you don't have to go to Florida to pick your own limes; regular lemons and limes will also make a delicious pie.

One-Crust 9-inch Baked Pie Shell (page 297)

1 can (14 oz) sweetened condensed milk

1 tablespoon grated lemon peel

¹/₂ teaspoon grated lime peel

¹/₄ cup lemon juice

¹/₄ cup lime juice

3 or 4 drops green food color

3 eggs, separated

¹/₄ teaspoon cream of tartar

1 Prepare pastry and bake pie shell.

2 Mix milk, lemon peel, lime peel, lemon juice, lime juice and food color. Beat egg yolks slightly; stir in milk mixture.

3 Beat egg whites and cream of tartar in 2¹/₂-quart bowl until stiff and glossy. Fold egg yolk mixture into egg whites.

4 Mound mixture in baked pie shell. Refrigerate until set, at least 2 hours before serving. Refrigerate any remaining pie.

1 Serving: Calories 328 (Calories from Fat 135); Fat 15g (Saturated 7g); Cholesterol 103mg; Sodium 235mg; Carbohydrate 41g (Dietary Fiber 1g); Protein 8g

Lemon Meringue Pie

8 servings | Prep time: 30 minutes | Start to Finish: 3 hours 45 minutes

Carefully measure the water and lemon juice in the filling. That way you'll get the right consistency for the pie to slice just right.

One-Crust 9-inch Baked Pie
Shell (page 297)

3 egg yolks

1½ cups sugar

⅓ cup plus 1 tablespoon
cornstarch

1½ cups water

3 tablespoon margarine or
butter

2 teaspoons grated lemon peel

½ cup lemon juice

2 drops yellow food color,
if desired

Meringue (below)

1 Prepare pastry and bake pie shell.

2 Heat oven to 400°F.

3 Beat egg yolks with fork in small bowl. Mix sugar and cornstarch in 2-quart saucepan. Gradually stir in water. Cook over medium heat, stirring constantly, until mixture thickens and boils. Boil and stir 1 minute.

4 Immediately stir at least half of the hot mixture into egg yolks; stir back into hot mixture in saucepan. Boil and stir 1 minute; remove from heat. Stir in margarine, lemon peel, lemon juice and food color. Pour into pie crust.

5 Make Meringue. Spoon onto hot pie filling. Spread over filling, carefully sealing meringue to edge of crust to prevent shrinking or weeping.

6 Bake 8 to 12 minutes or until meringue is light brown. Cool away from draft for 2 hours. Cover and refrigerate cooled pie until serving. Immediately refrigerate any remaining pie.

Meringue

3 egg whites
¼ teaspoon cream of tartar
6 tablespoons sugar
½ teaspoon vanilla

Beat egg whites and cream of tartar in medium bowl with electric mixer on high speed until foamy. Beat in sugar, 1 tablespoon at a time, and continue beating until stiff and glossy. Do not underbeat. Beat in vanilla.

1 Serving: Calories 425 (Calories from Fat 145); Fat 16g (Saturated 4g); Cholesterol 80mg; Sodium 210mg; Carbohydrate 66g (Dietary Fiber 0g); Protein 4g

Lemon Coconut Pie

8 servings   Prep time: 25 minutes   Start to Finish: 1 hour 5 minutes

Thin lemon slices are mixed into a sweet coconut filling in this rich, sweet-tart pie. Top with whipped cream for a heavenly treat.

Pastry for One-Crust 9-inch Pie (page 297)

2 large lemons

1 cup sugar

1 teaspoon salt

4 eggs

1 cup corn syrup

1 cup shredded coconut

1 cup whipped cream

Lemon peel or slices, if desired

1 Grate peel from lemons to measure 2 teaspoons. Pare lemons, removing all white membrane. Cut lemons into very thin slices. Sprinkle lemon peel, sugar and salt over lemon slices. Let stand at room temperature 2 hours.

2 Heat oven to 375°F. Prepare pastry.

3 Beat eggs and corn syrup. Stir in coconut. Pour coconut mixture over lemon slices and mix well. Pour into pastry-lined pie plate. Cover edge with 2- to 3-inch strip of aluminum foil to prevent excess browning.

4 Bake 40 to 50 minutes or until filling is set and pastry is golden brown. Remove foil during last 15 minutes of baking. Refrigerate until cold, at least 6 hours but no longer than 24 hours. Serve with whipped cream and garnish with lemon peel or slices. Refrigerate any remaining pie.

1 Serving: Calories 529 (Calories from Fat 232); Fat 26g (Saturated 14g); Cholesterol 153mg; Sodium 510mg; Carbohydrate 72g (Dietary Fiber 2g); Protein 6g

Black Bottom Pie

8 servings | Prep time: 55 minutes | Start to Finish: 3 hours 55 minutes

This triple-tiered treat of rich chocolate, smooth rum-flavored custard and whipped cream piled in a gingery crust is sure to be a hit!

Gingersnap Crust (below right)
1/2 cup granulated sugar
2 tablespoons cornstarch
1/4 teaspoon salt
2 cups milk
3 egg yolks
1 teaspoon vanilla
1 envelope unflavored gelatin
1/4 cup cold water
1 to 2 tablespoons rum or 1 teaspoon rum flavoring
3 oz semisweet chocolate, melted and cooled
3 egg whites
1/4 teaspoon cream of tartar
1/3 cup granulated sugar
1 cup whipping cream
2 tablespoons powdered sugar
Ground nutmeg, if desired

1 Make Gingersnap Crust; cool.

2 Mix 1/2 cup granulated sugar, the cornstarch and salt in 2-quart saucepan. Mix milk and egg yolks and gradually stir into sugar mixture. Cook over medium heat, stirring constantly, until mixture thickens and boils. Boil and stir 1 minute. Stir in vanilla. Remove 1 cup of the custard mixture; reserve.

3 Sprinkle gelatin on cold water to soften. Stir into custard mixture in saucepan until gelatin is dissolved. Stir in rum. Refrigerate about 10 minutes, stirring occasionally, until mixture mounds when dropped from a spoon.

4 Mix chocolate and reserved 1 cup custard mixture; pour into crust. Beat egg whites and cream of tartar in 2 1/2-quart bowl until foamy. Beat in 1/3 cup granulated sugar, 1 tablespoon at a time, and continue beating until stiff and glossy. Do not underbeat. Fold cooled custard mixture into meringue and spread over chocolate mixture. Refrigerate until set, at least 3 hours.

5 Beat whipping cream and powdered sugar in chilled 1 1/2-quart bowl until stiff. Spread over pie. Sprinkle with ground nutmeg. Immediately refrigerate any remaining pie.

Gingersnap Crust

1 1/2 cups crushed gingersnaps (24 cookies)
1/4 cup margarine or butter, melted

Heat oven to 350°F. Mix gingersnaps and margarine. Press firmly and evenly against bottom and side of ungreased pie plate, 9 inches. Bake 10 minutes.

1 Serving: Calories 460 (Calories from Fat 25); Fat 25g (Saturated 12g); Cholesterol 124mg; Sodium 338mg; Carbohydrate 52g (Dietary Fiber 1g); Protein 8g

Strawberry Glacé Pie *(bottom)* and Shaker Sugar Pie *(top)*

Strawberry Glacé Pie

8 servings | Prep time: 40 minutes | Start to Finish: 3 hours 40 minutes

When backyard gardens and farmer's markets flourish with summer fruits, look beyond strawberries for making this pie. Substitute 6 cups of raspberries or 5 cups of sliced fresh peaches for the strawberries.

Pastry for One-Crust 9-inch Baked Pie Shell (page 297)

1½ quarts strawberries

1 cup sugar

3 tablespoons cornstarch

½ cup water

1 package (3 oz) cream cheese, softened

1 Prepare pastry and bake pie shell.

2 Mash enough strawberries to measure 1 cup. Mix sugar and cornstarch in 2-quart saucepan. Gradually stir in water and mashed strawberries. Cook over medium heat, stirring constantly, until mixture thickens and boils. Boil and stir 1 minute; cool.

3 Beat cream cheese until smooth. Spread in pie shell. Fill shell with whole strawberries. Pour cooked strawberry mixture over top. Refrigerate about 3 hours or until set. Refrigerate any remaining pie.

1 Serving: Calories 315 (Calories from Fat 125); Fat 14g (Saturated 5g); Cholesterol 10mg; Sodium 180mg; Carbohydrate 47g (Dietary Fiber 3g); Protein 3g

Shaker Sugar Pie

12 servings | Prep time: 25 minutes | Start to Finish: 3 hours 20 minutes

Although this particular recipe has the Shaker touch (notice the traditional Shaker use of rose water), variations on the sugar pie theme were also enjoyed by pie lovers everywhere from Indiana to New England to the South.

Pastry for One-Crust 9-inch Pie (page 297)

1 cup packed brown sugar

½ cup butter or margarine, softened

2 tablespoons all-purpose flour

1½ cups whipping cream

1 teaspoon rose water or vanilla

1 egg

Ground nutmeg

1 Heat oven to 450°F. Make pastry.

2 Mix brown sugar, butter and flour until well blended. Spread in pastry shell.

3 Beat whipping cream, rose water and egg with hand beater until well blended. Pour over brown sugar mixture. Sprinkle with nutmeg.

4 Bake 10 minutes. Reduce oven temperature to 350°F. Bake 25 to 30 minutes longer or until knife inserted in center comes out clean. Cool 15 minutes. Refrigerate for 2 hours or until chilled. Refrigerate any remaining pie.

1 Serving: Calories 342 (Calories from Fat 223); Fat 25g (Saturated 14g); Cholesterol 83mg; Sodium 175mg; Carbohydrate 28g (Dietary Fiber 0g); Protein 2g

Strawberry-Rhubarb Pie

8 servings | Prep time: 30 minutes | Start to Finish: 2 hours 10 minutes

Heralded as the "pie plant" by early pioneers, this tart fruit was used in countless pies, sauces, jams and desserts. Early pink rhubarb provides a more mild flavor than the more mature red rhubarb. If fresh is out of season, you can use 4 cups unsweetened frozen rhubarb, thawed and drained.

Pastry for Two-Crust 9-inch Pie (page 297)

2 cups sugar

²/₃ cup all-purpose flour

1 teaspoon grated orange peel, if desired

3 cups sliced strawberries

3 cups cut-up rhubarb (½-inch pieces)

1 tablespoon margarine or butter

1 Heat oven to 425°F. Prepare pastry.

2 Mix sugar, flour and orange peel in large bowl. Stir in strawberries and rhubarb. Turn into pastry-lined pie plate. Dot with margarine. Cover with top pastry; seal and flute. Sprinkle with sugar if desired. Cover edge with 2- to 3-inch strip of aluminum foil to prevent excessive browning.

3 Bake about 55 minutes or until crust is brown and juice begins to bubble through slits in crust. Remove foil during last 15 minutes of baking. Cool in pie plate on wire rack.

1 Serving: Calories 560 (Calories from Fat 200); Fat 22g (Saturated 5g); Cholesterol 0mg; Sodium 310mg; Carbohydrate 88g (Dietary Fiber 3g); Protein 5g

Impossibly Easy Coconut Pie

6 to 8 servings | Prep time: 10 minutes | Start to Finish: 1 hour 5 minutes

To make this creamy coconut pie even more delicious, try pouring a little melted chocolate over each slice before serving.

2 cups milk

¼ cup margarine or butter, softened

4 eggs

¾ cup sugar

½ cup Original Bisquick

1½ teaspoons vanilla

1 cup flaked or shredded coconut

1 Heat oven to 350°F. Grease glass pie plate, 9 or 10 inches.

2 Stir all ingredients with fork until blended. Pour into pie plate.

3 Bake 50 to 55 minutes or until golden brown and knife inserted in center comes out clean. Refrigerate any remaining pie.

1 Serving: Calories 360 (Calories from Fat 160); Fat 18g (Saturated 8g); Cholesterol 150mg; Sodium 350mg; Carbohydrate 41g (Dietary Fiber 0g); Protein 8g

Pumpkin Pie

Be sure to use canned pumpkin and not pumpkin pie mix for this pie. The canned pumpkin is just puree, while the pie mix has spices already added to the puree. For a special garnish, cut leftover pastry into special shapes and bake separately on a cookie sheet until light golden brown. Arrange cutouts over baked filling.

Pastry for One-Crust 9-inch Pie (page 297)

2 eggs

1/2 cup sugar

1 teaspoon ground cinnamon

1/2 teaspoon salt

1/2 teaspoon ground ginger

1/8 teaspoon ground cloves

1 can (16 oz) pumpkin (not pumpkin pie mix)

1 can (12 oz) evaporated milk

Sweetened whipped cream

1 Heat oven to 425°F. Prepare pastry.

2 Beat eggs slightly in medium bowl with wire whisk or hand beater. Beat in remaining ingredients except sweetened whipped cream.

3 To prevent spilling, place pastry-lined pie plate on oven rack. Pour filling into pie plate. Bake 15 minutes.

4 Reduce oven temperature to 350°F. Bake about 45 minutes longer or until knife inserted in center comes out clean. Refrigerate about 4 hours or until chilled. Serve with sweetened whipped cream. Immediately refrigerate any remaining pie after serving.

1 Serving: Calories 295 (Calories from Fat 135); Fat 15g (Saturated 5g); Cholesterol 65mg; Sodium 330mg; Carbohydrate 34g (Dietary Fiber 1g); Protein 7g

COUNTRY COOKING WISDOM

Perfect Pastry

- A pastry blender makes easy work of cutting the shortening into the flour. If you don't have one, use two knives: With the blades almost touching, move knives back and forth in opposite directions in parallel cutting motion. The side of a fork or a wire whisk works, too.

- Don't mix too much once the water is added, or the pastry will be tough.

- Prepare pastry ahead to make rolling it easier. After shaping pastry dough into a flattened round, wrap it tightly and refrigerate for at least 15 minutes or even overnight.

- For a shiny top crust, brush the crust lightly with milk before baking.

- For a sugary top crust, moisten the crust lightly with water or milk, then sprinkle with sugar before baking.

Sweet Potato Pie

8 servings   Prep time: 25 minutes   Start to Finish: 5 hours 30 minutes

Cinnamon, ginger and cloves scent creamy sweet potatoes in this traditional Southern pie. Topped with whipped cream, it's a holiday favorite.

Pastry for One-Crust 9-inch Pie (page 297)

2 eggs

3/4 cup sugar

1 teaspoon ground cinnamon

1/2 teaspoon salt

1/2 teaspoon ground ginger

1/4 teaspoon ground cloves

1 can (23 oz) sweet potatoes, drained and mashed (1 3/4 to 2 cups)

1 can (12 oz) evaporated milk

Sweetened whipped cream, if desired

1 Heat oven to 425°F. Prepare pastry.

2 Beat eggs slightly in 2-quart bowl with hand beater. Beat in remaining ingredients except whipped cream. Place pastry-lined pie plate on oven rack and pour sweet potato mixture into plate. Cover edge with 2-inch strip of aluminum foil to prevent excessive browning.

3 Bake 15 minutes. Reduce oven temperature to 350°F. Bake 45 to 50 minutes or until knife inserted in center comes out clean. Remove foil during last 15 minutes of baking. Refrigerate at least 4 hours or until chilled. Serve with sweetened whipped cream. Immediately refrigerate any remaining pie.

1 Serving: Calories 340 (Calories from Fat 116); Fat 13g (Saturated 6g); Cholesterol 73mg; Sodium 536mg; Carbohydrate 48g (Dietary Fiber 2g); Protein 7g

Praline Sweet Potato Pie: Decrease second baking time to 35 minutes. Mix 1/3 cup packed brown sugar, 1/3 cup chopped pecans and 1 tablespoon margarine or butter, softened; sprinkle over pie. Bake about 10 minutes longer or until knife inserted in center comes out clean.

Pumpkin Pie: Substitute 1 can (16 oz) pumpkin (not pumpkin pie mix) for the sweet potatoes.

Kentucky Pecan Pie

8 servings   Prep time: 25 minutes   Start to Finish: 3 hours 15 minutes

Bourbon, a Kentucky favorite, and chocolate chips add richness to this pecan pie. When serving to children, just eliminate the bourbon and add peanut butter chips along with the chocolate ones. A sure crowd-pleaser either way.

Pastry for One-Crust 9-inch Pie (page 297)

²/₃ cup sugar

¹/₃ cup margarine or butter, melted

1 cup corn syrup

2 tablespoons bourbon, if desired

¹/₂ teaspoon salt

3 eggs

1 cup pecan halves or broken pecans

1 cup semisweet chocolate chips

1 Heat oven to 375°F. Prepare pastry.

2 Beat sugar, margarine, corn syrup, bourbon (if desired), salt and eggs with hand beater. Stir in pecans and chocolate chips. Pour into pastry-lined pie plate. Cover edge with 2- to 3-inch strip of foil to prevent excessive browning.

3 Bake 40 to 50 minutes or until set. Remove foil during last 15 minutes of baking. Refrigerate at least 2 hours or until chilled. Immediately refrigerate any remaining pie.

Chocolate Pecan Pie: Omit bourbon and chocolate chips. Melt 2 oz unsweetened chocolate with the margarine.

Pecan Pie: Omit bourbon and chocolate chips.

1 Serving: Calories 309 (Calories from Fat 34); Fat 34g (Saturated 10g); Cholesterol 86mg; Sodium 434mg; Carbohydrate 73g (Dietary Fiber 3g); Protein 6g

Honey Walnut Pie

8 servings   Prep time: 25 minutes   Start to Finish: 3 hours 25 minutes

A sweet syrup flavored with vanilla and honey surrounds flavorful walnuts in this delicious take on pecan pie.

Pastry for One-Crust 9-inch Pie (page 297)

¹/₂ cup packed brown sugar

¹/₂ cup corn syrup

¹/₂ cup honey

1 tablespoon all-purpose flour

1 tablespoon margarine or butter, melted

1 teaspoon vanilla

¹/₄ teaspoon salt

2 eggs

1¹/₂ cups walnut pieces

1 Heat oven to 350°F. Prepare pastry.

2 Beat brown sugar, corn syrup, honey, flour, margarine, vanilla, salt and eggs with hand beater. Stir in walnuts. Pour into pastry-lined pie plate. Cover edge with 2-inch strip of foil to prevent excessive browning .

3 Bake 45 to 55 minutes or until set. Remove foil during last 15 minutes of baking. Refrigerate at least 2 hours or until chilled. Immediately refrigerate any remaining pie.

1 Serving: Calories 443 (Calories from Fat 236); Fat 26g (Saturated 5g); Cholesterol 60mg; Sodium 267mg; Carbohydrate 39g (Dietary Fiber 2g); Protein 7g

Fried Jam Pie

12 servings | Prep time: 35 minutes | Start to Finish: 35 minutes

These delicious, handhelp pastries were a popular way to keep children quiet during long church services.

Pastry for Two-Crust 9-inch Pie (page 297)

3/4 cup jam, jelly or preserves

3/4 cup shortening

Powdered sugar

1 Make pastry through step 2. Divide evenly into 12 pieces. Roll each piece into ball. Flatten slightly (do not overwork pastry), then roll each ball into 4-1/2-inch circle on lightly floured cloth-covered surface with floured cloth-covered rolling pin.

2 Place 1 tablespoon jam on half of each circle. Moisten edge of pastry and fold pastry over jam. Seal edges with fork.

3 Heat shortening in 10-inch skillet over medium heat until melted. Fry pies about 2 minutes on each side or until golden brown. Drain on paper towels; cool slightly. Sprinkle with powdered sugar.

1 Serving: Calories 436 (Calories from Fat 214); Fat 24g (Saturated 9g); Cholesterol 9mg; Sodium 202mg; Carbohydrate 30g (Dietary Fiber 1g); Protein 2g

Streusel Peach Tarts

8 servings | Prep time: 30 minutes | Start to Finish: 1 hour

These tarts are a lovely way to feature fresh peaches. But sprinkled with a spiced streusel topping, they're just as good with canned peaches.

Pastry for Two-Crust 9-inch Pie (page 297)

1/2 teaspoon ground nutmeg

1/2 cup sugar

2 tablespoons all-purpose flour

2 tablespoons margarine or butter

1/4 teaspoon ground cinnamon

1/8 teaspoon ground nutmeg

4 fresh peaches, peeled, pitted and halved*

Whipping cream, if desired

1 Heat oven to 350°F. Prepare pastry as directed—except stir in 1/2 teaspoon nutmeg with the flour. Roll pastry into 15-inch circle. Cut into eight 4½-inch circles. Fit circles into individual tart pans or 6-oz custard cups, making pleats so pastry will fit closely; do not prick.

2 Mix sugar, flour, margarine, cinnamon and 1/8 teaspoon nutmeg until crumbly. Sprinkle half of the crumbly mixture in tart shells. Place 1 peach half, rounded side up, in each tart shell. Sprinkle remaining crumbly mixture over peaches.

3 Bake 25 to 30 minutes or until light brown. Serve warm with whipping cream.

8 canned peach halves, drained, can be substituted for the fresh peach halves.

1 Serving: Calories 375 (Calories from Fat 128); Fat 21g (Saturated 7g); Cholesterol 73mg; Sodium 325mg; Carbohydrate 43g (Dietary Fiber 2g); Protein 4g

Banana Cream Tart

8 servings | Prep time: 45 minutes | Start to Finish: 3 hours 45 minutes

If you are going to garnish with extra banana slices, dip them in lemon juice and put them on the tart just before serving, to keep them looking fresh.

1/2 cup granulated sugar

3 tablespoons cornstarch

1/4 teaspoon salt

2 1/4 cups milk

3 egg yolks

1 tablespoon margarine or butter, softened

1 teaspoon vanilla

Pastry for One-Crust 9-inch Pie (page 297)

2 bananas

1/2 cup whipping cream

1 tablespoon powdered sugar

Banana slices, if desired

1 Mix granulated sugar, cornstarch and salt in 1½-quart saucepan. Gradually stir in milk. Cook over medium heat, stirring constantly, until mixture thickens and boils. Boil and stir 1 minute.

2 Beat egg yolks until well blended. Stir at least half of the hot mixture gradually into egg yolks, then stir into hot mixture in saucepan. Boil and stir 1 minute; remove from heat. Stir in margarine and vanilla. Press plastic wrap onto filling in saucepan. Refrigerate 1 hour.

3 Heat oven to 475°F. Prepare pastry as directed—except roll into 11-inch circle. Fold pastry into fourths; unfold and ease into tart pan, 9 inches, pressing firmly against bottom and side. Trim any excess pastry by pressing against edge of pan. Prick bottom and side thoroughly with fork. Bake 10 to 12 minutes or until light brown; cool.

4 Spread ½ cup of the filling in tart shell. Slice bananas over filling. Spread remaining filling over bananas. Beat whipping cream and powdered sugar in chilled small bowl with electric mixer until stiff; spread over filling. Refrigerate at least 2 hours but no longer than 48 hours. Garnish with additional banana slices. Refrigerate any remaining tart.

1 Serving: Calories 353 (Calories from Fat 177); Fat 20g (Saturated 9g); Cholesterol 111mg; Sodium 272mg; Carbohydrate 39g (Dietary Fiber 1g); Protein 5g

Chocolate Hazelnut Tart

12 servings **Prep time: 20 minutes** **Start to Finish: 90 minutes**

The abundance of hazelnuts—or "filberts," as they are also called—led to their frequent use in old-time recipes. They are still quite popular. If you can't find them in your usual grocery store, try a gourmet shop.

Pastry for One-Crust 9-inch Pie (page 297)
1/3 cup margarine or butter
2 oz unsweetened chocolate
3 eggs
2/3 cup sugar
1/2 teaspoon salt
1 cup corn syrup
1 cup hazelnuts (filberts), skinned and coarsely chopped
Sweetened whipped cream, if desired

1 Move oven rack to lowest position. Heat oven to 475°F.

2 Make pastry as directed—except roll into 12-inch circle. Fold pastry into fourths; unfold and ease into springform pan, 9 × 3 inches, pressing firmly against bottom and side. Prick bottom and side thoroughly with fork. Bake 5 minutes; cool.

3 Reduce oven temperature to 350°F. Heat margarine and chocolate over low heat, stirring constantly, until chocolate is melted; cool slightly. Beat eggs, sugar, salt, corn syrup and chocolate mixture in medium bowl using hand beater. Stir in hazelnuts. Pour into pastry-lined pan.

4 Bake 65 to 70 minutes or until set; cool 10 minutes. Loosen tart from side of pan; remove side of pan. Serve with sweetened whipped cream. Refrigerate any remaining tart.

1 Serving: Calories 343 (Calories from Fat 184); Fat 21g (Saturated 6g); Cholesterol 57mg; Sodium 289mg; Carbohydrate 40g (Dietary Fiber 2g); Protein 5g

COUNTRY COOKING WISDOM

How to Skin a Hazelnut

Be sure to skin hazelnuts—their brown skin is quite bitter. To skin hazelnuts, heat the oven to 275°F. Spread hazelnuts in a single layer in ungreased shallow pan. Bake 20 to 25 minutes, shaking pan occasionally, until skins crack. Immediately wrap nuts in a kitchen towel and let steam for about 10 minutes. Rub nuts in the towel until the skins flake off.

Burnt Sugar-Almond Tarts

These individual tarts are bursting with a sweet caramelized filling and studded with almonds. They're delicious warm from the oven but just as tasty chilled the next day.

1½ cups sugar

½ cup boiling water

3 tablespoons margarine or butter

⅔ cup whipping cream

  Pastry for One-Crust 9-inch Pie (page 297)

⅔ cup slivered almonds, toasted

½ teaspoon vanilla

2 eggs

1 Heat 1 cup of the sugar in 10-inch heavy skillet over medium-low heat until sugar begins to melt. Continue cooking, stirring occasionally, until completely melted and medium brown; remove from heat.

2 Slowly stir in boiling water, mixing thoroughly. (If any lumps remain, return to heat until melted.) Cool 5 minutes; stir in margarine. Stir in whipping cream until well blended; cool.

3 Move oven rack to lowest position. Heat oven to 350°F. Prepare pastry as directed—except roll into 15-inch circle. Cut into eight 4½-inch circles. Reroll pastry scraps and cut into 4½-inch circle. Fit circles into individual tart pans or 6-oz custard cups, making pleats so pastry will fit closely; do not prick. Sprinkle almonds in tart shells.

4 Beat remaining ½ cup sugar, the vanilla, eggs and whipping cream mixture. Pour about ¼ cup mixture into each tart shell.

5 Bake 28 to 33 minutes or until set. Cool 15 minutes; remove from pans. Serve warm or chilled.

1 Serving: Calories 409 (Calories from Fat 209); Fat 23g (Saturated 8g); Cholesterol 77mg; Sodium 197mg; Carbohydrate 46g (Dietary Fiber 1g); Protein 5g

Chess Tart

8 servings | Prep time: 25 minutes | Start to Finish: 3 hours 40 minutes

Chess tarts owe their name to the fact that at one time the filling included cheese. The name chess (derived from "cheese") endures, although the cheese has been replaced by a lemon-flavored mixture.

Pastry for One-Crust 9-inch Pie (page 297)

4 eggs

1½ cups sugar

½ cup margarine or butter, softened

2 tablespoons yellow cornmeal

2 tablespoons half-and-half

2 tablespoons lemon juice

2 teaspoons vanilla

Dash of salt

1 Heat oven to 325°F. Prepare pastry.

2 Beat eggs, sugar and margarine in medium bowl with electric mixer on high speed, 3 minutes. Beat in remaining ingredients (mixture will look curdled).

3 Pour into pastry-lined pie plate. Bake about 1 hour or until set. Cool 15 minutes. Refrigerate for 2 hours or until chilled. Refrigerate any remaining tart.

1 Serving: Calories 438 (Calories from Fat 207); Fat 23g (Saturated 7g); Cholesterol 114mg; Sodium 334mg; Carbohydrate 52g (Dietary Fiber 1g); Protein 5g

Lemon Curd Tart

12 servings | Prep time: 40 minutes | Start to Finish: 2 hours 40 minutes

Fruit curds—a creamy mixture of juice, sugar and eggs—are often spread on scones and muffins. Here this thick, flavorful curd sits in a tender pastry crust as a lovely dessert offering.

Pastry for One-Crust 9-inch Pie (page 297)

3 eggs

1 cup sugar

¾ cup margarine or butter, softened

½ cup lemon juice

1 tablespoon grated lemon peel

Sweetened whipped cream, if desired

Fresh fruit, if desired

1 Heat oven to 475°F. Prepare pastry as directed—except roll into 11-inch circle. Fold pastry into fourths; unfold and ease into tart pan, 9 inches, pressing firmly against bottom and side. Trim any excess pastry by pressing against edge of pan. Prick bottom and side thoroughly with fork. Bake 8 to 10 minutes or until light brown; cool.

2 Beat eggs in 1½-quart saucepan until fluffy. Mix in remaining ingredients. Cook over medium-low heat 8 to 10 minutes, stirring constantly, until mixture is thick enough to coat a metal spoon; cool slightly. Pour into tart shell.

3 Cover and refrigerate at least 2 hours but no longer than 48 hours. Serve with sweetened whipped cream and fresh fruit. Refrigerate any remaining tart.

1 Serving: Calories 278 (Calories from Fat 165); Fat 18g (Saturated 5g); Cholesterol 57mg; Sodium 248mg; Carbohydrate 26g (Dietary Fiber 0g); Protein 3g

CHAPTER EIGHT

Icebox Creations

EVEN THOUGH WE USE REFRIGERATORS NOW, OUR GRANDPARENTS REMEMBER THE DAYS WHEN FOODS WERE KEPT COLD IN THE ICEBOX.

The iceman would deliver large blocks of ice that slowly melted into the drip pan, cooling the air in the icebox. There's something thrilling about a cold dessert, whether it's a gorgeous molded dessert, a wonderfully easy trifle or a rich, creamy ice cream. Perhaps our excitement stems from the anticipation—waiting for those fabulous desserts to come to the icebox.

Chocolate Chiffon Icebox Cake

8 servings | Prep Time: 60 minutes | Start to Finish: 6 hours

This airy chocolate, chiffon cake surrounds a creamy and rich filling seasoned with sweet chocolate and whipped cream.

3 tablespoons hot water

1 4-oz bar sweet baking chocolate

1 envelope unflavored gelatin

3 tablespoons cold water

1 cup milk, scalded

½ cup powdered sugar

1 teaspoon vanilla

½ Burnt Sugar-Chiffon Cake (page 269)

1½ cups whipping cream

Shaved chocolate, if desired

1 Heat hot water and chocolate over low heat, stirring constantly, until chocolate is melted. Cool to room temperature.

2 Sprinkle gelatin on cold water in medium bowl to soften. Stir in hot milk, powdered sugar and vanilla. Stir until gelatin is completely dissolved. Refrigerate about 45 minutes, stirring occasionally, until mixture is partially set.

3 Cut Burnt Sugar-Chiffon Cake into ½-inch slices; cut slices into 1-inch strips. Place strips on bottom and sides of loaf pan, 9 × 5 inches. Beat whipping cream in chilled medium bowl until stiff. Fold in chocolate mixture with wire whisk. Fold in gelatin mixture. Pour into cake-lined pan.

4 Cover and refrigerate about 5 hours or until firm. Unmold onto serving plate. Slice and garnish with whipped cream and shaved chocolate. Refrigerate any remaining dessert.

1 Serving: Calories 748 (Calories from Fat 334); Fat 38g (Saturated 17g); Cholesterol 159mg; Sodium 329mg; Carbohydrate 99g (Dietary Fiber 2g); Protein 8g

Dessert Wine Jelly

12 servings | Prep Time: 20 minutes | Start to Finish: 4 hours 20 minutes

Wine jelly has been an American favorite since the nineteenth century, when a gelatin dessert was referred to as a jelly.

4 envelopes unflavored gelatin

2 cups cold water

3 cups white or red grape juice

1 cup sugar

1 cup medium dry white wine

Sweetened whipped cream

1 Sprinkle gelatin on cold water in medium bowl to soften.

2 Heat grape juice to boiling. Stir grape juice and sugar into gelatin mixture until gelatin is dissolved. Stir in wine.

3 Pour into 6-cup mold. Refrigerate about 4 hours or until firm. Unmold onto serving plate. Serve with whipped cream.

1 Serving: Calories 130 (Calories from Fat 0); Fat 0g (Saturated 0g); Cholesterol 0mg; Sodium 10mg; Carbohydrate 27g (Dietary Fiber 0g); Protein 2g

Chocolate Chiffon Icebox Cake

Strawberry Crown

12 servings | Prep Time: 35 minutes | Start to Finish: 4 hours 15 minutes

Layers of strawberries and cream are nestled between layers of crunchy pecan mixture in this spectacular treat.

½ cup all-purpose flour

¼ cup chopped pecans or walnuts

¼ cup margarine or butter, softened

2 tablespoons packed brown sugar

1 envelope unflavored gelatin

½ cup cold water

1 quart strawberries, cut lengthwise into fourths

¾ cup granulated sugar

1 teaspoon lemon juice

Few drops red food color

1 cup whipping cream

1 Heat oven to 400°F.

2 Mix flour, pecans, butter and brown sugar until crumbly. Spread in ungreased square pan, 9 × 9 inches. Bake 12 to 15 minutes or until golden brown. Stir to break up.

3 Sprinkle gelatin on cold water to soften. Mash 1 cup of the strawberries in 1½-quart saucepan. Stir in granulated sugar and lemon juice. Heat to boiling over medium heat, stirring occasionally; remove from heat. Stir in gelatin until dissolved. Stir in food color.

4 Pour ¼ cup of the gelatin mixture into 7-cup mold. Arrange a few strawberry fourths, cut sides up, on gelatin mixture. Refrigerate until firm. Refrigerate remaining gelatin mixture about 40 minutes, stirring occasionally, until slightly thickened.

5 Beat whipping cream in chilled medium bowl until stiff. Fold in remaining strawberries and slightly thickened gelatin mixture.

6 Alternate layers of whipped cream mixture and crumb mixture in mold, beginning with whipped cream mixture and ending with crumbs. Refrigerate about 3 hours or until firm. Unmold onto serving plate. Refrigerate any remaining dessert.

1 Serving: Calories 214 (Calories from Fat 118); Fat 13g (Saturated 6g); Cholesterol 27mg; Sodium 55mg; Carbohydrate 24g (Dietary Fiber 1g); Protein 2g

COUNTRY COOKING WISDOM

Unmolding Gelatins

To remove a jelly or gelatin from its mold, run a knife dipped in warm water around the edge of the gelatin. Place the mold in warm water just to the rim of the mold, for about 15 seconds. Remove the mold from the water and place a serving plate on top of the mold. Invert the plate and mold and gently shake to loosen the gelatin. Remove the mold. If the gelatin does not release, repeat method.

Cranberry Refrigerator Dessert

8 servings | Prep Time: 25 minutes | Start to Finish: 5 hours 25 minutes

Tart cranberries scented with orange are layered with sweet cream and crushed saltine crackers. The flavors meld together, forming a delectable dessert.

1 cup sugar

¾ cup water

1 bag (12 oz) frozen cranberries (3½ cups)

1 teaspoon grated orange peel

2 cups whipping cream

¼ cup powdered sugar

1 cup finely crushed saltine crackers (29 squares)

¼ cup chopped nuts

1 Heat granulated sugar and the water to boiling, stirring occasionally. Stir in cranberries and heat to boiling; reduce heat. Cook over low heat about 10 minutes or until cranberries pop; remove from heat. Stir in orange peel. Cool about 1 hour or until room temperature.

2 Beat whipping cream and powdered sugar in chilled bowl until soft peaks form.

3 Spread ½ cup cracker crumbs in clear glass 8-cup bowl. Spoon about 1⅓ cups whipped cream mixture in small dollops over crumbs; spread carefully. Spoon ¾ cup cranberry mixture over whipped cream. Repeat twice. Sprinkle with nuts.

4 Cover and refrigerate 4 hours or until set. Serve with additional whipped cream, if desired.

1 Serving: Calories 407 (Calories from Fat 232); Fat 26g (Saturated 14g); Cholesterol 82mg; Sodium 141mg; Carbohydrate 44g (Dietary Fiber 3g); Protein 3g

COUNTRY COOKING WISDOM

Cooking Cranberries

When cooking cranberries, most recipes call for cooking them until they "pop." This doesn't mean you'll hear noises coming from the pan; it means the outer skin will burst as the berry expands. Fresh cranberry season is so short—late October to December—that you'll want to be sure to buy extra and freeze for use throughout the year.

Boysenberry-Apple Crumb Dessert

9 servings | Prep Time: 20 minutes | Start to Finish: 8 hours 20 minutes

Luscious fruit fills this cookies 'n cream dessert. If boysenberries aren't plentiful in your area, substitute blackberries or raspberries.

1½ cups crushed vanilla wafer cookies (about 40 cookies)

¼ cup margarine or butter, melted

½ cup margarine or butter, softened

1 cup powdered sugar

1 cup fresh boysenberries*

1 medium unpeeled eating apple, chopped

1 can (8 oz) crushed pineapple, well drained

¾ cup whipping cream

1 tablespoon powdered sugar

1 Mix wafer crumbs and melted margarine; reserve ½ cup. Press remaining crumb mixture firmly in ungreased square pan, 8 × 8 or 9 × 9 inches.

2 Beat softened margarine with electric mixer on medium speed until light and fluffy. Beat in 1 cup powdered sugar on low speed. Spread evenly over crumb mixture.

3 Mix boysenberries, apple and pineapple. Spoon evenly over butter mixture and press lightly into butter mixture.

4 Beat whipping cream and 1 tablespoon powdered sugar in chilled small bowl until stiff. Spread over fruit mixture.

5 Sprinkle reserved crumbs over top. Cover and refrigerate at least 8 hours. Refrigerate any remaining dessert.

*1 cup frozen boysenberries, thawed and drained, can be substituted for the fresh boysenberries.

1 **Serving:** Calories 400 (Calories from Fat 232); Fat 26g (Saturated 9g); Cholesterol 32mg; Sodium 301mg; Carbohydrate 41g (Dietary Fiber 1g); Protein 3g

Coconut Icebox Dessert

6 servings | Prep Time: 20 minutes | Start to Finish: 3 hours 20 minutes

You feel like you're in the Caribbean after just one bite! Toasted coconut and walnuts flavor vanilla pudding and whipped cream in this unforgettable elegant dessert.

¹/₃ cup sugar

2 tablespoons cornstarch

¹/₈ teaspoon salt

2 cups milk

2 egg yolks, slightly beaten

2 tablespoons margarine or butter, softened

1 teaspoon vanilla

1 cup whipping (heavy) cream

2 cups coarsely chopped vanilla wafer cookies

¹/₂ cup chopped walnuts

³/₄ cup toasted coconut

Candied cherries, if desired

1 Mix sugar, cornstarch and salt in 2-quart saucepan. Gradually stir in milk. Cook over medium heat, stirring constantly, until mixture thickens and boils. Boil and stir 1 minute.

2 Stir at least half of the hot mixture gradually into egg yolks; stir back into hot mixture in saucepan. Boil and stir 1 minute; remove from heat. Stir in margarine and vanilla. Pour into large bowl. Place waxed paper or plastic wrap directly on surface. Refrigerate about 1 hour or until cool.

3 Stir pudding slightly, if necessary, to soften. Beat whipping cream in chilled bowl until stiff. Fold whipped cream, vanilla wafers, walnuts and ½ cup of the coconut into pudding.

4 Spoon into 6-cup bowl. Sprinkle with remaining coconut and candied cherries. Cover and refrigerate 2 hours or until set. Serve with additional whipped cream, if desired.

1 Serving: Calories 320 (Calories from Fat 320); Fat 36g (Saturated 16g); Cholesterol 135mg; Sodium 282mg; Carbohydrate 44g (Dietary Fiber 1g); Protein 8g

COUNTRY COOKING WISDOM

Whip It right!

You'll get the best volume and flavor when whipping cream by following these simple techniques.

- Cold cream will whip the best. Chill your bowl and beaters if time permits, and keep the cream refrigerated until ready to use.

- When the cream begins to thicken as you beat it, reduce the mixer speed so you can watch carefully and beat just until soft peaks form. Overbeaten cream will look curdled.

- Cream will double when whipped, so for 1 cup whipped cream, start with ½ cup whipping cream.

- For sweetened cream, add 1 tablespoon sugar per ½ cup cream.

Peppermint Angel Food Dessert

9 servings   Prep Time: 35 minutes   Start to Finish: 2 hours 35 minutes

This recipe is perfect if you have leftover Angel Food Cake (page 277). You can also use a cake made from a packaged mix or a store-bought cake, with delicious results!

¼ cup sugar

¼ cup crushed peppermint candies

1 tablespoon cornstarch

Dash of salt

1 cup milk

1 egg yolk, slightly beaten

4 or 5 drops red food color

1 cup whipping cream

½ angel food cake

Crushed peppermint candy, if desired

1 Mix sugar, candies, cornstarch and salt in 1½-quart saucepan. Gradually stir in milk. Cook over medium heat, stirring constantly, until mixture thickens and boils. Boil and stir 1 minute.

2 Stir at least half of the hot mixture gradually into egg yolk; stir back into hot mixture in saucepan. Boil and stir 1 minute; remove from heat. Stir in food color. Refrigerate about 15 minutes, stirring occasionally, until mixture mounds slightly when dropped from a spoon.

3 Beat whipping cream in chilled large bowl until stiff. Fold peppermint mixture into whipped cream. Tear enough angel food cake into about 1½-inch pieces to measure 6 cups. Fold into peppermint mixture.

4 Spoon into ungreased square baking dish, 8 × 8 inches. Cover and refrigerate at least 2 hours or until set. Cut into squares. Serve with additional whipped cream and crushed peppermint candy.

1 Serving: Calories 240 (Calories from Fat 100); Fat 11g (Saturated 7g); Cholesterol 62mg; Sodium 286mg; Carbohydrate 32g (Dietary Fiber 0g); Protein 4g

COUNTRY COOKING WISDOM

Flavor Change

This recipe could easily become a butterscotch dessert by simply changing the candies to butterscotch ones and the food coloring to yellow. Another tasty variation would be watermelon candies with a drop of red food coloring. Any hard candy will do, so try your favorites!

Orange Mallow

6 servings | Prep Time: 15 minutes | Start to Finish: 2 hours 30 minutes

A treat for the kid in everyone, this delicious dessert is a take on the classic orange and cream ice cream bar. It's a breeze to prepare, as marshmallows are the base of the dish.

22 large marshmallows or 2 cups miniature marshmallows

1 teaspoon grated orange peel

²/₃ cup orange juice

1 cup whipping cream

1 Heat marshmallows, orange peel and orange juice over medium heat, stirring constantly, until marshmallows are melted. Cool about 15 minutes, or until thickened.

2 Beat whipping cream in chilled medium bowl until stiff. Stir marshmallow mixture to blend, then fold into whipped cream.

3 Divide among 6 dessert dishes. Refrigerate about 2 hours or until set. Refrigerate any remaining dessert.

1 Serving: Calories 234 (Calories from Fat 133); Fat 15g (Saturated 9g); Cholesterol 54mg; Sodium 36mg; Carbohydrate 26g (Dietary Fiber 0g); Protein 1g

Ginger-Cream Parfaits

4 parfaits | Prep Time: 10 minutes | Start to Finish: 5 hours 10 minutes

So simple yet so scrumptious! Crushed gingersnap cookies are folded into whipped cream, then chilled for hours so the flavors will meld. Yum!

1½ cups whipping cream

2 tablespoons powdered sugar

1 cup gingersnap cookie crumbs (16 cookies)

1 Beat whipping cream and powdered sugar in chilled medium bowl until stiff.

2 Layer crumbs and whipped cream in 4 parfait glasses, beginning with crumbs and ending with whipped cream. (Make about 4 layers of each.) Refrigerate at least 5 hours but no longer than 24 hours.

1 Serving: Calories 430 (Calories from Fat 322); Fat 36g (Saturated 21g); Cholesterol 122mg; Sodium 217mg; Carbohydrate 28g (Dietary Fiber 1g); Protein 3g

Raspberry Trifle

10 servings | Prep Time: 30 minutes | Start to Finish: 3 hours 30 minutes

The English did themselves proud by coming up with the trifle—a combination of ladyfingers or cake, fruit and custard.

1/2 cup sugar

3 tablespoons cornstarch

1/4 teaspoon salt

3 cups milk

1/2 cup dry sherry, dry white wine or apple juice

3 egg yolks, beaten

3 tablespoons margarine or butter, softened*

1 tablespoon vanilla

2 packages (3 oz each) ladyfingers

1/2 cup red raspberry preserves

1/2 cup slivered almonds

1 1/2 cups fresh raspberries** (reserve 10 raspberries for garnish)

1 cup whipping cream

2 tablespoons sugar

2 tablespoons slivered almonds

1 Mix 1/2 cup sugar, the cornstarch and salt in 3-quart saucepan. Gradually stir in milk and sherry. Heat to boiling over medium heat, stirring constantly. Boil and stir 1 minute.

2 Gradually stir at least half of the hot mixture into egg yolks; stir back into hot mixture in saucepan. Boil and stir 1 minute; remove from heat. Stir in margarine and vanilla. Cover and refrigerate pudding at least 3 hours.

3 Split ladyfingers lengthwise in half. Spread each half with raspberry preserves.

4 In 2-quart serving bowl, layer one-fourth of the ladyfingers, cut sides up, 1/4 cup of the almonds, half of the raspberries and half of the pudding; repeat. Arrange remaining ladyfingers around edge of bowl in upright position with cut sides toward center. (It may be necessary to gently ease ladyfingers down into pudding about 1 inch so that they remain upright.) Cover and refrigerate 30 minutes.

5 Beat whipping cream and 2 tablespoons sugar in chilled bowl until stiff; spread over dessert. Garnish with 2 tablespoons almonds and reserved raspberries.

*Do not use spread in this recipe.

**1 package (12 oz) frozen red raspberries, partially thawed, can be substituted for the 1 1/2 cups fresh raspberries.

1 Serving: Calories 394 (Calories from Fat 184); Fat 20g (Saturated 8g); Cholesterol 138mg; Sodium 262mg; Carbohydrate 45g (Dietary Fiber 2g); Protein 7g

COUNTRY COOKING WISDOM

Traditional Trifles

This British dessert is often served at Christmastime. Its presentation—traditionally made in a deep glass bowl so that you can see all the layers—is as important as its flavor. Garnish your trifle with fresh raspberries, almonds and even a mint sprig for a lovely holiday offering.

Chocolate Pudding Parfaits

6 servings   Prep Time: 25 minutes   Start to Finish: 3 hours 25 minutes

If you're rushed for time, prepare instant chocolate pudding and begin the recipe at step 2.

Chocolate Pudding (below right)

I cup whipping cream

I tablespoon powdered sugar

I cup flaked or shredded coconut, toasted (see Country Cooking Wisdom, page 288)

I to 1½ cups sliced fresh fruit

1 Make Chocolate Pudding—except do not pour into dessert dishes. Place waxed paper or plastic wrap directly on surface of pudding. Refrigerate until chilled.

2 Beat whipping cream and powdered sugar in chilled small bowl until stiff.

3 Alternate layers of pudding, coconut, fruit and whipped cream in 6 parfait glasses. (Make 2 layers of each.) Refrigerate until chilled.

I **Serving:** Calories 407 (Calories from Fat 245); Fat 27g (Saturated 17g); Cholesterol 141mg; Sodium 159mg; Carbohydrate 36g (Dietary Fiber 3g); Protein 6g

Chocolate Pudding

½ cup sugar	2 cups milk
⅓ cup cocoa	2 egg yolks, slightly beaten
2 tablespoons cornstarch	2 tablespoons butter or margarine
⅛ teaspoon salt	2 tablespoons vanilla

Mix sugar, cocoa, cornstarch and salt in 2-quart saucepan. Gradually sitr in milk. Cook over medium heat, stirring constantly, until mixture thickens and boils. Boil and stir 1 minute. Gradually stir at least half of the hot mixture into egg yolks; stir back into hot mixture in saucepan. Heat to boiling, stirring constantly. Boil and stir 1 minute; remove from heat. Stir in butter and vanilla. Pour into dessert dishes. Serve warm, or cover and refrigerate about 2 hours or until chilled. Refrigerate any remaining pudding.

COUNTRY COOKING WISDOM

Perfect Puddings

Custards and puddings use eggs to thicken and add richness. Tempering the eggs will prevent them from becoming scrambled when the hot pudding mixture is added to them. To temper, place the eggs in a bowl and beat well. Remove a small amount of the hot mixture from the pot and gradually add to the eggs while stirring constantly. Then stir the tempered egg mixture back into the pot, again stirring constantly. Voila! You'll have a rich, creamy sauce every time.

Icy Coffee Cream

8 servings | Prep Time: 25 minutes | Start to Finish: 8 hours 25 minutes

Refrigerating this mixture of vanilla, brown sugar and rich coffee allows the flavors to beautifully mingle. I'll remind you of ice cream!

1 envelope unflavored gelatin

¼ cup cold water

1½ cups strong coffee

¼ cup packed brown sugar

1½ cups whipping cream

¼ cup powdered sugar

½ teaspoon vanilla

1 Sprinkle gelatin on cold water in 1½-quart saucepan to soften. Stir in coffee and brown sugar. Heat over low heat, stirring constantly, until gelatin is dissolved. Place saucepan in bowl of ice and water about 10 minutes, or refrigerate about 30 minutes, stirring occasionally, just until mixture mounds slightly when dropped from spoon.

2 Beat whipping cream, powdered sugar and vanilla in chilled medium bowl until stiff. Fold coffee mixture into whipped cream.

3 Pour into square pan, 8 × 8 inches. Cover and freeze at least 8 hours or until firm. Let stand 10 minutes before serving.

1 Serving: Calories 199 (Calories from Fat 149); Fat 17g (Saturated 17g); Cholesterol 10mg; Sodium 22mg; Carbohydrate 12g (Dietary Fiber 0g); Protein 2g

Layered Fruit Dessert

6 servings | Prep Time: 40 minutes | Start to Finish: 4 hours 40 minutes

This simple dessert is especially pretty serving with whipped cream and garnished with lightly toasted sliced or slivered almonds.

Creamy Stirred Custard (page 335)

3 cups 1-inch cake pieces

2 cups cut-up fresh fruit

Prepare creamy stirred custard. Layer cake and fruit in 6 dessert dishes. Top with custard. Cover and refrigerate about 2 hours or until chilled.

1 Serving: Calories 234 (Calories from Fat 54); Fat 6g (Saturated 3g); Cholesterol 116mg; Sodium 285g; Carbohydrate 37g (Dietary Fiber 1g); Protein 9g

Cherry-Berries on a Cloud

10 to 12 servings | Prep Time: 25 minutes | Start to Finish: 9 hours

Lots of requests come in for this recipe, and it's no secret why! The juicy cherries and fresh fruit sit on a cloud of marshmallow and whipped cream, making this dessert irresistibly good.

Pastry Crust (below right)

1 package (8 oz) cream cheese, softened

3/4 cup sugar

1 teaspoon vanilla

2 cups whipping cream

2 1/2 cups miniature marshmallows

1 can (21 oz) cherry pie filling

1 teaspoon lemon juice

1 pint (2 cups) strawberries, sliced, or 1 bag (16 oz) frozen strawberries, thawed

1 cup fresh or frozen (thawed) sliced peaches

1 Prepare and bake Pastry Crust.

2 Beat cream cheese, sugar and vanilla in large bowl with electric mixer on medium speed until smooth.

3 Beat whipping cream in chilled medium bowl with electric mixer on high speed until stiff. Fold whipped cream and marshmallows into cream cheese mixture; spread over crust.

4 Cover and refrigerate at least 8 hours but no longer than 48 hours.

5 Mix pie filling, lemon juice, strawberries and peaches. Cut dessert into serving pieces; serve with fruit mixture. Cover and refrigerate any remaining dessert.

Pastry Crust

1 1/2 cups all-purpose flour
1 cup margarine or butter, softened
1/2 cup powdered sugar

Heat oven to 400°F. Beat all ingredients with electric mixer on low speed 1 minute, scraping bowl constantly. Beat on medium speed about 2 minutes or until creamy. Spread in ungreased rectangular pan, 13 × 9 inches. Bake 12 to 15 minutes or until edges are golden brown. Cool completely. (For quick cooling, place in freezer 10 to 15 minutes.)

1 Serving: Calories 650 (Calories from Fat 370); Fat 41g (Saturated 19g); Cholesterol 80mg; Sodium 310mg; Carbohydrate 67g (Dietary Fiber 2g); Protein 5g

COUNTRY COOKING WISDOM

Rescue Overwhipped Cream

Here's the best way to salvage overwhipped cream. When whipping heavy cream with an electric mixer, the cream often goes from soft peaks to overwhipped in seconds. When this happens, immediately stop whipping. Add more heavy cream, a tablespoon at a time, and gently stir with a whisk. This will bring the cream back to the soft peak stage.

Brandy Flans

6 servings   Prep Time: 25 minutes   Start to Finish: 4 hours 25 minutes

This creamy custard, scented with brandy and warm spices, is baked over a caramel syrup. To serve, turn the chilled custards onto individual plates and watch the caramel do the glazing. Decadent!

1¼ cups sugar

2 tablespoons water

2 eggs, slightly beaten

2 tablespoons brandy or
2 teaspoons brandy flavoring

½ teaspoon vanilla

¼ teaspoon ground nutmeg

¼ teaspoon ground cinnamon

¼ teaspoon ground allspice

Dash of salt

2 cups milk, scalded and
cooled

1   Heat ¾ of the cup sugar in heavy 1-quart saucepan over low heat, stirring constantly, until melted and golden brown. Gradually stir in water. Divide syrup evenly among six 6-oz custard cups. Allow syrup to harden in cups about 10 minutes.

2   Heat oven to 350°F.

3   Mix remaining ½ cup sugar, the eggs, brandy, vanilla, nutmeg, cinnamon, allspice and salt. Gradually stir in milk. Pour custard mixture over syrup. Place cups in rectangular pan, 13 × 9 inches, on oven rack. Pour very hot water into pan to within ½ inch of tops of cups.

4   Bake about 45 minutes or until knife inserted halfway between center and edges comes out clean. Remove cups from water. Refrigerate until chilled. Unmold at serving time.

1 Serving: Calories 247 (Calories from Fat 39); Fat 4g (Saturated 2g); Cholesterol 79mg; Sodium 80mg; Carbohydrate 46g (Dietary Fiber 0g); Protein 5g

COUNTRY COOKING WISDOM

Baking Baths

Why are custard desserts baked in a pan of water? This method, called a water bath, helps the custards bake gently and evenly. Without the hot water, the edges of the custard would cook too quickly.

Baked Honey Custard

5 servings | Prep Time: 10 minutes | Start to Finish: 50 minutes

This classic custard will stir up delicious memories of days gone by. It is a wonderfully simple treat served as is, but it's versatile and lends itself to use in many other desserts—among them parfaits and even dessert sauces.

2 eggs
1/3 cup honey
1/4 teaspoon salt
1/2 teaspoon vanilla
1 3/4 cups milk, scalded
Ground nutmeg

1 Heat oven to 350°F. Beat eggs slightly in medium bowl. Mix in honey, salt and vanilla. Gradually stir in milk. Pour into five 6-oz custard cups. Sprinkle with nutmeg.

2 Place cups in baking pan on oven rack. Pour very hot water into pan to within 1/2 inch of tops of cups.

3 Bake 40 to 50 minutes or until knife inserted halfway between center and edge comes out clean. Remove cups from water. Serve warm or cover and refrigerate about 3 hours or until chilled. Refrigerate any remaining custard.

1 Serving: Calories 151 (Calories from Fat 43); Fat 5g (Saturated 2g); Cholesterol 93mg; Sodium 179mg; Carbohydrate 23g (Dietary Fiber 0g); Protein 4g

Creamy Stirred Custard

5 servings | Prep Time: 30 minutes | Start to Finish: 2 hours 30 minutes

The French call this creamy custard sauce crème anglaise. Serve it over cake, fruit or other desserts. It is used in Layered Fruit Dessert (page 331).

3 eggs
1/3 cup sugar
Dash of salt
2 1/2 cups milk
1 teaspoon vanilla

1 Beat eggs slightly in 2-quart heavy saucepan. Stir in sugar and salt. Gradually stir in milk. Cook over medium heat 15 to 20 minutes, stirring constantly, until mixture just coats a metal spoon; remove from heat. Stir in vanilla.

2 Place saucepan in cold water until custard is cool. (If custard curdles, beat vigorously with hand beater until smooth.) Cover and refrigerate at least 2 hours. Refrigerate any remaining custard.

1 Serving: Calories 171 (Calories from Fat 63); Fat 7g (Saturated 3g); Cholesterol 139mg; Sodium 120mg; Carbohydrate 19g (Dietary Fiber 0g); Protein 8g

Individual Lime Schaum Tortes

6 servings | Prep Time: 40 minutes | Start to Finish: 14 hours 40 minutes

A schaum torte may be either an unadorned meringue or a more complicated dessert such as this one. These pretty little tortes have appeared in different versions in Betty Crocker cookbooks through the years, dating all the way back to the first *Betty Crocker's Cookbook,* published in 1950.

Meringue Shells (below right)
- ³/₄ cup sugar
- 3 tablespoons cornstarch
- ¹/₈ teaspoon salt
- ³/₄ cup water
- 3 egg yolks, slightly beaten
- 1 tablespoon margarine or butter
- 1 tablespoon grated lime peel
- ¹/₃ cup lime juice
- Few drops green food color
- 1 cup whipping cream

1 Prepare Meringue Shells.

2 Mix sugar, cornstarch and salt in 1½-quart saucepan. Gradually stir in water. Cook over medium heat, stirring constantly, until mixture thickens and boils. Boil and stir 1 minute. Stir at least half of the hot mixture gradually into egg yolks; stir back into hot mixture in saucepan. Boil and stir 1 minute; remove from heat.

3 Stir in margarine, lime peel, lime juice and food color. Cool 15 minutes. Refrigerate until room temperature. Spoon into shells, cover and refrigerate at least 12 hours.

4 Beat whipping cream in chilled small bowl until stiff. Spread over filling. Refrigerate any remaining tortes.

Meringue Shells

- 3 egg whites
- ¹/₄ teaspoon cream of tartar
- ³/₄ cup sugar

1 Heat oven to 275°F.

2 Cover cookie sheet with heavy brown paper. Beat egg whites and cream of tartar in medium bowl with electric mixer on high speed until foamy. Beat in sugar, 1 tablespoon at a time, and continue beating until stiff and glossy. Do not underbeat.

3 Shape meringue on brown paper into six 3½-inch circles with back of spoon, building up sides. Bake 45 minutes. Turn off oven; leave meringues in oven with door closed 1 hour. Remove from oven; finish cooling meringues away from draft.

1 Serving: Calories 365 (Calories from Fat 169); Fat 19g (Saturated 10g); Cholesterol 157mg; Sodium 119mg; Carbohydrate 50g (Dietary Fiber 0g); Protein 4g

Tart Lemon Pudding

4 servings | Prep Time: 15 minutes | Start to Finish: 2 hours 15 minutes

This rich pudding is bursting with flavor from fresh lemon juice and zest. For a special touch, garnish with fresh berries and a mint sprig.

2 cups sugar

1/2 cup cornstarch

2 cups water

4 egg yolks, slightly beaten

1/4 cup margarine or butter

2 teaspoons grated lemon peel

2/3 cup lemon juice

1 Mix sugar and cornstarch in 2-quart saucepan. Gradually stir in water. Cook over medium heat, stirring constantly, until mixture thickens and boils. Boil and stir 1 minute.

2 Gradually stir at least half the hot mixture into egg yolks; stir back into hot mixture in saucepan. Heat to boiling, stirring constantly. Boil and stir 2 minutes; remove from heat. Stir in margarine, lemon peel and lemon juice.

3 Pour into dessert dishes. Refrigerate about 2 hours or until chilled. Refrigerate any remaining pudding.

1 Serving: Calories 613 (Calories from Fat 141); Fat 16g (Saturated 4g); Cholesterol 205mg; Sodium 146mg; Carbohydrate 119g (Dietary Fiber 0g); Protein 3g

COUNTRY COOKING WISDOM

Meringue Magic

A froth of egg white, sugar and air, meringues can make a melt-in-your-mouth soft topping for pies or a hard, crispy shell to cradle cream fillings, fruit or ice cream. Here's all you'll need to know for making successful meringues every time.

- Start with cold eggs—they're easier to separate—and separate them very carefully. Even a speck of yolk in the whites will keep them from achieving the volume needed during beating.

- For better volume, let egg whites stand at room temperature for 30 minutes before beating. Or put the whites in a microwavable bowl and microwave uncovered on High for about 10 seconds per egg white to bring them to room temperature. If you heat them too long, however, they'll cook through.

- Beat in sugar gradually, about 1 tablespoon at a time, so that your meringue will be smooth and not gritty. Continue beating until the meringue stands in stiff peaks when you lift the beaters out of the mixture.

Apricot Mousse

12 servings | Prep Time: 25 minutes | Start to Finish: 5 hours 10 minutes

Mousse is a French term for "froth" or "foam." These airy desserts are made frothy by folding a fruit puree into whipped cream or beaten egg whites. Here sweet apricots and brandy, laced with a hint of almond, are turned into an exquisite dessert.

2 cups sliced peeled apricots (6 medium)*

¼ cup sugar

2 envelopes unflavored gelatin

4 eggs

3 egg yolks

¼ cup brandy or 2 teaspoons brandy flavoring

¼ teaspoon almond extract

2 cups whipping (heavy) cream

Sweetened whipped cream, if desired

1 Place apricots in blender. Cover and blend on high speed about 1 minute or until smooth.

2 Mix sugar and gelatin in 2-quart saucepan.

3 Beat eggs and egg yolks in medium bowl with electric mixer on high speed about 5 minutes or until thick and lemon colored. Stir eggs into gelatin mixture. Heat to boiling over medium heat, stirring constantly; remove from heat. Stir in apricot puree, brandy and almond extract.

4 Refrigerate just until mixture mounds slightly when dropped from a spoon.

5 Beat whipping cream in chilled large bowl until stiff. Fold apricot mixture into whipped cream. Pour into 8-cup mold. Refrigerate at least 4 hours or until firm; unmold. Serve with sweetened whipped cream. Refrigerate any remaining mousse.

1 can (30 oz) apricot halves, drained, can be substituted for the 2 cups fresh apricot slices.

1 Serving: Calories 219 (Calories from Fat 158); Fat 18g (Saturated 10g); Cholesterol 176mg; Sodium 43mg; Carbohydrate 9g (Dietary Fiber 1g); Protein 5g

Strawberry-Rhubarb Flummery

4 servings | **Prep Time: 20 minutes** | **Start to Finish: 2 hours 20 minutes**

Flummeries were originally thickened with oatmeal, although we now use cornstarch or flour. They were particularly popular among Shakers.

3 cups ¹/₂-inch pieces fresh rhubarb*

I cup sugar

¹/₄ cup cold water

3 tablespoons cornstarch

I cup sliced fresh strawberries**

Few drops red food color

Whipping cream

1 Heat rhubarb, sugar and 1 tablespoon of the water to boiling in 2-quart saucepan; reduce heat. Simmer uncovered about 5 minutes, stirring occasionally, until rhubarb is tender.

2 Mix cornstarch and remaining water. Stir into rhubarb mixture. Heat to boiling, stirring constantly. Boil and stir 1 minute. Stir in strawberries and food color.

3 Spoon into dessert dishes. Cover and refrigerate about 2 hours or until chilled. Serve with whipping cream.

*1 package (16 oz) frozen unsweetened rhubarb, thawed and drained, can be substituted for the fresh rhubarb.

**1 package (10 oz) frozen strawberries, thawed and drained, can be substituted for the fresh strawberries.

1 Serving: Calories 249 (Calories from Fat 3); Fat 0g (Saturated 0g); Cholesterol 0mg; Sodium 5mg; Carbohydrate 63g (Dietary Fiber 3g); Protein 1g

Frozen Torte

Crisp meringue layers are filled with luscious mocha cream—absolutely delicious! Be sure to pick a cool, dry day to make this recipe. If it's humid or raining, the sugar in the meringue will absorb moisture, making for sticky, spongy meringues.

4 egg whites
1/2 teaspoon cream of tartar
1 cup sugar
Mocha Filling (below right)
Shaved chocolate, if desired

1 Heat oven to 275°F. Cover 2 cookie sheets with heavy brown paper.

2 Beat egg whites and cream of tartar in large bowl with electric mixer on high speed until foamy. Beat in sugar, 1 tablespoon at a time, and continue beating until stiff and glossy. Do not underbeat.

3 Divide meringue into 3 parts. Place 1 part on 1 cookie sheet and shape into 6-inch circle. Place remaining 2 parts on second cookie sheet and shape each part into 6-inch circle.

4 Bake 45 minutes. Turn off oven; leave meringues in oven with door closed 1 hour. Remove from oven. Finish cooling meringues away from draft.

5 Stack meringues, spreading filling between layers and on top of torte. Decorate with shaved chocolate. Freeze uncovered at least 3 hours or until filling on top is firm. (For ease in cutting, dip knife into hot water and wipe after cutting each slice.)

Mocha Filling

1/4 cup sugar
3 tablespoons cocoa
2 tablespoons powdered instant coffee
2 cups whipping cream

Beat all ingredients in chilled medium bowl until stiff.

1 Serving: Calories 443 (Calories from Fat 268); Fat 30g (Saturated 18g); Cholesterol 109mg; Sodium 68mg; Carbohydrate 44g (Dietary Fiber 1g); Protein 5g

Peppermint Bavarian

8 servings | Prep Time: 15 minutes | Start to Finish: 5 hours 55 minutes

Hard candy flavors this decadent dessert! To give it a streaked look, food coloring is folded into the whipped cream mixture before placing in the mold, making for a lovely presentation.

1 envelope unflavored gelatin

¼ cup cold water

3 eggs

¼ cup sugar

⅓ cup crushed peppermint candies

¼ teaspoon salt

1 cup milk

1 cup whipping cream

3 tablespoons sugar

Few drops red food color

1 Sprinkle gelatin on cold water to soften; reserve.

2 Mix eggs, ¼ cup sugar, the candies and salt in 2-quart heavy saucepan. Gradually stir in milk. Cook over medium heat 7 to 10 minutes, stirring constantly, until mixture thickens and just begins to boil; remove from heat. Stir in reserved gelatin until dissolved.

3 Place saucepan in ice and water about 15 minutes or in refrigerator about 30 minutes, stirring occasionally, until mixture mounds when dropped from spoon. (If mixture is too thick, place saucepan in warm water and stir until smooth. Refrigerate about 10 minutes or until mixture mounds when dropped from spoon.)

4 Beat whipping cream and 3 tablespoons sugar in chilled medium bowl until stiff. Fold gelatin mixture into whipped cream. Gently fold in food color just until streaked with color.

5 Pour into 4-quart mold. Cover and refrigerate 5 hours or until set. Quickly dip mold into hot water and unmold on serving plate. Refrigerate any remaining Bavarian cream dessert.

1 Serving: Calories 206 (Calories from Fat 126); Fat 14g (Saturated 1g); Cholesterol 123mg; Sodium 126mg; Carbohydrate 16g (Dietary Fiber 0g); Protein 5g

Orange Bavarian

8 servings | Prep Time: 20 minutes | Start to Finish: 5 hours

Cool and custardy, Bavarians have been enjoyed for years. These rich desserts are a blend of gelatin, flavorings and whipped cream.

1 cup boiling water

1 package (4-serving size) orange-flavored gelatin

½ cup sugar

1 tablespoon grated orange peel

1 cup orange juice

1 cup whipping cream

1 Pour boiling water on gelatin in medium bowl; stir until gelatin is dissolved. Stir in sugar, orange peel and orange juice. Refrigerate, stirring occasionally, until mixture mounds slightly when dropped from a spoon.

2 Beat whipping cream in chilled medium bowl until stiff. Beat gelatin mixture until foamy. Fold gelatin mixture into whipped cream.

3 Pour into 4-cup mold or individual dessert dishes. Cover and refrigerate 4 hours or until firm; unmold.

1 Serving: Calories 204 (Calories from Fat 100); Fat 11g (Saturated 7g); Cholesterol 41mg; Sodium 51mg; Carbohydrate 26g (Dietary Fiber 0g); Protein 2g

Peach Ice Cream

Nothing tastes as good in the summer as fresh peach ice cream! Using local ripe peaches produces the most flavorful ice cream, so schedule time during peak peach season to make some.

1 cup sugar

1 cup milk

¼ teaspoon salt

3 egg yolks, beaten

2 cups whipping cream

1 tablespoon vanilla

2 cups mashed peeled peaches
(4 to 5 medium)

1 Mix ½ cup of the sugar, the milk, salt and egg yolks in 1-quart saucepan. Cook over medium heat, stirring constantly, just to boiling (do not boil). Refrigerate uncovered in chilled bowl 1 to 1 hour 30 minutes or until room temperature.

2 Stir whipping cream and vanilla into milk mixture. Mix peaches and remaining ½ cup sugar; stir into cream mixture.

3 Pour into 1-quart ice-cream freezer. Freeze according to manufacturer's directions.

Times will vary depending on manufacturer's directions.

1 Serving: Calories 1,364 (Calories from Fat 223); Fat 25g (Saturated 15g); Cholesterol 162mg; Sodium 111mg; Carbohydrate 33g (Dietary Fiber 1g); Protein 4g

Strawberry Ice Cream

Great summertime memories are made when you bring out the ice-cream maker. Look for berries with a deep red color and no white. The riper the strawberries, the more flavorful this ice cream will be!

1 quart fresh strawberries,
washed and hulled

¾ cup sugar

2 cups whipping cream

1 cup milk

½ teaspoon vanilla

2 eggs

1 Mix strawberries and ½ cup of the sugar in bowl. Let stand about 1 hour, stirring occasionally. Mash strawberries.

2 Whisk together whipping cream, milk, vanilla, eggs and remaining ¼ cup sugar. Cook in medium saucepan over low heat about 8 minutes, stirring constantly, until mixture thickens. Stir in strawberry mixture.

3 Chill mixture about 2 hours. Pour into ice-cream freezer. Freeze according to manufacturer's directions.

Times will vary depending on manufacturer's directions.

1 Serving: Calories 330 (Calories from Fat 215); Fat 24g (Saturated 15g); Cholesterol 135mg; Sodium 55mg; Carbohydrate 27g (Dietary Fiber 2g); Protein 4g

Apple Ice Cream

12 (½ cup) servings | Prep Time: 20 minutes | Start to Finish: 3 hours 20 minutes*

This unusual flavor is delicious for Thanksgiving and Christmas. Feel free to add a little cinnamon or even pumpkin pie spice for a real holiday treat!

1 cup sugar

1 cup milk

¼ teaspoon salt

3 egg yolks, beaten

2 cups whipping cream

1 teaspoon vanilla

3 or 4 drops red or green food color, if desired

3 medium peeled eating apples, cored and cut up

1 tablespoon lemon juice

1 Mix ½ of the cup sugar, the milk, salt and egg yolks in 1-quart saucepan. Cook over medium heat, stirring constantly, just to boiling (do not boil). Refrigerate uncovered in chilled bowl 1 to 1 hour 30 minutes or until room temperature.

2 Stir whipping cream, vanilla and food color into milk mixture.

3 Place half of the apples, remaining ½ cup sugar and the lemon juice in blender or food processor. Cover and blend, using quick on-and-off motions, until coarsely chopped. Add remaining apples. Cover and blend until finely chopped but not mashed. Stir into milk mixture.

4 Pour into 2-quart ice-cream freezer. Freeze according to manufacturer's directions.

Times will vary depending on manufacturer's directions.

1 Serving: Calories 243 (Calories from Fat 148); Fat 16g (Saturated 10g); Cholesterol 108mg; Sodium 74mg; Carbohydrate 23g (Dietary Fiber 0g); Protein 2g

Caramel Crunch Ice Cream

8 (½ cup) servings | Prep Time: 20 minutes | Start to Finish: 3 hours 20 minutes*

You will certainly taste the Southern influence in this special ice cream. The mix of Caramel Crunch and pecans imitates the flavor of the praline, a Southern favorite. Like this ice cream, pralines are made with brown sugar and pecans.

½ cup sugar
1 cup milk
¼ teaspoon salt
3 egg yolks, beaten
Caramel Crunch (below right)
½ cup chopped pecans
2 cups whipping cream
1 tablespoon vanilla

1 Mix sugar, milk, salt and egg yolks in 1-½-quart saucepan. Heat over medium heat, stirring constantly, just to boiling (do not boil). Refrigerate uncovered in chilled bowl at least 2 hours.

2 Prepare Caramel Crunch.

3 Stir Caramel Crunch, pecans, whipping cream and vanilla into milk mixture. Pour into 1-quart ice-cream freezer. Freeze according to manufacturer's directions.

Caramel Crunch

1 tablespoon margarine or butter, softened
⅓ cup packed brown sugar

1 Spread butter on cookie sheet, 15 × 12 inches, leaving 1½-inch border on all sides. Sprinkle brown sugar evenly over buttered area.

2 Set oven control to broil. Broil 3 to 4 inches from heat 1 to 2 minutes or until brown sugar is melted. (Watch closely as mixture burns quickly.)

3 Cool slightly; remove from cookie sheet with spatula. Break into pieces.

Times will vary depending on manufacturer's directions.

1 Serving: Calories 395 (Calories from Fat 297); Fat 33g (Saturated 21g); Cholesterol 122mg; Sodium 70mg; Carbohydrate 15g (Dietary Fiber 0g); Protein 2g

Philadelphia Ice Cream

8 (½ cup) servings   Prep Time: 5 minutes   Start to Finish: 1 hour 5 minutes*

Simple and creamy, this classic vanilla ice cream will be a hit every time you prepare it.

½ cup sugar

3 cups whipping cream

4½ teaspoons vanilla

⅛ teaspoon salt

1 Mix all ingredients until sugar is dissolved.

2 Pour into 1-quart ice-cream freezer. Freeze according to manufacturer's directions.

Times will vary depending on manufacturer's directions.

1 Serving: Calories 363 (Calories from Fat 297); Fat 33g (Saturated 21g); Cholesterol 122mg; Sodium 70mg; Carbohydrate 15g (Dietary Fiber 0g); Protein 2g

COUNTRY COOKING WISDOM

Incredible Ice Cream

Marco Polo is rumored to have brought back a recipe for an ice-cream confection from Asia, but ice cream did not become widely known in Europe until the late seventeenth century. Ice cream became popular in the American colonies toward the end of the next century—it seems that even George Washington was quite fond of it!

Ice cream in Europe was made with a custard base. Philadelphia, the birthplace of our Constitution, was also the birthplace of a special kind of ice cream. Made without egg custard, Philadelphia Ice Cream is both rich and simple. First Lady Dolley Madison, who served ice cream frequently at the White House, is credited with making ice cream the popular American treat it remains today.

Fresh Lemon Sherbet

8 (½ cup) servings   Prep Time: 5 minutes   Start to Finish: 1 hour 5 minutes*

Lighter than ice cream, sherbets use either milk or, as in this recipe, half-and-half instead of heavy cream. They are also flavored with fruit—often citrus fruits.

1¼ cups sugar

2 cups half-and-half

⅓ cup lemon juice

1 to 2 tablespoons lemon peel

1 or 2 drops yellow food color

1 Mix all ingredients until sugar is dissolved.

2 Pour into 1-quart ice-cream freezer. Freeze according to manufacturer's directions.

Times will vary depending on manufacturer's directions.

1 Serving: Calories 202 (Calories from Fat 163); Fat 7g (Saturated 4g); Cholesterol 22mg; Sodium 25mg; Carbohydrate 35g (Dietary Fiber 0g); Protein 2g

Three-Fruit Ice

8 (½ cup) servings   Prep Time: 15 minutes   Start to Finish: 1 hour 15 minutes*

Unlike ice cream and sherbet, an ice contains no cream or milk but instead is a frozen fruit puree. Here you'll find a mélange of 3 fruits—banana, orange and lemon. Simply delicious!

1 cup sugar

⅛ teaspoon salt

1¼ cups water

½ cup orange juice (1 medium orange)

3 tablespoons lemon juice (1 lemon)

2 ripe bananas, mashed (¾ cup)

1 Heat sugar, salt and half of the water to boiling in 1-quart saucepan. Remove from heat.

2 Stir in remaining water, orange juice, lemon juice and bananas.

3 Pour into 1-quart ice-cream freezer. Freeze according to manufacturer's directions.

Times will vary depending on manufacturer's directions.

1 Serving: Calories 131 (Calories from Fat 1); Fat 0g (Saturated 0g); Cholesterol 0mg; Sodium 38mg; Carbohydrate 34g (Dietary Fiber 1g); Protein 0g

Helpful Nutrition and Cooking Information

Nutrition Guidelines

We provide nutrition information for each recipe that includes calories, fat, cholesterol, sodium, carbohydrate, fiber and protein. Individual food choices can be based on this information.

Recommended intake for a daily diet of 2,000 calories as set by the Food and Drug Administration

Total Fat	Less than 65g
Saturated Fat	Less than 20g
Cholesterol	Less than 300mg
Sodium	Less than 2,400mg
Total Carbohydrate	300g
Dietary Fiber	25g

Criteria Used for Calculating Nutrition Information

- The first ingredient was used wherever a choice is given (such as ⅓ cup sour cream or plain yogurt).

- The first ingredient amount was used wherever a range is given (such as 3 to 3½-pound cut-up broiler-fryer chicken).

- The first serving number was used wherever a range is given (such as 4 to 6 servings).

- "If desired" ingredients and recipe variations were not included (such as sprinkle with brown sugar, if desired).

- Only the amount of a marinade or frying oil that is estimated to be absorbed by the food during preparation or cooking was calculated.

Ingredients Used in Recipe Testing and Nutrition Calculations

- Ingredients used for testing represent those that the majority of consumers use in their homes: large eggs, 2% milk, 80%-lean ground beef, canned ready-to-use chicken broth and vegetable oil spread containing not less than 65 percent fat.

- Fat-free, low-fat or low-sodium products were not used, unless otherwise indicated.

- Solid vegetable shortening (not butter, margarine, nonstick cooking sprays or vegetable oil spread as they can cause sticking problems) was used to grease pans, unless otherwise indicated.

Equipment Used in Recipe Testing

We use equipment for testing that the majority of consumers use in their homes. If a specific piece of equipment (such as a wire whisk) is necessary for recipe success, it is listed in the recipe.

- Cookware and bakeware without nonstick coatings were used, unless otherwise indicated.

- No dark-colored, black or insulated bakeware was used.

- When a pan is specified in a recipe, a metal pan was used; a baking dish or pie plate means ovenproof glass was used.

- An electric hand mixer was used for mixing only when mixer speeds are specified in the recipe directions. When a mixer speed is not given, a spoon or fork was used.

Strawberry Shortcakes (page 283)

Cooking Terms Glossary

Beat: Mix ingredients vigorously with spoon, fork, wire whisk, hand beater or electric mixer until smooth and uniform.

Boil: Heat liquid until bubbles rise continuously and break on the surface and steam is given off. For rolling boil, the bubbles form rapidly.

Chop: Cut into coarse or fine irregular pieces with a knife, food chopper, blender or food processor.

Cube: Cut into squares ½ inch or larger.

Dice: Cut into squares smaller than ½ inch.

Grate: Cut into tiny particles using small rough holes of grater (citrus peel or chocolate).

Grease: Rub the inside surface of a pan with shortening, using pastry brush, piece of waxed paper or paper towel, to prevent food from sticking during baking (as for some casseroles).

Julienne: Cut into thin, matchlike strips, using knife or food processor (vegetables, fruits, meats).

Mix: Combine ingredients in any way that distributes them evenly.

Sauté: Cook foods in hot oil or margarine over medium-high heat with frequent tossing and turning motion.

Shred: Cut into long thin pieces by rubbing food across the holes of a shredder, as for cheese, or by using a knife to slice very thinly, as for cabbage.

Simmer: Cook in liquid just below the boiling point on top of the stove; usually after reducing heat from a boil. Bubbles will rise slowly and break just below the surface.

Stir: Mix ingredients until uniform consistency. Stir once in a while for stirring occasionally, often for stirring frequently and continuously for stirring constantly.

Toss: Tumble ingredients (such as green salad) lightly with a lifting motion, usually to coat evenly or mix with another food.

metric conversion guide

VOLUME

U.S. UNITS	CANADIAN METRIC	AUSTRALIAN METRIC
¼ teaspoon	1 mL	1 ml
½ teaspoon	2 mL	2 ml
1 teaspoon	5 mL	5 ml
1 tablespoon	15 mL	20 ml
¼ cup	50 mL	60 ml
⅓ cup	75 mL	80 ml
½ cup	125 mL	125 ml
⅔ cup	150 mL	170 ml
¾ cup	175 mL	190 ml
1 cup	250 mL	250 ml
1 quart	1 liter	1 liter
1½ quarts	1.5 liters	1.5 liters
2 quarts	2 liters	2 liters
2½ quarts	2.5 liters	2.5 liters
3 quarts	3 liters	3 liters
4 quarts	4 liters	4 liters

WEIGHT

U.S. UNITS	CANADIAN METRIC	AUSTRALIAN METRIC
1 ounce	30 grams	30 grams
2 ounces	55 grams	60 grams
3 ounces	85 grams	90 grams
4 ounces (¼ pound)	115 grams	125 grams
8 ounces (½ pound)	225 grams	225 grams
16 ounces (1 pound)	455 grams	500 grams
1 pound	455 grams	0.5 kilogram

MEASUREMENTS

INCHES	CENTIMETERS
1	2.5
2	5.0
3	7.5
4	10.0
5	12.5
6	15.0
7	17.5
8	20.5
9	23.0
10	25.5
11	28.0
12	30.5
13	33.0

TEMPERATURES

FAHRENHEIT	CELSIUS
32°	0°
212°	100°
250°	120°
275°	140°
300°	150°
325°	160°
350°	180°
375°	190°
400°	200°
425°	220°
450°	230°
475°	240°
500°	260°

NOTE: The recipes in this cookbook have not been developed or tested using metric measures. When converting recipes to metric, some variations in quality may be noted.

Index

Page numbers in *italics* indicate photographs.

Complete your cookbook library with these *Betty Crocker* titles

Betty Crocker **Baking for Today**

Betty Crocker's **Best Bread Machine Cookbook**

Betty Crocker's **Best Chicken Cookbook**

Betty Crocker **Christmas Cookbook**

Betty Crocker's **Best of Baking**

Betty Crocker's **Best of Healthy and Hearty Cooking**

Betty Crocker's **Best-Loved Recipes**

Betty Crocker's **Bisquick® Cookbook**

Betty Crocker **Bisquick® II Cookbook**

Betty Crocker **Bisquick® Impossibly Easy Pies**

Betty Crocker **Celebrate!**

Betty Crocker's **Complete Thanksgiving Cookbook**

Betty Crocker's **Cook Book for Boys and Girls**

Betty Crocker's **Cook It Quick**

Betty Crocker **Cookbook, 10th Edition—**
The **BIG RED** *Cookbook*®

Betty Crocker **Cookbook, Bridal Edition**

Betty Crocker **Cookbook, Heart Health Edition**

Betty Crocker **Cookie Book**

Betty Crocker **Baking Basics**

Betty Crocker **Cooking Basics**

Betty Crocker's **Cooky Book, Facsimile Edition**

Betty Crocker **Decorating Cakes and Cupcakes**

Betty Crocker's **Diabetes Cookbook**

Betty Crocker **Dinner Made Easy with Rotisserie Chicken**

Betty Crocker **Easy Everyday Vegetarian**

Betty Crocker **Easy Family Dinners**

Betty Crocker's **Easy Slow Cooker Dinners**

Betty Crocker's **Eat and Lose Weight**

Betty Crocker's **Entertaining Basics**

Betty Crocker's **Flavors of Home**

Betty Crocker **4-Ingredient Dinners**

Betty Crocker **Grilling Made Easy**

Betty Crocker **Healthy Heart Cookbook**

Betty Crocker's **Healthy New Choices**

Betty Crocker's **Indian Home Cooking**

Betty Crocker's **Italian Cooking**

Betty Crocker **Just the Two of Us Cookbook**

Betty Crocker **Kids Cook!**

Betty Crocker's **Kitchen Library**

Betty Crocker's **Living with Cancer Cookbook**

Betty Crocker **Low-Carb Lifestyle Cookbook**

Betty Crocker's **Low-Fat, Low-Cholesterol Cooking Today**

Betty Crocker **More Slow Cooker Recipes**

Betty Crocker's **New Chinese Cookbook**

Betty Crocker **One-Dish Meals**

Betty Crocker's **A Passion for Pasta**

Betty Crocker's **Picture Cook Book, Facsimile Edition**

Betty Crocker **Quick & Easy Cookbook**

Betty Crocker's **Slow Cooker Cookbook**

Betty Crocker **30-Minute Meals for Diabetes**

Betty Crocker **Ultimate Bisquick® Cookbook**

Betty Crocker's **Ultimate Cake Mix Cookbook**

Betty Crocker **Whole Grains Cookbook**

Betty Crocker **Why It Works**

Betty Crocker **Win at Weight Loss Cookbook**